Business Digital Transformation

Alex Zarifis • Despo Ktoridou
Leonidas Efthymiou • Xusen Cheng
Editors

Business Digital Transformation

Selected Cases from Industry Leaders

palgrave
macmillan

Editors
Alex Zarifis
School of Business, University of Nicosia
Nicosia, Cyprus

Cambridge Center for Alternative Finance
University of Cambridge
Cambridge, UK

Leonidas Efthymiou
School of Business, University of Nicosia
Nicosia, Cyprus

Despo Ktoridou
School of Business, University of Nicosia
Nicosia, Cyprus

Xusen Cheng
School of Information
Renmin University of China
Beijing, China

ISBN 978-3-031-33664-5 ISBN 978-3-031-33665-2 (eBook)
https://doi.org/10.1007/978-3-031-33665-2

This Palgrave Macmillan imprint is published by the registered company Springer Nature Switzerland AG.
The registered company address is: Gewerbestrasse 11, 6330 Cham, Switzerland

Paper in this product is recyclable.

Contents

Contributors

Theodor Andersson Agency for Digital Government (DIGG), Sundsvall, Sweden

Mads Jørgsholm Bierrings Copenhagen Business School, Frederiksberg, Denmark

Xusen Cheng School of Information, Renmin University of China, Beijing, China

Andrew Crean Supponor, Ltd., London, UK

Fabio Cuzzolin Visual AI Lab, Oxford Brookes University, Oxford, UK

Paraskevi Dekoulou Aristotle University of Thessaloniki, University Campus, Thessaloniki, Greece

Leonidas Efthymiou School of Business, University of Nicosia, Nicosia, Cyprus

Despo Ktoridou School of Business, University of Nicosia, Nicosia, Cyprus

Ambika Kulshrestha Rectangle Consulting, Hyderabad, India

Sandeep Kulshrestha Rectangle Consulting, Hyderabad, India

Yianna Orphanidou School of Business, University of Nicosia, Nicosia, Cyprus

Steve Plunkett Supponor, Ltd., London, UK

Alexander Rast Visual AI Lab, Oxford Brookes University, Oxford, UK

Eleftherios Sdoukopoulos Hellenic Institute of Transport - Centre for Research and Technology Hellas, Marousi, Greece

Vivek Singh Visual AI Lab, Oxford Brookes University, Oxford, UK
Supponor, Ltd., London, UK

Gerishanth Sivakumar Copenhagen Business School, Frederiksberg, Denmark

M. C. Omar C. Vargas-González Instituto Tecnológico de México, Campus Cd. Guzmán, Cd. Guzman, Jalisco, Mexico

José G. Vargas-Hernández Postgraduate and Research Division, Tec MM Campus Zapopan. Instituto Tecnológico José Mario Molina Pasquel y Henríquez, El Bajio, Zapopan, Jalisco, Mexico

Nico Wunderlich IT University of Copenhagen, Copenhagen, Denmark

Alex Zarifis School of Business, University of Nicosia, Nicosia, Cyprus
Cambridge Centre for Alternative Finance, University of Cambridge, Cambridge, UK

List of Figures

List of Graphs

List of Tables

1

Sustainable Digital Transformation in Finance, Tourism, Transport, Entertainment and Social Innovation

Alex Zarifis, Leonidas Efthymiou, and Xusen Cheng

1.1 Introduction

There is an ongoing digital transformation with an increasing diffusion of technologies that are acting as a catalyst for business advancement. The first chapter discusses the importance of sustainable digital transformation at this point in time and explains why each case was chosen, the

A. Zarifis (✉)
School of Business, University of Nicosia, Nicosia, Cyprus

Cambridge Centre for Alternative Finance, University of Cambridge, Cambridge, UK
e-mail: zarifis.a@unic.ac.cy

L. Efthymiou
School of Business, University of Nicosia, Nicosia, Cyprus
e-mail: efthymiou.l@unic.ac.cy

X. Cheng
School of Information, Renmin University of China, Beijing, China
e-mail: xusen.cheng@ruc.edu.cn

A. Zarifis et al. (eds.), *Business Digital Transformation*,
https://doi.org/10.1007/978-3-031-33665-2_1

common threads and some key findings. Each case brings a different piece of the puzzle, but it also serves to test and verify our current understanding of digital transformation. There are common lessons across all cases, along with the specific lessons some cases offer for those specific sectors of the economy. The research presented here is practical, with directly applicable lessons for organizations, but it also raises broader questions about how digital transformation is shaping the workplace, our private lives and society in general. There are cases of sustainable digital transformation in finance, tourism, transport, entertainment and social innovation that inform this discussion.

The main theme of the research presented here is to address organizational challenges and pitfalls experienced during the implementation of, and experimentation with, digital transformation. The research here aims to reveal an eclectic mix of examples, experiences and best practices in the business sector, where the seeds of digital transformation are set. The research here aims to provide historical cases as well as taxonomies of digital transformation in the business sector, along with their impact on selected corporate entities. It includes cases and best practices from industry leaders in the technology and implementation of digital transformation. The interrelation among people, technology and organizational structures are significant themes of the research presented here. The use of new and emergent Artificial Intelligence (AI) tools to achieve digital transformation in businesses, as well as future trends in AI, is the dominant characteristic of this research. The target audience of this research is all the stakeholders engaged in this process such as managers, software developers and researchers.

The nine main themes identified here are as follows: (1) Digital transformation leaders will constantly innovate, while digital transformation laggards will have a stop-start approach. (2) There are no simple answers, or a single way to go forward, with digital transformation. (3) Each sector of the economy has its own opportunities, challenges and must find its own path forward. (4) Changes in one sector of the economy, such as the financial sector, will send a ripple of change across other sectors of the economy. (5) Change needs a shared vision, and digital transformation needs leaders to create the shared vision. (6) Digital transformation needs trust and cooperation on every level: Teams, organizations, governments and super-organizations like the EU. (7) People will still have a role: Staff, customers and other stakeholders are still important. (8) There is a dark side to digital transformation that may not have been fully revealed to us yet. (9) Digital transformation should happen hand in hand with sustainability and resilience.

The next section argues that sustainable digital transformation is an opportunity with far-reaching consequences. The third section builds on the cases presented here and finds nine common themes of successful digital transformation across the cases. Lastly the fourth section gives an overview of the fascinating chapters presented here.

1.2 The Importance of Sustainable Digital Transformation

Sustainable digital transformation is a term that is being used frequently in the last few years (Shi et al., 2022). It involves the union of technological change and innovative technologies. Digital transformation with Artificial Intelligence can offer scalability not seen before. It involves constant innovation, evolution and acceleration. It is true that technology is an enabler of digital transformation, but transformation often involves people, technology and new business models. How are these interlinked? Do they function individually or together to make digital transformation a success? Is one force more decisive than others, or are they equally important? With the increasing capabilities of AI and the speed of automated services that can be delivered, is human involvement still necessary? Will we keep human involvement out of nostalgia, so we have something to do, or will roles evolve so that the human involvement still adds value?

Leaders in large and small, public and private organizations appreciate the transformational impact of new technologies such as Artificial Intelligence, big data, cloud computing, Internet of Things (IoT), blockchain and 5G but are unclear on what their organization should look like in the future and how to get there (Pflaum et al., 2019; Zarifis et al., 2021). The environment they find themselves in, with almost daily steps towards, and away from, globalization, new local and international regulation, further adds to this uncertainty (Herbert et al., 2019). These leaders are therefore looking for successful cases of digital transformation, in a variety of contexts, to guide them (Alt et al., 2018; Bátiz-Lazo & Efthymiou, 2016; Zarifis & Cheng, 2023).

While the unstoppable march of technology and the global instability may seem like enough of a challenge for a leader to understand, these are by no means the only forces driving digital transformation. There are also some more subtle, but still influential, forces at play. The post-pandemic worker is not as willing to sacrifice their quality of life for the promise of career advancement and the status that comes with it (Gupta & Mukherjee, 2022). With this mindset, the promise of digital transformation delivering a more efficient machine may not be enough, and people want to know where they fit into this picture. This zeitgeist is reflected in the increased interest in sustainability in its many facets (Purvis et al., 2019).

These forces pushing and pulling digital transformation, but also holding it back, bring us to one overarching question: What is the destination of the digital transformation journey? While some companies automate their processes one by one, when the opportunity arises, as we see with AI chatbots (Zarifis et al., 2021), there should be a clear idea of where this journey will take an organization. Taking all this into account, the leader of digital transformation should act like a true leader, taking staff, customers and other stakeholders with them on this journey.

Despite the challenges of a complex, ill-defined problem, there are also reasons to be optimistic (Vial, 2019). What emerges strongly from the research findings presented here and other literature reviewed here is the willingness to work together and learn from each other (Thrassou et al., 2022a). Leaders in digital transformation must become experts of technology in their context but also be receptive of the solutions found in adjacent contexts or even further away. A leader of digital transformation must disassemble the technology, processes, business models and strategies involved and then put together their own collage of what they want to achieve and their own montage of the journey there.

1.3 Common Themes Across the Chapters

As was touched on already, there were some common themes and key findings that came out strongly in this research that will be discussed in more detail here. The common themes from the chapters are also areas for future research to further explore (Table 1.1).

Major theme 1: Digital transformation leaders will constantly innovate, while digital transformation laggards will have a stop-start approach. Digital transformation leaders will rapidly innovate going through regular iterative evolutions of their technologies, moving through repeated cycles of agile developments metaphorically forming a 'spiral' or a 'spring'. New innovations and in-house skills are built up in this process of constant innovation. Continuing with the metaphor this tightly coiled 'spring' will store 'energy' propelling the organization forward. Digital

Table 1.1 The major themes in digital transformation based on eight cases

Cases in digital transformation	Major themes in sustainable digital transformation
Entertainment (live broadcasts)	1. Digital transformation leaders will constantly innovate, while digital transformation laggards will have a stop-start approach.
Transport and tourism (airports)	2. There are no simple answers, or a single way to go forward, with digital transformation.
Finance (Fintech business models and trust)	3. Each sector of the economy has its own opportunities, challenges and must find its own path forward.
Transport and tourism (seaports and cruise ships)	4. Changes in one sector of the economy, such as the financial sector, will send a ripple of change across other sectors of the economy.
	5. Change needs a shared vision, and digital transformation needs leaders to create the shared vision.
Finance (Central Bank Digital Currencies and trust)	6. Digital transformation needs trust and cooperation on every level: Teams, organizations, governments and super-organizations like the EU.
Local government (information privacy)	7. People will still have a role: Staff, customers and other stakeholders are still important.
Service sector (Indian context)	8. There is a dark side to digital transformation that may not have been fully revealed to us yet.
Social innovation (sustainable development)	9. Digital transformation should happen hand in hand with sustainability and resilience.

transformation laggards will have a stop-start approach copying certain solutions of the leaders but not keeping up. Metaphorically a far less tightly coiled 'spring', more like a line touching the leader's tightly coiled 'spring' at some points and missing other points. Digital transformation followers will create less innovations and not build up in-house capabilities as much (Fig. 1.1).

Major theme 2: There are no simple answers, or a single way to go forward, with digital transformation. If this were purely a case of technology adoption, then there would be some typical approaches such as selecting the best of breed for each application, or by adopting a tried and tested Enterprise Resource Planning system (ERP). The importance of each context limits the availability of generalizable solutions. The availability of data is vastly different for different organizations. Due to the far-reaching consequences of digital transformation, it comes up against legal and regulatory limitations more often, and these are very context specific (Slok-Wodkowska & Mazur, 2021).

Major theme 3: Each sector of the economy has its own opportunities, challenges and must find its own path forward. Following on from the previous point, while it is difficult to identify generalizable solutions, there are more specific approaches that show promise. We see here examples from using machine learning to manipulate video in real time, blockchain being utilized in a supply chain and how to build trust in Fintech. These solutions have often emerged after a variety of alternatives were

Fig. 1.1 The tightly coiled 'spring' of digital transformation leader's innovation and the followers

explored. They are valuable lessons in digital transformation that can help a leader move forward with digitization and automation faster, more sustainably and with lower risk of failure.

Major theme 4: Changes in one sector of the economy, such as the financial sector, will send a ripple of change across other sectors of the economy. Digital transformation may be happening at different speeds, and change may not be happening in lockstep between sectors in the economy, but some changes in one place send ripples across business and society. For example, finance is a part of many other organizations' value chain, and beyond that has responsibilities to the economy and the people where it is active. Changes brought by Fintech, such as greater accessibility to banking and loans, make it easier for small businesses, particularly in rural areas, to have access to credit and grow. The barriers to accessing finance and technology are being reduced in many cases. While it is asking too much from a leader to predict when and how a change somewhere else will impact them, they should be able to react quickly and should not be caught flat-footed.

Major theme 5: Change needs a shared vision, and digital transformation needs leaders to create the shared vision. Digital transformation requires changes to the organizational structure and culture of an organization. While machine learning may offer a solution for scalability and diversification, this also requires broader co-ordination to implement. The division between business and technology must be reduced, and a more innovative agile approach must be ingrained into people (Panetta, 2016; Vial, 2019). A transformational leader is needed that will support the development of a new shared vision based on values that resonate with people. In most cases, these shared values include customer focus, ease of use, sustainability and resilience. In practice this means running more operations of a business as projects and taking advantage of the ecosystem around the organization.

Major theme 6: Digital transformation needs trust and cooperation on every level: Teams, organizations, governments and super-organizations like the EU. There is evidence that organizations are appreciating the magnitude and far-reaching nature of digital transformation, and they are trying to reach some consensus in how to move forward. There are aspects of digital transformation that are opportunities to gain a competitive advantage, but there are also areas that need co-ordination and collaboration between competitors, regulators and other stakeholders. The collaboration will need trust so that there is openness between competitors on the challenges they face and even sharing of data, for example, for machine learning to be trained. The increasing role of technology not only requires more collaboration but also offers the means to do this by providing more immersive environments in virtual worlds, also known as the metaverse.

Major theme 7: People will still have a role: Staff, customers and other stakeholders are still important. This is not just about work, but many other aspects of our lives including digital transformation (Thrassou et al., 2022b). There are pitfalls to over-relying on technology and data. There is a long history of data being created and interpreted in a misleading way leading to tragic consequences (Hodson & Quaglia, 2009). The financial models that led to the 2008 economic crash often presented new investments as secure because the data on them did not go far back enough to include the previous busts in the almost inevitable boom-bust cycle. While the capabilities of machine learning are impressive, it does not escape the old adage of garbage in, garbage out. Despite the increased role of technology, it will not lead, and it will not dictate what will happen. Even in a scenario where the leaders of an organization are sufficiently enamoured with AI to let this happen, there will be pushback from the increasingly knowledgeable and actively engaged consumer.

Major theme 8: There is a dark side to digital transformation that may not have been fully revealed to us yet. The research presented here presents several effective implementations but also some failures that could be useful lessons. However, all the research here, while acknowledging the occasional error of humans engaged in this process, illustrates the value of being 'in the loop', influencing decisions and learning from them. Being fully engaged on a daily basis is necessary so that people with skills and judgement are there to deal with the negative implications of digital transformation that are here and those that will come later. The negative implications that resonate most currently are the ethical issues and personal information privacy concerns. An artificial agent's automated reasoning may make judgements that are not acceptable by humans (Bonnemains et al., 2018). When we are looking at a simple case of cause and effect, this may be easy to resolve, but this becomes more challenging with interrelated processes that have indirect outcomes. For example, in the research we present here, particularly the research on Fintech and video augmentation, we see some indirect and unexpected consequences.

Most of us have heard the metaphors such as data being the new oil, the new gold and so on. What some people may not fully appreciate yet is how much personal information is being used and how invasive the insights can be. Most people are comfortable with data being collected on their purchases, but when the insight gained on them extends into their health and information on their beliefs that can be manipulated, this becomes harder to accept. The expansion of digital transformation and the data collected on staff and other stakeholders increases the power of those controlling the data, typically the employer, and reduces the power of the staff and others whose data was collected. There are two extremes to dealing with this. The first is to push digital transformation and 'force' staff to accept it. In a similar way to how an authoritarian leader would do. The second approach is to act with a more inclusive spirit and co-create the digital transformation.

Major theme 9: Digital transformation should happen hand in hand with sustainability and resilience. Digital transformation and sustainability are, rightly, two of the most researched topics in recent years. Both can be implemented in a small scale at the organizational level but require broader collaboration to harness the greatest benefits possible. AI and automated processes need to operate in a sustainable way (van Wynsberghe, 2021), as there are limited resources. Sustainable AI must not harm the environment and be fair to society (van Wynsberghe, 2021). Similarly, many approaches to achieving sustainability, such as the circular economy, benefit from AI and automation (Wilson et al., 2022). The social, economic and environment pillars of sustainability will benefit from the way AI removes the barriers of scalability.

1.4 Overview of the Chapters

Chapter 2 The second chapter 'What Are We Automating? On the Need for Vision and Expertise When Deploying AI Systems' by Alexander Rast, Vivek Singh, Steve Plunkett, Andrew Crean and Fabio Cuzzolin offers a fascinating case of a cutting-edge application of machine learning. This research illustrates capabilities of machine learning that few people know about. This research offers a glimpse into the development of advanced AI solutions, but it also gives some useful lessons on the process of deployment. The process of deploying the AI solution involves the interplay of the developers, the business purchasing it and their clients. Along with many new insights this research reinforces some very familiar and repeating themes in digital transformation such as the importance of data and the limitations that insufficient data sets on a system.

Chapter 3 Like the second chapter, the third chapter provides another case of applying new technologies to solve a business problem. Many of us have had problems with our baggage when travelling, so this is a chapter that resonates with many of us on a very personal level. The research is on 'Blockchain in the Aviation Industry: A Decentralized Solution to the Transparency Issue in Baggage Handling', and it is by Mads Jørgsholm Bierrings, Gerishanth Sivakumar and Nico Wunderlich. Airline travel is expanding drastically, and legacy systems are struggling to keep up. The existing legacy systems have proven over the years that they cannot be optimized beyond a certain point, and they have their inherent limitations. The attributes of blockchain and RFID technologies can improve many of the processes in an airport, particularly the baggage handling as we see in this case. With low-cost airlines having very low profit margins and low flexibility to resolve customer problems, having a more reliable system will be beneficial. With blockchain and RFID as the underlying technologies, transparency is enhanced, and the value of data extracted from tracking luggage can be unlocked.

Chapter 4 In the fourth chapter we move from the application of specific innovative technology to a taxonomy of business models. The chapter 'The Five Emerging Business Models of Fintech for AI Adoption, Growth and Building Trust' is by Alex Zarifis and Xusen Cheng. The five Fintech business models are (a) disaggregating and focusing on one part of the value chain, (b) utilizing AI in the current processes without changing the business model, (c) finance incumbent extending their model to utilize AI and access new customers and data, (d) a startup finance disruptor only getting involved in finance, and (e) a tech company adding finance to their existing portfolio of services. For all five Fintech models the way trust is built should be part of the business model. Trust is not always built at the same point in the value chain or by the same type of organization. The trust building should happen where the customers are attracted and onboarded. The five Fintech business models give an organization five proven routes to AI adoption and growth. The five distinct approached identified also make it easier for a company in finance to understand what their competitors are doing. Simlarly, regulators in this area can benefit from the clarity the taxonomy offers.

Chapter 5 The fifth chapter explores the improvements technology can bring to seaports and the cruise industry, complementing the chapter on airports nicely. The chapter 'Digital Transformation and System Interoperability in EU Seaports: A Platform Facilitating Supply Chain in the Cruise Industry' is by Leonidas Efthymiou, Paraskevi Dekoulou, Yianna Orphanidou and Eleftherios Sdoukopoulos. The analysis examines the implementation of the National Maritime Single Window (NMSW), the adoption of a European Maritime Single Window (EMSW) and how these systems support the development of a supply-chain platform in the cruise industry. The findings suggest that digital transformation through NMSWs and EMSW contributes to data transfer in real time. Also, the interoperability of systems creates a digital environment where other systems co-exist, facilitating connectivity between the public and private sectors. However, more formalized strategizing is needed, to leverage cooperation between public and private stakeholders in the ever-changing digitized environment.

Chapter 6 The sixth chapter looks at the application of a new technology with far-reaching consequences. 'The Six Ways to Build Trust and Reduce Privacy Concern in a Central Bank Digital Currency (CBDC)' is by Alex Zarifis and Xusen Cheng. A Central Bank Digital Currency (CBDC) offers many potential benefits for governments and citizens, such as faster transactions at a lower cost and richer information on consumers' behaviour. It is important however that the consumer's perspective on the adoption of CBDCs is not neglected. A CBDC needs consumers to trust and use it, to avoid either a complete failure or a partial failure, leading to CBDCs being part of two parallel systems. This research identifies the six ways to build trust in a CBDC so it can be successfully adopted: (1) Trust in the government and the central bank issuing a CBDC, (2) expressed guarantees for the user of a CBDC, (3) the positive reputation of existing CBDCs active elsewhere, (4) automation and reduced human involvement achieved by a CBDC technology, (5) trust building functionality of a CBDC, and (6) privacy features of the CBDC wallet app and back-end processes such as anonymity.

Chapter 7 The seventh chapter explores the sensitive issue of personal information privacy and puts forward some innovative and practical solutions, illustrating the important role that the public sector has in digital transformation. The chapter 'Insight and Control over Personal Data: A View from Sweden' is by Theodor Andersson. The research explores ways to increase citizen engagement and knowledge of the value and use of personal information as a way to offer better and more individualized services. There are some legal challenges that need to be investigated further so that they can be overcome, and an ecosystem can be implemented offering increased individual insight and control. The main focus of this research is on the potential conflict between an individual's right to gain further insight and control and the prerequisites and incentives for authorities to realize such insight and control. This research can inform a workable and sustainable solution for all the stakeholders on this important issue.

Chapter 8 Several chapters have identified how important the context is to digital transformation, so it is useful to see in this chapter the context of the service sector in India being explored. The chapter 'Digital Transformation in the Indian Service Sector: Benefits, Challenges and Future Implications' is by Ambika Kulshrestha, Sandeep Kulshrestha, Leonidas Efthymiou and Despo Ktoridou. The chapter examines the impact of digital transformation in four areas of the organization, namely culture, processes, people and business model. The findings show that positives outweigh the negatives, hence it can be deduced that technology was as per the expectations of most managers. However, considering the impact on each individual 'area', it can be easily deciphered that digitalization had neither a good nor a bad impact on the organizations. Interestingly, those who experience a positive impact by digitization are mostly chief executives and senior managers, whereas those who experience a negative impact are managers in middle and junior positions. Such findings reveal that digitization is experienced differently by people in different roles.

Chapter 9 The social implications of digital transformation are in the periphery of several of the other chapters, so it is beneficial that in this chapter they take centre stage. The chapter 'The Impact of Digital Transformation on the Sustainable Development of Social Innovation, Socio-ecological Resilience and Governance' José G. Vargas-Hernández, M. C. Omar C. Vargas-González and Leonidas Efthymiou. This chapter examines how digital transformation influences Social Innovation, along with its impact on socio-ecological resilience and governance. The analysis departs from the assumption that Social Innovation has a strong dependence relationship with socio-ecological resilience and governance. However, confronted with the imperatives of an increasingly digital work, social systems are challenged to maintain coherence and simultaneously explore innovating and sustainable paths. Therefore, we have to look more closely at Social Innovation alongside digital transformation. It is concluded that digital transformation is itself a form of Social Innovation. This is because digitization facilitates a framework of enhanced communication, problem-solving and knowledge sharing. Within this framework, digital transformation becomes a driver of Social Innovation, while it enables greater interconnection with socio-ecological resilience and governance.

References

Alt, R., Beck, R., & Smits, M. T. (2018). FinTech and the Transformation of the Financial Industry. *Electronic Markets, 28*(3), 235–243). Springer Verlag. https://doi.org/10.1007/s12525-018-0310-9

Bátiz-Lazo, B., & Efthymiou, L. (2016). The Book of Payments: Historical and Contemporary Views on the Cashless Society. In *The Book of Payments: Historical and Contemporary Views on the Cashless Society*. Palgrave Macmillan. https://doi.org/10.1057/978-1-137-60231-2

Bonnemains, V., Saurel, C., & Tessier, C. (2018). Embedded Ethics: Some Technical and Ethical Challenges. *Ethics and Information Technology, 20*(1), 41–58. https://doi.org/10.1007/s10676-018-9444-x

Gupta, A. S., & Mukherjee, J. (2022). Long-Term Changes in Consumers' Shopping Behavior Post-Pandemic: An Exploratory Study. *International Journal of Retail and Distribution Management, 50*(12), 1518–1534. https://doi.org/10.1108/IJRDM-04-2022-0111

Herbert, I., Milne, A., & Zarifis, A. (2019). Data Technologies and Next Generation Insurance Operations. *Journal of Financial Transformation, 50*, 110–117.

Hodson, D., & Quaglia, L. (2009). European Perspectives on the Global Financial Crisis: Introduction. *Journal of Common Market Studies, 47*(5), 939–953. https://doi.org/10.1111/j.1468-5965.2009.02029.x

Panetta, K. (2016). *10 management techniques from Born-Digital Companies*. https://www.gartner.com/smarterwithgartner/10-management-techniques-from-born-digital-

Pflaum, A., Prockl, G., Bodendorf, F., & Chen, H. (2019). *The Digital Supply Chain of the Future: Technologies, Applications and Business Models*. Proceedings of the 52nd Hawaii international conference on system sciences, January. https://doi.org/10.24251/hicss.2019.618

Purvis, B., Mao, Y., & Robinson, D. (2019). Three Pillars of Sustainability: In Search of Conceptual Origins. *Sustainability Science, 14*(3), 681–695. https://doi.org/10.1007/s11625-018-0627-5

Shi, L., Mai, Y., & Wu, Y. J. (2022). Digital Transformation: A Bibliometric Analysis. *Journal of Organizational and End User Computing, 34*(7), 1–20. https://doi.org/10.4018/JOEUC.302637

Slok-Wodkowska, M., & Mazur, J. (2021). The EU's Regional Trade Agreements: How the EU Addresses Challenges Related to Digital Transformation. *International Journal of Management and Economics, 57*(2), 105–120. https://doi.org/10.2478/ijme-2021-0009

Thrassou, A., Buhalis, D., Shahriar, A., & Efthymiou, L. (2022a). Tourism and Hospitality in the Digital Era: Technology and Its (im)Possibilities. *Euromed Journal of Business.*

Thrassou, A., Vrontis, D., Efthymiou, L., Weber, Y., Riad, S. M., & Tsoukatos, E. (2022b). In A. Thrassou, D. Vrontis, L. Efthymiou, Y. Weber, S. M. R. Shams, & E. Tsoukatos (Eds.), *Business Advancement Through Technology Volume II.* Springer International Publishing. https://doi.org/10.1007/978-3-031-07765-4

van Wynsberghe, A. (2021). Sustainable AI: AI for Sustainability and the Sustainability of AI. *AI and Ethics, 1*(3), 213–218. https://doi.org/10.1007/s43681-021-00043-6

Vial, G. (2019). Understanding Digital Transformation: A Review and a Research Agenda. *Journal of Strategic Information Systems, 28*(2), 118–144). Elsevier B.V. https://doi.org/10.1016/j.jsis.2019.01.003

Wilson, M., Paschen, J., & Pitt, L. (2022). The Circular Economy Meets Artificial Intelligence (AI): Understanding the Opportunities of AI for Reverse Logistics. *Management of Environmental Quality: An International Journal, 33*(1), 9–25. https://doi.org/10.1108/MEQ-10-2020-0222

Zarifis, A., & Cheng, X. (2023). AI Is Transforming Insurance With Five Emerging Business Models. In *Encyclopedia of Data Science and Machine Learning* (pp. 2086–2100). IGI Global. https://doi.org/10.4018/978-1-7998-9220-5.ch124

Zarifis, A., Kawalek, P., & Azadegan, A. (2021). Evaluating If Trust and Personal Information Privacy Concerns Are Barriers to Using Health Insurance That Explicitly Utilizes AI. *Journal of Internet Commerce, 20*(1), 66–83. https://doi.org/10.1080/15332861.2020.1832817

2

What Are We Automating? On the Need for Vision and Expertise When Deploying AI Systems

Alexander Rast, Vivek Singh, Steve Plunkett, Andrew Crean, and Fabio Cuzzolin

2.1 Introduction

The last two decades in business computing have seen the extraordinary development of Artificial Intelligence (AI) from a set of specialised techniques for niche applications to a mainstream set of tools. Deploying Artificial Intelligence (AI) solutions in a business context has become extremely fashionable but can easily be done without a critical appraisal of what the underlying use case is. *What is AI going to do* that cannot be

A. Rast (✉) • F. Cuzzolin
Visual AI Lab, Oxford Brookes University, Oxford, UK
e-mail: arast@brookes.ac.uk

V. Singh
Visual AI Lab, Oxford Brookes University, Oxford, UK

Supponor, Ltd., London, UK

S. Plunkett • A. Crean
Supponor, Ltd., London, UK

A. Zarifis et al. (eds.), *Business Digital Transformation*,
https://doi.org/10.1007/978-3-031-33665-2_2

achieved just as effectively by more mature (and arguably more transparent) technologies? A 'top-down' answer is typically not enough; it is, for instance, insufficient to say 'this AI will allow us to discover more profitable trading patterns' or 'that AI will enable a dynamic Web site with content tuned to the needs of a particular customer'. Discussion of end goals like this may motivate considering AI-based solutions, but they do not constitute the kind of formal specification that makes it possible to evaluate whether, much less what implementation of, an AI system will realise its high-level goals (Calegari et al., 2020). AI solutions tend to be narrowly domain specific, data dependent, and sensitive to implementation details. The crucial point to be understood here is that AI systems are not guaranteed to solve anything.

Because of this sensitivity, a business aiming to deploy AI successfully generally has to have, or develop, substantial in-house expertise even before beginning the design process. This is a crucial step in digital transformation. Most modern artificial intelligence methods use powerful but extremely nuanced mathematical techniques, and the in-house team will need to be, at least, conversant in these mathematical algorithms (and their associated pitfalls) to be able to make rational design choices. The first step in the design of a working AI system is (or perhaps, should be) the enumeration of the mathematical, data, and application assumptions involved; and this will need to be referred to often in order to make sure such assumptions are not being violated (or taken for granted). Most prominent in modern systems in the chain of assumptions are those about the nature and distribution of the data (Marcus, 2020).

An empirical approach to data collection or algorithm development generally yields inconsistent results. Design by trial and error tends to produce apparently working systems that then fail spectacularly when they encounter conditions outside the range of what had been thought of or tested ab initio (Cai & Koutsoukos, 2020). Data sensitivity is the most well known of these pathologies; even large companies have fallen afoul of this in situations that lead to serious PR embarrassments (The Guardian, 2018). Scaling is another major source of problems; it cannot be assumed that a system developed at prototype scale with a limited dataset will work at all, much less well, when scaled to a production environment (Brigato & Iocchi, 2020). The converse is true as well; attempts to scale down large systems to a streamlined, efficient solution do not always succeed; and the results are often problem dependent (Passalis & Tefas, 2018). Another emerging issue is cross-domain transfer and generalisability; it is almost hypnotically alluring to attempt to apply a working AI solution developed for one domain to another, which may even appear to be relatively similar—for example, to transfer the knowledge from a music recommendation system to one designed to recommend books. But again, results have often been uneven (Long et al., 2015b; Tan et al., 2017; Ramirez et al., 2019). The pattern that seems to emerge is that (well-designed) AI systems can transfer knowledge relatively well with *very* large systems and datasets, but smaller systems are less effective at such transfer (Hoefler et al., 2021). Quite aside from the fact that the largest-scale systems are out of scope for all but the largest, most well-resourced firms, a dilemma emerges: expend the resources, manpower, and development time to create one large 'omnibus' AI or develop a set of specialised AIs for each specialised task. Hence we return to the problem noted at the outset: *what is AI going to do*?

It is worth listing the major challenges involved in creating and deploying a successful AI system:

- Application scoping
- Problem specification
- Data acquisition, annotation, and curation
- Platform selection
- Model selection
- Model tuning
- System validation

This study will examine the practical implementation of a complex AI system in a real business case—a firm engaged in real-time media delivery for sporting events, transitioning from an older, physically based system to an AI-based approach. It will analyse the above challenges with a particular focus on the data acquisition, annotation, and curation problem (which turns out to dominate the considerations).

2.2 The General Background of AI

Before describing the specifics, it is useful to describe the general background of Artificial Intelligence to put solutions in context. As a computational discipline, the roots of practical AI extend back to the late 1950s, the 'traditional' birth date being the Dartmouth Workshop of 1956 (McCarthy et al., 1955). However, despite several start-stop waves of AI adoption involving various techniques, the modern era of AI did not truly start to take shape until the emergence and eventual dominance of neural network techniques, based largely on the so-called deep networks. What it means for a network to be 'deep' is somewhat vaguely defined, but it refers, in general, to a network with considerably more 'layers' (arrays of neurons) that either the two originally introduced in the Perceptron (Rosenblatt, 1958) (and later shown to be seriously limited by Minsky in 1969 (Minsky & Papert, 1969)) or the three shown to be sufficient to implement a universal function approximator (Hornik, 1991). Neural networks are often represented diagrammatically as large-scale parallel systems (Fig. 2.1); this provides a convenient conceptual understanding, but in fact, most computers represent neural networks as linear algebra operations over very large matrices.

Although they have a 'different' parallelism than their diagrammatic counterparts, such operations are very naturally suited to parallel systems and have become routinely implemented on specialised hardware, typically, Graphics Processing Units (e.g. nVIDIA RTX series) (https://www.nvidia.com/en-us/design-visualization/ampere-architecture/), (https://www.nvidia.com/en-gb/design-visualization/rtx-a6000/) that efficiently compute matrix-vector products, the core of neural networks in modern implementations. It is now understood that neural networks are an alternative formulation of Bayesian machine learning (Hoefler et al., 2021), which itself derives from the Bayesian reasoning systems that dominated AI in the early 2000s. Bayesian and other machine learning approaches still have significant applications and deployments in modern AI systems. In either case, similar challenges apply, but the deep neural network case can conveniently be used to illustrate many of the features of modern AI systems and indicate the main considerations.

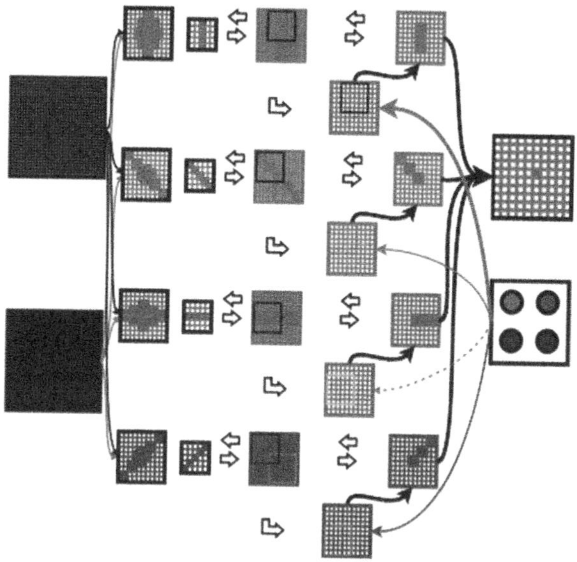

Fig. 2.1 A 'typical' modern deep convolutional neural network (CNN). Layers alternate between match-to-template convolutional layers and grouping 'max-pooling' layers, ending in fully connected layers to the 'heads'

Deep networks themselves have grown from relatively 'shallow' (in modern terms) networks involving 'only' 8–16 layers (Krizhevsky et al., 2012) to very large-scale systems with 100+ layers (He et al., 2016; Justus et al., 2018) (Fig. 2.2). The most popular forms of modern neural network are Convolutional Neural Networks (CNNs)—which internally do a complex match-to-template with the data (LeCun et al., 1998), and Transformers—which correlate data elements across sequences of data (Vaswani et al., 2017). Many other models exist, each offering some tradeoff of different capabilities for different classes of problem, but CNNs, in particular, are widely used in machine vision applications (Jiao et al., 2019; Abirami et al., 2020), which is completely rational considering their original inspiration in the visual cortex of humans and other mammals (Al-Aidroos et al., 2012). It is not thought CNNs actually implement the processing the visual cortex does, but the structural similarities do suggest some affinity. Most CNNs for real applications can be split into three structures. The 'backbone' is the early layers of the network

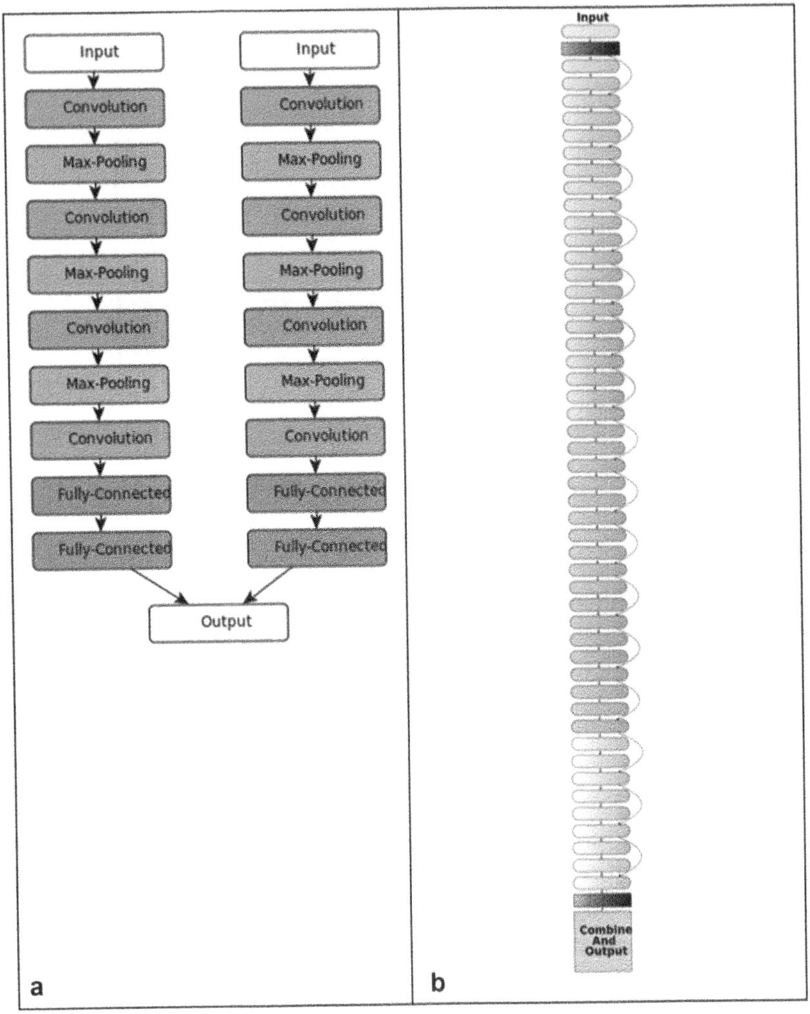

Fig. 2.2 CNN development. The network on the left has only 11 layers; by contrast the network on the right has 50 layers (and larger versions of the same ResNet architecture have up to 152). (**a**) A 'shallow' siamese CNN (Koch et al., 2015). (**b**) A 'deep' CNN (ResNet50) (He et al., 2016)

and is used for changing the input data representation into one the later network can use efficiently. Backbone networks are highly standard and go by names like AlexNet (Krizhevsky et al., 2012), VGG (Simonyan &

Zisserman, 2015), or ResNet (He et al., 2016). The 'neck' is the component that computes the statistical distributions and correlations that map input spaces to output spaces, for example, 'features' to 'classes' or 'blocks' to 'regions'. Neck structures are typically tuned to suit the application but remain general (and reusable) since their purpose is to produce universal representations. Typically a developer does not entirely hand-craft the neck but customises it from an off-the-shelf neck component. The 'head(s)' transforms the general patterns represented in the neck to the specific output representations needed for the particular application, for example, a set of labels such as 'ball', 'player', and 'grass'. There may be several heads (Masaki et al., 2021) representing different label classes or properties—and these are entirely designed by the developer for the specific use. It should thus be seen that in essence, what CNNs are actually doing is nothing more than juggling the representation. The entire process of a CNN consists of finding an output representation that efficiently encodes the latent information desired from the input data.

What has led, arguably, to the widespread adoption of CNNs and other deep neural networks is the emergence of 'frameworks', integrated toolchains that link naturally with hardware platforms like nVIDIA and allow a high-level specification to be compiled directly down into code heavily optimised for the hardware. Frameworks not only reduce the design cycle by allowing networks to be assembled in 'building-block'-like fashion from a library of standard components but also greatly improve the resultant performance by using powerful automated optimisations that replace what would otherwise be possibly months of hand-tuning. Popular frameworks include TensorFlow (https://www.tensorflow.org), PyTorch (https://pytorch.org), and Keras (https://keras.io) (names that may be familiar to many readers). These tools allow rapid application development and may appear to make neural network development entirely straightforward but feature significant quirks which must be dealt with and require considerable experience (Dai et al., 2022), (https://www.knowledgehut.com/blog/data-science/pytorch-vs-tensorflow). First, these frameworks are typically dependent on a very specific computer and operating system environment including particular versions of support libraries, hardware, and environment variables. Merely configuring a system to run any framework for the first time can take up to a week (or more). Environment-manager software like Conda (https://conda.io) can, at least, manage the software dependencies reasonably, but hardware is another matter—and typically the user or developer must match their framework version and installation to the hardware they actually have on their system. Second, different framework versions can yield different performance for the same networks, and this means that an AI developed on one system does not necessarily migrate neatly to another; indeed, it is frequently the case that older versions or hardware might yield better performance than newer versions (Shahriari et al., 2022). This, in turn, leads to a third quirk: results may not be reproducible; one cannot, for example, rely on published benchmark studies to decide upon networks because the performance (or even functionality!) reported in such articles may depend upon a particular setup ((Elshawi et al., 2021), and see, e.g. (https://pytorch.org/docs/stable/notes/randomness.html)). Overall, then, frameworks are an essential but temperamental part of modern AI development, rather like a Formula 1 race car: a high-performing vehicle but one which requires a competent driver and continuous maintenance by an expert crew.

It has already been noted that CNNs are really doing nothing more than finding efficient data representations. For them to do so, they need data, a LOT of data. The problem is more subtle than it may initially seem; essentially, since large-scale neural networks contain many millions or billions of weights (commonly called 'parameters' in modern terminology), they may have the representational power to encode the *entire* dataset, if the dataset is small (Hoefler et al., 2021). Therein lies the problem: if they do encode the entire dataset, the system is nothing more than a complex, opaque look-up table; the same results could have been had by simply storing the inputs as (input, class) pairs. This is useless; there is no 'intelligence' in this case because the network is not representing general properties of the system but simply mirroring the data, the well-known problem known as 'overfitting' (Shorten & Koshgoftaar, 2019). Overtraining happens whenever a suitably large network is presented with a suitably 'small' dataset for a long enough training time. For billions of weights, corresponding billions of data values need to be presented. But now this in turn creates a pair of related problems. First, training takes time; billions of data items may take weeks of time to process (Thompson et al., 2020), with enormous energy cost as well (Patterson et al., 2021), and this is likely entirely beyond the resources of most smaller firms, whilst being inefficient for larger firms (unless the result has unusually widespread application) (Brown et al., 2020). Second and more critically, using *supervised* learning methods, a very substantial chunk of this data needs to be annotated data—marked up with 'correct' identifications—and annotation is generally a tedious, labour-intensive manual process (Hinterstoisser et al., 2019). There are partial solutions from unsupervised or 'semi-supervised' learning methods (Ouali et al., 2020; Li et al., 2022), but these are not usually complete, are typically less accurate, and involve even longer training times. Solving the data problem is now being discovered to be perhaps the crux issue in AI deployment, as indeed will be seen in the case study presented here.

2.3 Case Study: Background

The company to be considered, Supponor, Ltd. (http://www.supponor.com), is an emerging market leader in the field of targeted advertising provision. Specifically, Supponor operates at sporting events, to take LED billboards or other advertising placement points on the field or venue of play, and substitute the locally visible content for content more suitably targeted to the regions or countries where the event is being broadcast live via television. The problem is very dynamic: Supponor's systems must be able to detect the regions of advertising content from the video stream, blank out these regions, and substitute different content without accidentally blanking out critical video, such as players and balls. All of this must be done in real time, at full frame rate, whilst considering problems of, for example, distortion in the image, altered aspect ratio due to camera angle, transient occlusions, weather, and lighting contrast across the scene. Supponor initially entered into the market using proprietary physical technology directly installed on the field of play to be able to perform the real-time substitutions. However, the system was cumbersome, installation and setup time was significant, cost to the sporting organisation was considerable, and the system represented a fixed capital investment with significant risks. As time went on it was clear there were further problems with diversification and expansion: a system installed for a given venue or sport did not easily transfer to different venues or sports; progressive changes within the sport either to play or to venue facilities could mean opportunities lost and/or costly changes to the installed system; the approach relied on long-term commitments from sporting organisations (generally, the leagues or associations in the relevant country for the relevant sport); the system was vulnerable to physical faults or disruptions; and perhaps most critically, the start-up costs were more than all but the most well-resourced organisations (generally, the 'premier' leagues in big-market sports) could afford. In short, the fixed-installation nature of their existing technology prevented an agile business model. Supponor decided, therefore, to consider the possibility of full digital replacement, based purely on the video data as processed by an AI for video scene understanding. Their experience provides a good example of digital transformation in practice.

The company was put in contact with leading experts from Oxford Brookes University with a strong background in scene understanding; in particular, members of the Visual AI Lab (VAIL) (https://www.brookes.ac.uk/research/units/tde/groups/visual-artificial-intelligence-laboratory), led by Prof. Fabio Cuzzolin. The VAIL team outlined a programme of work aimed at exploring the feasibility of using digital replacement approaches—technology that could not only substitute for the existing system but add additional capabilities, such as the ability to transfer directly to new sports or venues with little start-up time, or to overlay advertisements not just on the raw video, but potentially on that supplied by third-party broadcasters who have already overlain additional data layers (e.g. a running 'score ticker' at the bottom of the screen). The groups agreed to develop a Knowledge Transfer Partnership (KTP) with a dual purpose: on the one hand, to explore state-of-the-art AI video replacement solutions, and on the other to promote the development of the necessary in-house expertise in AI noted in the introduction to permit Supponor to continue forward with further developments. KTPs are a particular funding route supported by UK Research and Innovation (UKRI) (https://www.ukri.org/opportunity/knowledge-transfer-partnership/), the UK's national research funding body, to support close collaborations between industry and academia, particularly for de-risking exercises and/or development of in-house knowledge in leading-edge research at the margins of commercial viability. The project was eminently suited to this type of funding arrangement; work began in September 2021.

Forming such partnerships, however, takes time, and in the period between the initial contact between Supponor and Brookes, and the start of the actual project, Supponor itself had already begun the preliminary development of all-digital replacement technology. Much of this was in recognition of the clear limits of the original physical approach. But additional drivers included further developments in their target sports, particularly football, Supponor's initial primary area of focus (and in which they have by far the largest market penetration). There, the introduction of features like second rows of billboards and advertising 'carpets' placed directly on the pitch offered new opportunities that could not be exploited with the existing system. Furthermore, diversification into additional sports such as basketball (in the NBA) and hockey (the NHL) presented a complex roll-out roadmap with considerable start-up time for organisations eager to go 'live' early and at a large scale. Only all-digital replacement could solve these problems, and so Supponor built its own internal technical development group and an initial all-digital system, borrowing heavily from the existing technology, with a plan to transition away from the physical installations as quickly as the AI-based technology could mature. The state-of-play at the beginning of the project was thus that Supponor had what could be considered a prototype all-digital system (albeit in real deployments), but with significant limitations to its use or future potential.

2.4 The Supponor Experience

In spite of the extremely early nature of the new digital solution, Supponor's initial experience was reasonably positive. Deployments in football largely worked as a drop-in replacement for the physical technology with minimal start-up time; perhaps this was not surprising given Supponor's extensive experience and deployments in football. Viewer familiarity with the displayed effects also no doubt played a role; it is considerably easier to deploy replacement technologies with marginally different behaviour to an audience already familiar with the overall effect than it is to introduce hitherto unseen technologies to completely inexperienced audiences not expecting significant changes to their existing experience.

An object lesson in how this can come into play was encountered in deployment to the NHL. Supponor itself was, in fact, well aware of the limitations and potential for teething problems and strongly recommended a cautious roll-out, but NHL management was eager to get the system live at full scale across the league early and opted for a very aggressive roll-out plan. Given that there were no immediate technology concerns, just a *general* sense at Supponor that an ambitious deployment schedule would be inviting trouble, the groups proceeded with immediate roll-out. As things happened, the technical issues encountered revolved not around the AI components, which generally worked acceptably, but on integration issues such as video format, display resolution, and hardware. These generated a spike of technical support load for Supponor, but the larger problem was how these relatively minor issues affected the viewer experience. Although the roll-out was by and large successful, it produced something of an Internet backlash amongst die-hard NHL fans who felt that the resulting effects were too visually intrusive or noticeable (Nixon, 2022). In turn, this wave of outrage generated a group of fans using their own video tools to isolate and characterise particular artefacts in the video stream which would probably pass for unnoticed to the casual observer, but pointed out in this way, suddenly became very distracting. As a consequence, Supponor was bombarded by a wave of online criticism, arguably unfairly directed at them, because they had already been keenly aware of the limitations of the existing system. This demonstrates that it is not only important that a company have in-house expertise in AI but also that they need to be able to communicate this effectively to their user base so that users do not end up with unrealistic expectations.

A level-headed analysis suggests that what was necessary in this situation was to temper expectations carefully for all parties. Undoubtedly, the NHL moved extremely aggressively and underestimated the strength of fan discontent, particularly with regard to heavily intrusive or distracting advertisements that quite literally drew attention to themselves. This is to be contrasted with the cautious plan adopted by the Bundesliga in Germany, which requires extensive system validation *and* continuous analysis following each match to retain certification. Perhaps surprisingly, Supponor itself may have ended up being aided by the NHL experience because fan response provided an unforeseen torrent of debugging information. In essence, the group of disgruntled fans provided free identification of artefacts at scale without being so overwhelming in number as to colour the largely positive experience of the majority. Further disruptions are likely to decrease in scale as viewers become 'acclimatised' and the identified issues are ironed out. However, these transitions could have been made more smoothly if the roll-out had been preceded by a period of pilot trials and perhaps focus groups amongst the fan base—lessons which apply equally to any would-be deployer of state-of-the-art AI solutions.

Teething pains aside, Supponor's immediate transition to AI technology has been surprisingly rapid and successful. At the end of 2021 the company was just starting to transition, and their combined physical/virtual deployments amounted to 800, up from about 150 from the previous year. By contrast, at the end of 2022, the company foresees 3000 deployments (matches/events covered), the greatest part of the increase coming from the NHL deployment of approximately 1400 games (it should be noted that the scale of this roll-out alone, compared to the comparatively conservative growth in football roll-outs the previous year, indicates the ambitiousness of the NHL schedule). However, the jump from 150 to 800 and then subsequently to 3000 was entirely driven by the virtual technology—demonstrating how rapidly AI has overtaken the physical technology. Revenue growth was likewise strong, a gain of 140% between the 2021–22 and 2022–23 financial years. The company has now started to work with Formula 1, which, following the more cautious approach recommended, has seen a successful pilot project form the basis of talks for a more long-term, wide-scale deployment. AI will be particularly important here because the international nature of F1 and the extremely unique, individual nature of each venue more-or-less necessitate off-site processing not tied to a physical installation—something the virtual solution enables which had previously been infeasible. The question then may be—what is left for the KTP to explore? Has not Supponor negotiated the learning curve in the digital transformation successfully, and do they not, as a result, have the required in-house expertise already?

2.5 Crafting State-of-the-Art Solutions

At first glance, it may seem like Supponor has already solved most, if not all, of the major issues involved in transitioning to an AI virtualisation solution. However, the truth—hinted at in who Supponor is working with—is that this process is still relatively expensive and resource intensive. The AI must, in essence, be hand-crafted for each new sport, and less potential has been observed for cross-domain transfer than might have been hoped under the existing approach. Sports with relatively similar game play and venue setup like hockey and football might, for example, offer hope that the system could be generalised to work with an arbitrary such 'players on a pitch' format, yet the systems themselves are individual for each. F1, meanwhile, presents an entirely new class of sport with little expectation of direct transfer, and developing what is in essence a new system from the ground up requires considerable compute as well as human resources over many months. What is needed is an approach that can somehow generalise across sports, to the overall *class* of video infilling, and this involves moving from simple video segmentation (bounding different objects in a scene) to true video understanding (identifying the type of object bounded and being able to characterise—and predict—its behaviour). If then, the original aim of the KTP was to build expertise and develop a proof-of-concept, the goal has now changed: a proof-of-concept exists together with some in-house expertise, but what is wanted now is a more general system and a shift of design approach away from ad-hoc, hand-crafted AIs towards ones based on more universal, generalisable methods.

Originally the analysis focussed on so-called whole-scene understanding. Supponor's existing virtual AI method trains only on cropped or masked patches of the original video stream—isolating the areas thought to be of interest and then implementing limited scene segmentation within those areas. This has strong similarities with the '2-stage' models (He et al., 2017) often used in perception systems for applications like autonomous driving: an initial model separates regions and a second stage of processing segments within the region by applying class labels. However, recent research suggests such 2-stage models may be discarding global information across the scene that can inform segmentation, in other words, that can provide further conditioning on the posterior region probabilities. 'End-to-end' systems (Long et al., 2015a) produce segmented objects without any division into regions; this is particularly useful for the case of relatively slow-moving objects which, over a series of frames, smoothly change position in the visual field; many sports have this characteristic, and so an end-to-end system based on full semantic segmentation of the scene appears to make sense (Fig. 2.3). It was also thought that this might allow better cross-domain transfer, as the network is learning general properties of segmentable shapes, rather than properties of objects of a specific expected size or shape within the visual field.

However, it became quickly apparent that traditional full-scene segmentation faced a daunting barrier: the need for labelled data. For semantic segmentation to work, typical systems require training using large

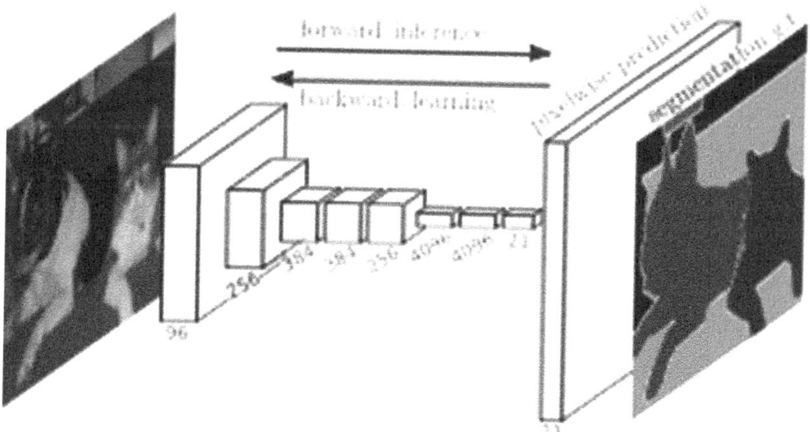

Fig. 2.3 End-to-end convolutional network for semantic segmentation. (From Long et al. (2015a))

datasets annotated with the ground truth for both regions and labels. Thus, for example, a player on the pitch has to be given both an outline and a label indicating this object is of class 'player'. It does not take long to realise that with complex, variable shapes like players, labelling video images will be a tedious and time-consuming process; many players in many postures and locations will have to be hand-annotated, the pixel boundaries may not be clear-cut, and if two objects intersect on the field, it is not immediately obvious how they should be segmented, particularly if prediction is desired for the next frame. Existing training data was, for the most part, only partial frames, which makes sense in the case of Supponor's first-generation AI system but would not be useful to develop a full-scene understanding model. For new generations of AI to be deployed, some method of generating labelled data rapidly, cheaply, and at scale would be essential, and it became very apparent that this challenge, indeed, would dominate the entire process of transitioning to a virtual AI system.

2.6 The Data Gap

The basic problem—the 'data gap'—is starting to be understood throughout the AI industry as one of the most formidable ones to overcome. Generating large, *labelled* datasets is both labour intensive and time consuming. There are firms that specialise in manual annotation of datasets, typically by outsourcing the annotation to a contract labour pool, for example, Mindy (https://mindy-support.com/services-post/data-annotation-services) and Qualitas Global (https://www.qualitas-global.com), but for the scale of annotation that makes effective training possible, costs remain significant. Quotes for annotation of only 2000 frames of data for Supponor ranged from about $11,000 to about $27,000; and it was generally thought that this volume of labelled frames is not sufficient in itself (i.e. without the use of other 'data augmentation' methods) to train a full-scene understanding system to a production standard.

This is a cost often overlooked in the deployment of AI systems. Research articles often quote impressive state-of-the-art performance figures for tasks like semantic segmentation (Chen et al., 2018), but these articles often conceal two hard truths. In the first instance, many articles are written focussing on established standard benchmark datasets. Such datasets have typically been assembled by large teams or consortia over many years and reflect a very large prior investment (Lin et al., 2014). Furthermore, standard benchmark datasets may be somewhat informative as to *abstract* performance capabilities of a system but are typically not tuned to *specific* application requirements and are not suitable for training models for production applications. Some cross-domain transfer is possible, but results are often disappointing (Zhang & Davison, 2020; Zhang et al., 2021). In the second instance, state-of-the-art figures are often quoted in articles (Chen et al., 2020; Wang et al., 2021a) by large research teams working for the very largest firms in the field, for example, Google, Amazon, or Microsoft, who are lavishly resourced in computer hardware, staffing, and access to data sources. Such a level of data access is not generally available to most firms. Indeed, many times access to data is blocked behind paywalls, as companies, increasingly aware of the value of data, understandably attempt to monetise their assets. Frequently, this is at rates that, while reflecting the labour involved in their creation, remain utterly inaccessible to small- and medium-sized enterprises (SMEs). When one considers that even how much value the dataset would have to the customer company may not be easily assessable without prior access to the data itself and some pilot trials, it becomes hard to justify what looks like a risky fixed investment in what could turn out to be a 'pig in a poke'.

For *specialised* domains such as Supponor's video-infill case, useful data may be unavailable even if the company has the resources to purchase it from an external source. Existing datasets, whether open-access or pay-for-play, tend to focus on general scene understanding for generic scenes or videos—the sort of application most useful, for example, to label photos on an Internet picture gallery or provide annotations for a film database. This may be useful to mass-market content providers but is of less interest to domain specialist companies, especially those whose business model is primarily B2B focussing on the needs of client organisations rather than end consumers. A quick inspection made it clear that there was very, very little in the way of pre-existing datasets for the Supponor case. Hence there was a decision to be made: spend the time and money on extensive hand annotation or look for alternative methods to bridge the data gap.

2.7 Solutions to the Data Gap

Efforts examined a variety of approaches. These include using standard automated 'data augmentation' strategies (Shorten & Koshgoftaar, 2019) to expand Supponor's existing labelled datasets; use of simulation to create complete 'virtual worlds' that come automatically available with ground-truth information (because it is inherent to the simulation itself'); hybrid approaches combining both limited full-scene understanding and local scene segmentation similar to Supponor's existing system; unsupervised and 'semi-supervised' (Wang et al., 2019; Chen et al., 2020) learning techniques that can bootstrap the learning to the point where a smaller labelled dataset is sufficient to fine-tune the system; enhanced annotation tools that permit faster and more automated manual annotation and simply 'biting the bullet' and outsourcing a large dataset to an annotation firm.

Even the most cursory look at the costs involved in hand annotation—as seen above—quickly eliminated the full-annotation approach at the outset. Much more than $20K would not have been economically justified given uncertainty of outcomes—nor was it within the budget of the KTP. Data augmentation and hybrid strategies were also quickly eliminated, in part by early trials that performed poorly, but more realistically, because transferring a partial-scene dataset to full-scene dataset would be complex, error prone, and dependent on prior assumptions. The simulation approach was looked at more seriously; the existence of game engines that, for example, include football and hockey hinted at the possibility of progress. As a future research direction for the general annotation problem, such simulation-based approaches look promising because, in principle, they can automatically generate arbitrary volumes of labelled data with almost infinite permutations (Hinterstoisser et al., 2019). However, again, a realistic appraisal concluded that game engines and other simulation platforms are complex systems with steep learning curves, the required expertise lay outside the skill sets of the team, and it was not at all immediately clear that off-the-shelf or even fully bespoke in-house simulation would be sufficiently similar to the real world to be useful for training. Simulation remains a very promising avenue for future exploration but in the present is too dependent on personnel with matching skills.

The remaining options were to leverage special-purpose annotation tools and to explore unsupervised and partially supervised methods. Supponor developed contacts with V7 Labs (https://www.v7labs.com), a firm offering a semi-automated annotation tool that promises dramatic reduction in annotation time. Although it was not yet definitely clear that it would reduce the costs to annotate significantly, it was reasoned that, given that the tool could potentially improve annotations for the *production* team working on Supponor's existing AI solution as well as for the *research* team in the KTP, a trial was justified. A quick series of tests followed and resulted in the following conclusions. First, it was found that indeed the annotation time dropped significantly—from hours per frame to around 45 minutes per frame. Second, the annotator could be used to edit frames automatically annotated using other AI methods to produce accurate ground-truth data efficiently using a combination of automatic and manual methods. Finally, it was also concluded that whilst these results were effective and certainly justified the purchase of the V7 tool, they would still be inadequate for the extent of data required.

Almost inevitably, then, the group was looking at using unsupervised/semi-supervised methods. As it happened, such approaches were already built into the project, so these already looked like attractive options, but they were brought significantly forward in the project timeline by the pressing need to be able to use a minimum of hand-labelled data. Very recently, 'self-supervised' techniques which use information metrics to extract latent data have suddenly gained traction and seen promising reported results in the literature (Lai et al., 2020; Wang et al., 2021b). In part, this may be because the limitations of hand annotation and supervised learning are now becoming very evident to all research AI practitioners. Nevertheless, it is an emerging field, not one where many firms have existing in-house expertise, and indeed, it lies entirely outside the experience of the existing Supponor technical team. By contrast, the KTP

Fig. 2.4 Example of preliminary results from self-supervised learning on benchmark datasets. From presentation to KTP LMC4 meeting presentation, 29 November 2022

partners at Brookes were already looking into these methods intensively and have some preliminary results, so it has proven a natural fit to extend these methods into the Supponor project, with the aim not only to improve the system but to embed the knowledge and expertise brought to the in-house team and create a core capability extending Supponor's competitive advantage. Results (Fig. 2.4) thus far have been confined to benchmark datasets but already suggest that a semi-supervised learning stage can automate annotations to about 65% accuracy—not enough, yet, for production-quality full-scene understanding but enough to reduce the manual annotation requirements to a few thousand frames.

A staged path of development has been established with a network successively augmented by self-supervised pre-training, partially supervised training, and fine-tuned training with full manual annotation using the V7 tools (Fig. 2.5).

It is still early to conclude exactly how effective this pipeline will be. It is, however, abundantly clear that this would not have been possible without the KTP partnership to transfer research expertise to the commercial environment.

2.8 Conclusions

The overall experience of both Supponor and Brookes in the KTP powerfully reinforces how critical it is for firms to understand fully the technical as well as business implications of automation using AI. In-house expertise is vital if initiatives are to be successful; without it, a company

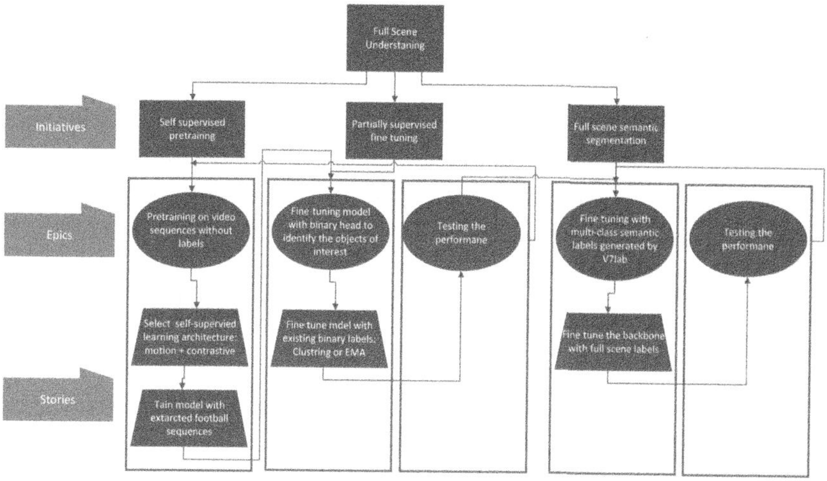

Fig. 2.5 Development path. The system is being evolved from a self-supervised initial setup to a network ultimately implementing full-scene segmentation with a combination of annotated and unannotated data pre-trained using self-supervised learning. From presentation to KTP LMC4, 29 November 2022

on the one hand is ill-prepared to handle the unexpected pitfalls of AI development, and on the other unable to take advantage of recent developments in a field still rapidly advancing. Indeed, Supponor has quickly recognised the importance of this and as a result has begun forming an in-house *research* team (based in France) to supplement the *development* team (based in Finland). The two teams have complementary roles; the development team is responsible for day-to-day deployments, bugfixes, and maintenance of the existing system, whilst the research team is responsible for taking recent advances from the academic research community and translating them into a strategic technology roadmap for the future. The Supponor-Brookes KTP, meanwhile, is a direct link into academic research at the edge of the state-of-the-art—an information conduit that gives Supponor access to skills and technologies beyond the commercial horizon. Where this leads to remains to be seen, but it seems clear that Supponor is now on a rapidly ascending trajectory with its wholehearted embrace of a fully virtual AI content infill technology.

The entire process has also put the spotlight strongly on the data-generation problem. It appears that for AI development of the future, this will dominate research, over and above even the creation of new models. In the past AI was thought about mostly as automating the problem of data *processing*; the future appears headed towards data *creation*. Both the research and the software pipeline under investigation in the Supponor-Brookes KTP now look more like a process to automate the generation of information using AI and machine learning methods than it is to automate their interpretation. Perhaps fittingly, this is where Supponor started: the entire business is based on creative content infill; it now appears that their AI systems of the future will be performing content infill on themselves. In the end, AI may work best when it embodies the intelligence built into the company deploying it.

References

Abirami, R. N., Vincent, P. M. D. R., Srinivasan, K., Tariq, U., & Chang, C.-Y. (2020). Deep CNN and Deep GAN in Computational Visual Perception-Driven Image Analysis. *Complexity, 2021*, 5541134.

Al-Aidroos, N., Said, C. P., & Turk-Browne, N. B. (2012). Top-Down Attention Switches Coupling Between Low-Level and High-Level Areas of Human Visual Cortex. *Proceedings of the National Academy of Sciences of the United States of America, 109*(35), 4.

Brigato, L., & Iocchi, L. (2020). *A Close Look at Deep Learning with Small Data.* Proceedings of 25th International Conference on Pattern Recognition (ICPR 2020).

Brown, T., et al. (2020). Language Models are Few-Shot Learners. *arXiv:2005.14165*.

Cai, F., & Koutsoukos, X. (2020). *Real-time Out-of-distribution detection in Learning-Enabled Cyber-Physical Systems.* Proceedings of the 11th ACM/IEEE International Conference on Cyber-Physical Systems (ICCPS).

Calegari, R., Ciatto, G., Denti, E., & Omicini, A. (2020). Logic-Based Technologies for Intelligent Systems: State of the Art and Perspectives. *Information, 11*, 167.

Chen, L.-C., Zhu, Y., Papandreou, G., Schroff, F., & Adam, H. (2018). *Encoder-Decoder with Atrous Separable Convolution for Semantic Image Segmentation.*

Proceedings of 2018 European Conference on Computer Vision (ECCV 2018).

Chen, L.-C., Lopes, R. G., Cheng, B., Collins, M. D., Cubuk, E. D., Zoph, B., Adam, H., & Shlens, J. (2020). *Naive-Student: Leveraging Semi-Supervised Learning n Video Sequences for Urban Scene Segmentation.* Proceedings of 2020 European Conference on Computer Vision (ECCV 2020).

Dai, H., Peng, X., Shi, X., He, L., Xiong, Q., & Jin, H. (2022). Reveal Training Performance Mystery Between TensorFlow and PyTorch in the Single GPU Environment. *Science China: Information Sciences, 65*, 112103.

Elshawi, R., Wahab, A., Barnawi, A., & Sakr, S. (2021). DLBench: A Comprehensive Experimental Evaluation of Deep Learning Frameworks. *Cluster Computing, 24*, 2017.

He, K., Zhang, X., Ren, S., & Sun, J. (2016). *Deep Residual Learning for Image Recognition.* Proceedings of 2016 International Conference on Computer Vision and Pattern Recognition (CVPR 2016).

He, K., Gkioxari, G., Dollár, P., & Girshick, R. (2017). *Mask R-CNN.* Proceedings of 2017 IEEE International Conference on Computer Vision and Pattern Recognition (CVPR 2017).

Hinterstoisser, S., Pauly, O., Heibel, H., Marek, M., & Bokeloh, M. (2019). *An Annotation Saved is an Annotation Earned: Using Fully Synthetic Training for Object Detection.* Proceedings of 2019 International Conference on Computer Vision (ICCV 2019).

Hoefler, T., Alistarh, D., Ben-Nun, T., Dryden, N., & Peste, A. (2021). Sparsity in Deep Learning: Pruning and Growth for Efficient Inference and Training in Neural Networks. *Journal of Machine Learning Research, 23*, 1.

Hornik, K. (1991). Approximation Capabilities of Multilayer Feedforward Networks. *Neural Networks, 4*(2), 251.

Jiao, L., Zhang, F., Liu, F., Yang, S., Li, L., Feng, Z., & Qu, R. (2019). A Survey of Deep Learning-Based Object Detection. *IEEE Access, 7*, 1.

Justus, D., Brennan, J., Bonner, S., & McGough, A. S. (2018). *Predicting the Computational Cost of Deep Learning Models.* Proceedings of the 2018 IEEE International Conference on Big Data.

Koch, G., Zemel, R., & Salakhutdinov, R. (2015). *Siamese Neural Networks for One-Shot Image Recognition.* Proceedings of 32nd International Conference on Machine Learning (ICML 2015).

Krizhevsky, A., Sutskever, I., & Hinton, G. E. (2012). *ImageNet Classification with Deep Convolutional Neural Networks.* Advanced Neural Information Processing Systems 25 (NIPS 2012).

Lai, Z., Lu, E., & Xie, W. (2020). *MAST: A Memory-Augmented Self-Supervised Tracker*. Proceedings of 2020 IEEE Conference on Computer Vision and Pattern Recognition (CVPR 2020).

LeCun, Y., Bottou, Y., Bengio, Y., & Haffner, P. (1998). Gradient-Based Learning Applied to Document Recognition. *Proceedings of the IEEE, 86*(11), 2278.

Li, L., Zhou, T., Wang, W., Yang, L., Li, J., & Yang, Y. (2022). *Locality-Aware Inter-and Intra-Video Reconstruction for Self-Supervised Correspondence Learning*. Proceedings of 2022 IEEE Conference on Computer Vision and Pattern Recognition (CVPR 2022).

Lin, T.-S., Maire, M., Belongie, S., Hays, J., Perona, P., Ramanan, D., Dollár, P., & Zitnick, C. L. (2014). *Microsoft COCO: Common Objects in Context*. Proceedings of 2014 European Conference on Computer Vision (ECCV 2014).

Long, J., Shelhamer, E., & Darrell, T. (2015a). *Fully Convolutional Networks for Semantic Segmentation*. Proceedings of 2015 International Conference on Computer Vision and Pattern Recognition (CVPR 2015).

Long, M., Cao, Y., Wang, J., & Jordan, M. I. (2015b). *Learning Transferable Features with Deep Adaptation Networks*. Proceedings of 32nd International Conference on Machine Learning (ICML 2015).

Marcus, G. (2020). *The Next Decade in AI: Four Steps Towards Robust Artificial Intelligence*. arXiv:2002.06177.

Masaki, S., Hirakawa, T., Yamashita, T., & Fujiyoshi, H. (2021). *Multi-Domain Semantic-Segmentation using Multi-Head Model*. Proceedings of 2021 IEEE Intelligent Transportation Systems Conference (ITSC 2021).

McCarthy, J., Minsky, M. L., Rochester, N., & Shannon, C. E. (1955). *Proposal for the Dartmouth Summer Research Project on Artificial Intelligence*. Tech. Rep., Dartmouth College.

Minsky, M. L., & Papert, S. (1969). *Perceptrons: An Introduction to Computational Geometry*. MIT Press.

Nixon, G. (2022, 15 Oct). The Ads Are Virtual, But for Some NHL Fans, the Irritation is Real. *Canadian Broadcasting Company (CBC) News*.

Ouali, Y., Hudelot, C., & Tami, M. (2020). *Semi-Supervised Semantic Segmentation with Cross-Consistency Training*. Proceedings of 2020 Conference on Computer Vision and Pattern Recognition (CVPR 2020).

Passalis, N., & Tefas, A. (2018). *Learning Deep Representations with Probabilistic Knowledge Transfer*. Proceedings of 2018 European Conference on Computer Vision (ECCV 2018).

Patterson, D., Gonzalez, J., Le, Q., Liang, C., & Munguia, L.-M. (2021). *Carbon Emissions and Large Neural Network Training*. arXiv:2104.10350.

Ramirez, P. Z., Tonioni, A., Salti, S., & Di Stefano, L. (2019). *Learning Across Tasks and Domains*. Proceedings of 2019 International Conference on Computer Vision (ICCV 2019).

Rosenblatt, F. (1958). The Perceptron: A Probabilistic Model for Information Storage and Organization in the Brain. *Psychological Review, 65*(6), 386.

Shahriari, M., Ramler, R., & Fischer, L. (2022). How Do Deep-Learning Framework Versions Affect the Reproducibility of Neural Network Models? *Machine Learning and Knowledge Extraction, 4*, 888.

Shorten, C., & Koshgoftaar, T. M. (2019). A Survey on Image Data Augmentation for Deep Learning. *Journal of Big Data, 6*, 60.

Simonyan, K., & Zisserman, A. (2015). *Very Deep Convolutional Networks for Large-Scale Image Recognition*. Proceedings of 2015 International Conference on Learning Representations.

Tan, B., Zhang, Y., Pan, S. J., & Yang, Q. (2017). *Distant Domain Transfer Learning*. Proceedings of 31st AAAI Conference on Artificial Intelligence (AAAI17).

The Guardian. (2018). Google's Solution to Accidental Algorithmic Racism: Ban Gorillas. *The Guardian*.

Thompson, N. C., Greenewald, K., Lee, K., & Manso, G. F. (2020). The Computational Limits of Deep Learning. *MIT Initiative on the Digital Economy Research Brief*, 4.

Vaswani, A., Shazeer, N., Parmar, N., Uszkoreit, J., Jones, L., Gomez, A. N., Kaiser, L., & Polosukhin, I. (2017). *Attention Is All You Need*. Advances in Neural Information Processing Systems 31 (NIPS 2017).

Wang, W., Song, H., Zhao, S., Shen, J., Zhao, S., Hoi, S., & Ling, H. (2019). *Learning Unsupervised Video Object Segmentation Through Visual Attention*. Proceedings of 2019 IEEE Conference on Computer Vision and Pattern Recognition (CVPR 2019).

Wang, H., Jiang, X., Ren, H., Hu, Y., & Bai, S. (2021a). *SwiftNet: Real-time Video Object Segmentation*. Proceedings of 2021 IEEE Conference on Computer Vision and Pattern Recognition (CVPR 2021).

Wang, N., Zhou, W., & Li, H. (2021b). *Contrastive Transformation for Self-Supervised Correspondence Learning*. Proceedings of 35th AAAI Conference on Artificial Intelligence (AAAI-21).

Zhang, Y., & Davison, B. D. (2020). *Impact of ImageNet Model Selection on Domain Adaptation*. Proceedings of 2020 IEEE Winter Applications of Computer Vision Workshops (WACVW 2020).

Zhang, G., Zhao, H., Yu, Y., & Poupart, P. (2021). *Quantifying and Improving Transferability in Domain Generalization*. Advances in Neural Information Processing Systems 35 (NeurIPS 2021).

Alexander Rast is Senior Lecturer in Computer Science at Oxford Brookes University. He is a member of the Artificial Intelligence and Robotics research group and affiliated with the Visual AI Laboratory. He has close partnerships with several other research groups including the Autonomous Driving and Intelligent Transport group and the Institute for Ethical AI. His research interests focus on neural networks, with an emphasis on hardware implementations of spiking neural systems (neuromorphic chips). He is particularly concerned with embedded and robotic applications of neural networks (both spiking and nonspiking) and has worked on perception, visual attention, language grounding, and neuromorphic-robotic integration. Along with Fabio Cuzzolin he is one of the two academic supervisors for the Brookes-Supponor Knowledge Transfer Partnership.

Vivek Singh is the Knowledge Transfer Partnership (KTP) Associate for the Brookes-Supponor KTP. His background includes previous work with the Visual AI Laboratory on models for visual semantic segmentation in the surgical operating theatre under the SARAS project. His research focusses on scene understanding, semantic scene segmentation, object and action detection and recognition, and facial expression analysis.

Steve Plunkett is the Chief Product Officer for Supponor, Ltd. and has overall technical responsibility for Supponor's AIR digital replacement technology. He is the KTP company supervisor for the project and has day-to-day responsibility for managing progress.

Andrew Crean is the Chief Financial Officer for Supponor and is the Chairman of the KTP Local Management Committee (LMC), with overall oversight of the entire project. He sets strategic directions for the project and ensures research objectives are matched with Supponor technical and market requirements.

Fabio Cuzzolin is Professor of Computing at Oxford Brookes University and the director of the Visual AI Laboratory. He is the lead academic in the Brookes-Supponor Knowledge Transfer Partnership and is currently PI for eight funded projects with a total budget of £5,000,000. Professor Cuzzolin's research focusses on artificial intelligence and its applications to computer vision and robotics. As founder in 2012 of OBU's Visual Artificial Intelligence Laboratory he has been conducting work at the boundaries of computer vision. In particular the Lab is world-leading in deep learning for detecting and recognising human actions, as evidenced by some of the best detection accuracies to date and the first system (2017) able to detect multiple action instances in a streaming video in real time. The work has been highly cited in the field and has led publications in top computer vision journals such as IEEE PAMI and IJCV. Parts of the technology are being spun off as the foundations for a start-up company. The team's focus has now shifted towards issues at the boundaries of visual AI, such as the modelling via deep learning of complex activities performed by multiple people and agents, the predicting of future events and intentions, and the creation of a machine theory of mind.

3

Blockchain in the Aviation Industry: A Decentralized Solution to the Transparency Issue in Baggage Handling

Mads Jørgsholm Bierrings, Gerishanth Sivakumar, and Nico Wunderlich

3.1 Baggage Handling as a Constraint of Growth in the Aviation Industry

The aviation industry has experienced tremendous growth in recent decades and is expected to recover and surpass pre-covid traveller numbers by 2024 (IATA, 2018, 2022a). This expansion has put additional strain on airport capacity and operations. However, one of the most important aspects of the flying experience—secure and reliable baggage handling—continues to rely on legacy technology from the previous century. Baggage handling, as to many other operations in the aviation

---

M. J. Bierrings (✉) • G. Sivakumar
Copenhagen Business School, Frederiksberg, Denmark
e-mail: madsbierrings@gmail.com; geri.sivakumar@live.com

N. Wunderlich
IT University of Copenhagen, Copenhagen, Denmark
e-mail: nicw@itu.dk

A. Zarifis et al. (eds.), *Business Digital Transformation*,
https://doi.org/10.1007/978-3-031-33665-2_3

industry, involves many stakeholders. These stakeholders collaborate to maintain a complex logistic chain of distributed activities at international locations, integrating multiple companies and airports and coordinating decentralized subcontractors. To accommodate the growing number of passengers, this chapter presents a transformative prototype of blockchain-based baggage handling in airport logistics. As a consequence, the digitally re-designed baggage handling process may provide transparency through decentralized stakeholder management and real-time traceability.

Baggage handling is the process of transporting the passengers' luggage from check-in to arrival, which entails a plurality of cross-border processes, stakeholders, and information systems. In 2018, 24.8 million bags were mishandled, of which 77% constituted delayed, 5% lost/stolen, and 18% damaged. These mishandled bags provide the aviation industry with a yearly bill of USD 2.4 billion (SITA, 2019). In addition, failed luggage also creates dissatisfied passengers that on average waste 1.7 days of their vacation or business trip waiting for the mishandled bag (Ahmed et al., 2013). On top of that, passengers may be discouraged to buy checked-in luggage to avoid risks of losing it and minimize overall travel time. Under the current conditions, it is the responsibility of the airline to pay the compensation to the customer, as the flight carrier is legally responsible for the transfer of the customer's property. Considering the industry dynamics as well as the current technological infrastructure, it is necessary to reconsider how the problem of mishandled luggage can be solved. Check-in, loading onto the aircraft, transfer, and arrival are the overall steps in the handling process, with transfer representing the critical bottleneck in mishandled luggage (SITA, 2019). Based on extant literature and primary data collection, we identify the lack of transparency in this baggage transfer as a problem to be solved by developing and testing a transformative IT artefact for intervention and change in the air transport organizations involved (Hevner et al., 2004).

In this chapter, we present and evaluate a prototype as well as insightful activities for carrying out a digital transformation of an airport's baggage handling process. When IATA announced a baggage tracking resolution (753) for all members to implement by June 2018, airlines were required to comply with a minimum number of baggage registration points at check-in, flight on-loading, transfer, and arrival (IATA, 2019b). Nonetheless, each airport bears some responsibility for how this standard is implemented (IATA, 2022b). We seek to understand the aviation industry's transparency problem through a case study of an international hub airport as represented by one of the largest baggage service providers operating on-site. We arrive at a decentralized luggage management solution as a transformative IT artefact. Building on RFID and blockchain as the underlying digital technologies, the instantiation has the potential to revitalize the way we think about transparency and unlock the value of data extracted from tracking luggage. In Sect. 3.2, we investigate the problem in detail through a detailed problem definition and research motivation. Section 3.3 presents and organizes digitized baggage handling activities in a process sequence. We evaluate a transformative prototype of blockchain-based RFID scanning and state executable business implications in Sect. 3.4. Section 3.5 summarizes our findings and brings this book chapter to a close with a brief reflection.

3.2 The Digital Transformation of Baggage Handling

Problem Definition

Following the ongoing discontent with mishandled luggage, it was necessary to first establish the design problem. To provide a solid foundation for the comprehension of the case, relevant scientific research articles were incorporated into the process of formulating probable concerns with baggage mishandling, where airport infrastructure and customer service were determined to be the most critical factors. Regarding the first issue, Zhang et al. (2008) conducted a case study at Beijing Capital International Airport and attributed the problem of mishandled luggage to the inefficient existing barcode system, which Singh et al. (2016). D. Mishra and A. Mishra (2010) cite IATA research in which barcode reading issues and the failure to receive baggage status alerts account for 20% of mishandled luggage.

From the passengers' viewpoint, luggage is expected to be delivered on time and at the right place; a need which is emphasized by Fitantri et al. (2017). Through a case study at Soekarno-Hatta Airport, Fitantri et al. (2017) find satisfactory baggage handling to be a decisive factor for passengers' overall satisfaction. Furthermore, the lack of knowledge into where lost luggage is located is a concern for airlines not only financially but also in terms of passengers' perceived service quality of airlines. According to Wyld et al. (2005), baggage delivery is a "all or nothing" occurrence in which passengers seeking information about the projected delivery of lost luggage are provided unambiguous responses. A more transparent solution could increase customer service levels and operational efficiency. Researchers agree on the importance of optimizing the luggage handling process and recommend radio frequency identification (RFID) technology to do so.

Although the rate of mishandled luggage is decreasing annually (SITA, 2019), the air traffic industry is not utilizing the most recent technical advancements to further reduce this rate. Due to the interconnected structure of the baggage handling process, the interdependence and complexity of the parties place huge demands on the global coordination of actors and systems. However, transparency is essential for a successful baggage handling process. This was highlighted in particular by a team leader from one of the airport's luggage service providers, who explicated a deficiency which turned out to be a great frustration for the interviewed team leader.

> And the worst of it is that the outstation cannot see that we have sent it [the luggage], because there is no scanning point when the luggage is loaded onto the plane. And a lot of stations cannot see that it has been scanned on arrival either.
>
> — Team Leader, Baggage Service Provider

Research Motivation

Stakeholders in luggage handling may be affected by the transparency issue heterogeneously, therefore pragmatic, and hedonic needs may differ.

Consequently, the applied IT artefacts should involve and connect stakeholders to approach the problem from various perspectives. A solution is thus intended to involve the stakeholders of *airports, passengers, airlines,* and *handling companies*. The overall goal is to enhance the user experience (Djamasbi et al., 2016; Sein et al., 2011, p. 2). As a result, it is critical to comprehend how the incorporation of digital technology in the handling procedure reflects the logic of more satisfied clients. The research question addressed in this chapter thus focuses on the digital transformation of the handling process in the aviation industry:

> How can the implementation of digital technology improve the baggage handling process?

At the process level, transparency is important to handling companies, as evidenced by an interview with the team leader of the baggage service provider in question.

> Being able to track bags from start to finish and identify where something went wrong — that would be the absolute biggest.
> — Team Leader, Baggage Service Provider

However, the perspectives of ground handlers who carry out the daily processes to implement transparency may vary. Consequently, the proposed digital transformation of the handling process determines the potential transparency benefits from an increased number of registration points. In this digital transformation project, we deploy the following technologies of blockchain, RFID, digital dashboards, and mobile apps.

1. Blockchain technology
   Blockchain provides the backbone for baggage transparency and tracking and represents the crucial transformative technology applied in this case. Each luggage piece is recorded as transactions along the transfer journey and becomes validated against the pre-defined smart contracts, wherein policies and validation mandates are set.
   Blockchain technology, like distributed ledger technologies in general, allows for decentralized business provisioning. Blockchain's technical

properties enable distributed stakeholders to connect for mutual transactions without prior knowledge of each other. Blockchain, which is frequently touted as a trust-free technology, can replace a central market maker, which typically safeguards transactions and validates the identities of the actors. Blockchain, in turn, provides digitally enabled consensus mechanisms, smart contracts, and distributed databases, all of which enable decentralized transaction processing. This decentralization is only possible because of newer blocks added to the chain as a result of consistent tracking of transactions and identification of ownership. Since decentralized databases provide comparable copies of prior transactions maintained at multiple nodes in a network, the present status, location, and ownership of a transferred object, such as luggage, may be transparently monitored by anybody with access to blockchain data. Several blockchain types define actors who can read or write on a blockchain, such as public or private blockchains. Following a stakeholder analysis, establishing a blockchain can thus facilitate the decentralized handling of luggage in an autonomous and transparent manner to all stakeholders engaged in the process, including customers, airports, and luggage carriers.

2. RFID

   RFID is the automated identification technology employed in this case to identify baggage. Through the RFID scanning points, luggage pieces can be tracked as they are transferred from the departure airport check-in to the destination airport baggage conveyor belt.

   Radio frequency identification (RFID) technology permits a touch-free tracking and tracing of objects through electromagnetic waves. RFID readers, sensors, or transponders, for instance, log the location of an object passing by, which generates data to be forwarded digitally. The location of an object, such as a piece of luggage, can thus be tracked without manual interference of physical contact, which supports automatic processing. Collecting and processing the transmitted location data can thus offer a seamless tracing of objects in their journey along a supply chain, such as baggage handling. RFID technology proves efficiency in scanning high volume and size of objects at short time. Apart from that, compared to the legacy technology of barcode scanning, RFID can be set up easier and at lower cost and requires less manual correction of sources of error. RFID is thus preferred for the handling of critical objects in high-reliability processes to ensure consistent and scalable tracing along critical transfer points.

3. Digital Dashboards

   Digital dashboards are suggested in the given case to monitor baggage handling transparently. As an artefact, digital dashboards are needed to help internal airport operations with real-time data on, inter alia, baggage handling with key metrics to monitor and manage baggage handling operations.

   Digital dashboards enable business users to monitor and analyse their most important data sources in real time and in a digestible, presentational format, resulting in better decision-making. By providing a quick and easy way to visualize and understand complex data, the business decision-making process can be partially automated. When compared to traditional report-based analysis, the time spent analysing data is drastically reduced. In general, organizations struggle with gathering data, retrieving information, and making decisions based on the information retrieved (Hansoti, 2010). In contrast, digital dashboards provide quick, transparent, and consistent access to data. A digital dashboard is an interface that allows organizations to have data available in the right form at the right time, which contributes to efficient internal processes and reduces decision-making delays.

4. Mobile Applications

   In this case, a mobile application is provided as an IT artefact for end customers. A mobile application allows them to track and be notified of key events as their luggage pieces are transferred along the transfer journey from check-in to arrival.

   Mobile apps, also called mobile application programs, offer limited functionality for a specific task at a maximum of usability. The limited functionality ensures that only essential features are provided, allowing the user to maintain an overview and avoid becoming overwhelmed by too many options. As a result, the design of mobile apps is optimized for touch screens and can even be personalized by the customer. Mobile apps benefit from reduced but necessary functionality and integration into mobile operating systems for real-time usage requirements. The latter provide quick access to APIs, allowing for the quick and efficient synchronization of data stored on external (cloud) databases with the app's status. Thus, any user who accesses the app can receive real-time information about tracked transactions. Mobile apps are often rolled out free of charge, to increase the user base easily without payment barriers that hinder its adoption. A wide-spread use of an app accelerates the utilization of the offered service and provides feedback mechanism from completed transactions to increase user satisfaction in future periods.

3.3 Digital Process Transformation

In the following, we develop components of digital technology that serve as the foundation for a digitally transformed baggage handling process. We rely on primary interview data with stakeholders, scientific research publications, and external, industry-specific sources to gain a thorough understanding of the wicked transparency problem. For idea generation, sketching is iteratively used to explore several aspects of action design in collaboration with the stakeholders (Bellamy et al., 2011). Based on our divergent thinking, we thus seek to explore alternative ways of designing transparency to discover possibilities and realize constraints (Gallagher, 2017; Bellamy et al., 2011). As we become increasingly aware of the wicked problem as well as the diverse understanding and importance of transparency, we intend to adopt convergent thinking to narrow down the definition of and solution to the problem. According to our analysis, transparency is a problem whose importance varies depending on the individual actor in the baggage handling process, which we have also attempted to incorporate as part of the sketched process components and their implementation below.

Component 1: A blockchain- and RFID-based decentralized luggage management solution that redefines transparency and coordination through two key elements:

1. Changing the client/server architecture to a peer-to-peer architecture that allows for increased collaboration and autonomous settlement between the stakeholders and through
2. Replacing inefficient barcode technology with RFID for baggage tracking

Component 2: An internal software as a service (SaaS) which displays a data-driven dashboard to be used by luggage handlers for real-time monitoring of baggage handling operations, that is, designing transparency for luggage handlers.

Component 3: A mobile application enables customers to track their luggage using the baggage management data generated by baggage scanning, hence creating transparency for passengers.

Digital Process: Following a process perspective, we illustrate the digital solution's various states and key events based on its three components. This facilitates an appreciation of the need for transparency and temporality of user behaviour when transporting luggage from departure to arrival.

Digitized Process Components

The intention of the sketched process components is to demonstrate how to design transparency through implementing digital technology.

Component 1: Blockchain and RFID for Autonomous Baggage Tracking

The baggage handling procedure in the aviation industry is under increased pressure (SITA, 2019). To meet the need for more effective coordination between involved actors and information systems, the entire ecosystem may be designed to be transparent. Therefore, we have designed a baggage management solution based on a peer-to-peer architecture as opposed to the conventional client/server architecture.

To construct the solution, we utilized the analogy of framing as prescribed by Dorst (2011), which resulted in a combination of RFID tags and blockchain technology, a combination that has already been proven effective in the shipping industry. Using RFID, for instance, global logistics companies can track containers from departure to arrival using a blockchain-based ecosystem. The problem arises in the air transportation industry when passengers arrive and wait for their luggage on the conveyor belt. This issue is recast in the context of the shipping industry, where a recipient may wait for a container to arrive at the destination port. A well-established global logistics company, for example, encountered similar container-disappearance issues but was unable to investigate the causes. The logistics company implemented RFID tags to identify and track containers in real-time to solve this transparency issue (Shi et al., 2011). As with the logistics company's intention to connect all parties in the blockchain-based ecosystem, the blockchain architecture could be envisioned to connect all luggage handling parties, that is, cross-border actors and systems, thereby simplifying the coordination and settlement processes.

For the present aviation scenario, Fig. 3.1 illustrates how RFID transponders record a suitcase on the blockchain continuously throughout the journey. As a result, smart contracts can trigger compensation payouts in the event of mishandled luggage, providing an alternative to the cumbersome claim process. Smart contracts are programmable contracts that, enabled by blockchain, specify the rules that must be followed to validate a transaction (Mougayar & Buterin, 2016).

Component 2: Dashboard to Improve Internal Operations

One way to define and comprehend transparency is through the lens of baggage handlers. A dashboard may enable baggage handlers to (1) manage operations by simulating the pressure experienced on multiple parameters during baggage handling operations and (2) act if luggage is mishandled by identifying the registration point where the luggage was most recently registered. For the former, the provided insight may allow handlers to plan and prioritize resources in response to fluctuating passenger demand. If 100 bags are checked in at the desk, but only 80 are registered at registration point number 5, the latter could be explained with a hypothetical example. In such a scenario, the remaining 20 bags

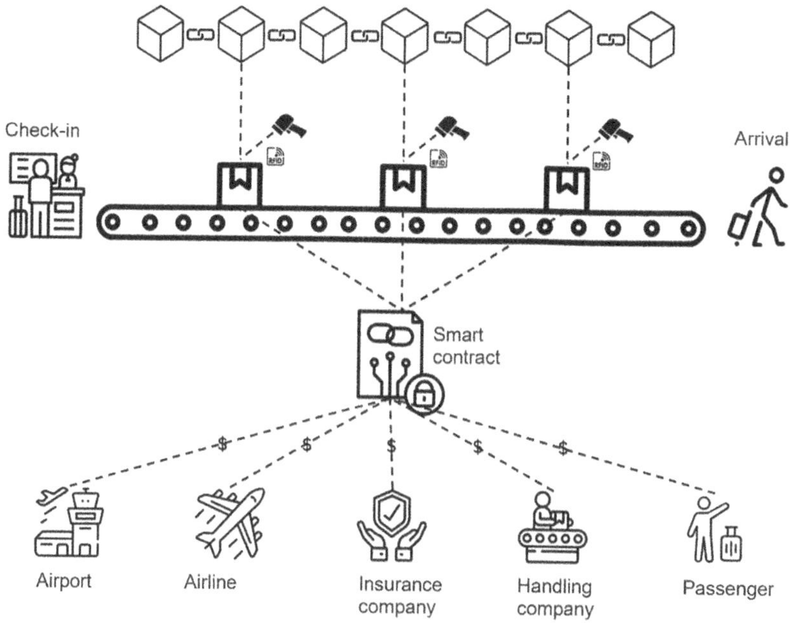

Fig. 3.1 Decentralized blockchain and RFID luggage handling solution

may be delayed or lost, and the dashboard allows the handlers to quickly identify the range in which a particular bag is mishandled.

Regarding Fig. 3.2, the dashboard solution may appear simple at first glance. Still, it may be adequate for managing resources required for baggage handling and identifying intervention-required processes, resulting in a more efficient method for handling luggage. The current lack of registration points in the handling process is a major problem in terms of lack of transparency (Team Leader, Baggage Service Provider, 2019). If the number of registration points increases in accordance with Resolution 753 of the International Air Transport Association, the dashboard may help increase transparency even further. The collection of data may also allow handling suppliers to use it for data analytics, such as the application of machine learning to advise handlers on the allocation of resources across operational activities.

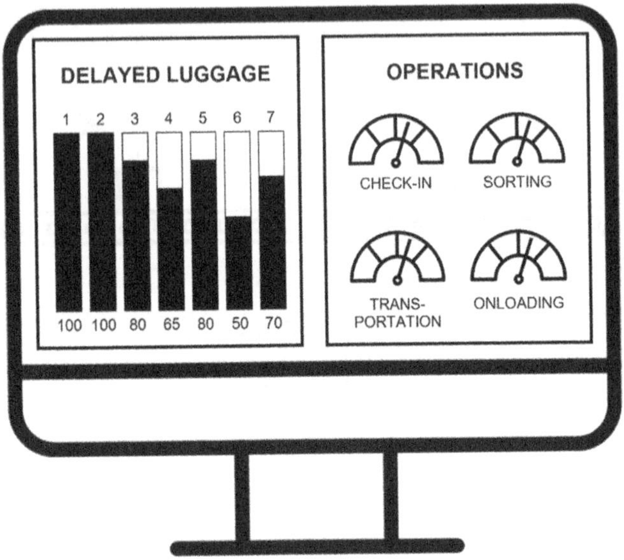

Fig. 3.2 Dashboard for luggage tracking

Component 3: Mobile Application for Increased Passenger Satisfaction Another technique for creating transparency is from the passengers' perspective. In addition to the transparency of baggage tracking, passengers find the process of claiming compensation for a mishandled bag to be cumbersome and frustrating (Team Leader, Baggage Service Provider, 2019). A mobile application with improved user experience should make it possible for passengers to claim compensation without having to contact handling staff members directly. This scenario is depicted in Fig. 3.3 to demonstrate our reasoning.

A Digital Process of Baggage Handling

We present a time-sequenced perspective on how to integrate digital technology into baggage handling. The activities described below are combined into a single digital process (Fig. 3.4), relying on the three introduced technical components. With the blockchain-based luggage

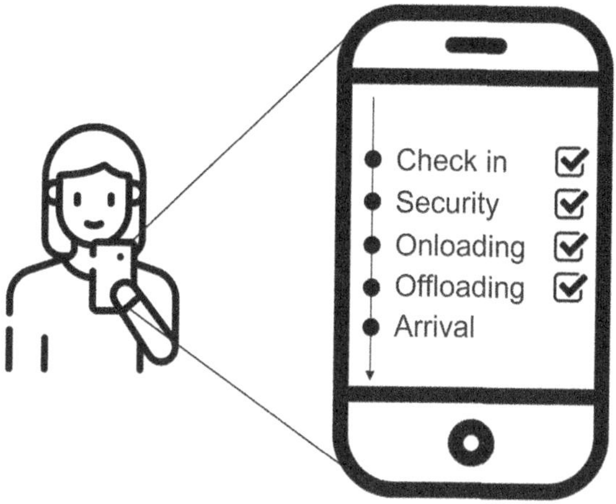

Fig. 3.3 Mobile application for passengers

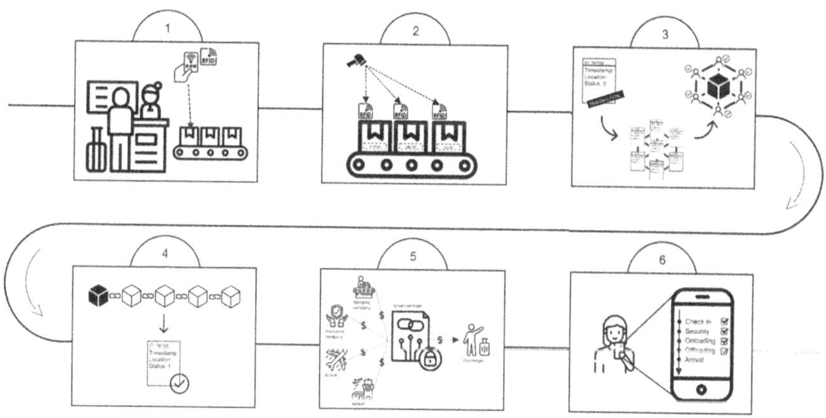

Fig. 3.4 Digital process of baggage handling along six activities

management system, the process is structured according to identified key activities.

Activity (1) The process begins when a passenger checks in their luggage, which causes the transaction to be recorded on the blockchain network. The RFID tag is printed at the check-in desk and attached to the luggage, allowing it to be tracked from departure to arrival.

Activity (2) Throughout the process, the RFID tags attached to the luggage are scanned several times, including at the check-in desk, luggage distribution centre, loading/unloading points, arrival distribution centre, and so on (Fig. 3.5).

Activity (3) Transactions from the described scanning points are aggregated into a block and affirmed by peers with validation rights. This means that every time a piece of luggage is scanned along the way, it is securely validated and stored in the blockchain.

Activity (4) Validated transaction blocks are added to the blockchain, ensuring that no data is lost and the status of each transaction is undisputed (Fig. 3.6).

Activity (5) Transactions are validated against smart contracts defined in the blockchain, which may result in additional actions. Handling companies, insurance companies, airlines, airports, passengers, and other stakeholders are all involved in the defined smart contract. This agreement and documentation ensure that responsibility is undeniably and clearly delegated among the parties involved, providing the passenger with a sense of security in the event of lost or damaged luggage. It also makes it easier and faster for the companies involved to reach an agreement when, for example, compensation must be calculated and settled.

Activity (6) Throughout the journey from the departure airport to the arrival airport, the customer can track the luggage in real time via a mobile application linked to the decentralized luggage handling sys-

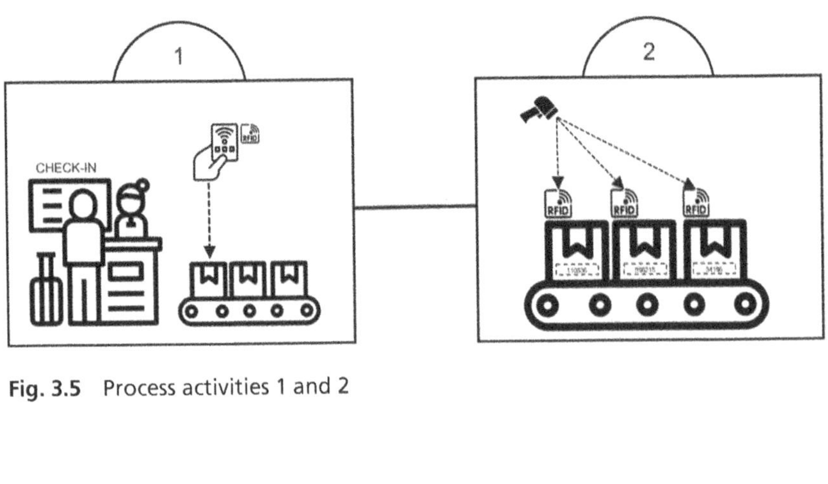

Fig. 3.5 Process activities 1 and 2

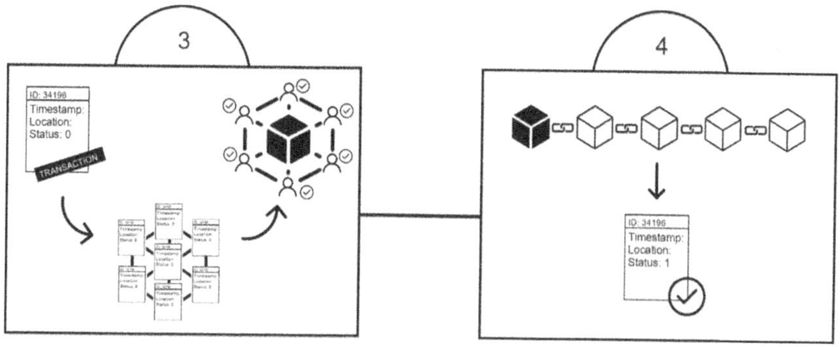

Fig. 3.6 Process activities 3 and 4

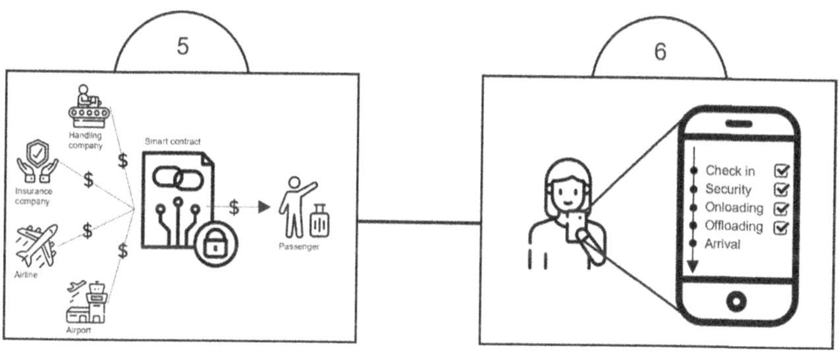

Fig. 3.7 Process activities 5 and 6

tem. From the passenger's perspective, this increases transparency because the passenger can track the luggage through several scanning points and know ahead of time if, for example, the luggage was not loaded onto the aircraft from the departure airport (Fig. 3.7).

In comparison to the conventional baggage handling process, a blockchain-based solution offers increased transparency, security, efficiency, and cost savings for all parties involved. The combination of RFID and blockchain enables the secure and efficient identification and registration of baggage based on a transparent and traceable log of each step of the baggage handling process. This means that passengers can easily track their bags, and airlines can easily identify potential problems with bag handling. The decentralized nature of blockchain technology guarantees that records are secure and cannot be altered without the consensus of validating parties. The availability of real-time data on the location and status of bags enables faster and more efficient baggage handling, thereby reducing the risk of delays or lost bags. Finally, the streamlined process reduces the need for manual intervention, allowing airlines to reduce operational costs and improve their bottom line, which would otherwise be constrained.

3.4 Prototype Evaluation and Business Implications

In the sketched digital process transformation, we illustrated and systematized several ways to increase transparency in baggage handling. In the following section, we focus on the blockchain and RFID-based solution, which we derive from using empirical data from a baggage service provider, aviation industry reports, and relevant research from identified scientific publications. In this section, we evaluate a prototype that illustrates the registration of a piece of luggage on a private blockchain, which motivates us to deduce the business implications of the examined case. The implications extrapolate illuminating examples from the prototype illustrating how a luggage transaction is recorded on a private blockchain.

Prototype Evaluation: Recording Luggage on a Private Blockchain

This section is intended to illustrate our prototype hypothesis of registering baggage items on a blockchain. First, we describe the materials and tools employed, followed by a fairly technical, step-by-step review of the described procedure and a unit test to determine its dependability. The result demonstrates the successful registration of luggage items on the blockchain, providing a starting point for further research into how the aviation industry can use the technology to simplify the otherwise complex and rather unreliable luggage handling process.

To demonstrate how the suggested process activities enhance baggage handling, we begin the evaluation with a testable hypothesis to demonstrate the prototype's contribution to the solution. The hypothesis serves as a prerequisite for the subsequent business implications and is stated as follows:

Prototype hypothesis: *The system registers baggage items on the blockchain in an autonomous and reliable manner.*

The example prototype is a decentralized application (Dapp) based on blockchain technology, a peer-to-peer-based ledger that is distributed among all actors in the ecosystem (Wang et al., 2018), which would be the baggage handling ecosystem in this case. Since Ethereum provides a blockchain platform that is renowned for its integration with smart contracts, our prototype is a locally running Dapp based on a private Ethereum blockchain, where only selected participants have permission to enter and transact, in contrast to a public blockchain such as Bitcoin, where everyone has access and validation rights (Mougayar & Buterin, 2016, p. 112).

Materials and Tools

The materials used to compile the example prototype include different frameworks, tools, and programming languages. The tools used are described in the following and includes *Ganache*, *Truffle*, *Solidity* and *Metamask* (Dapp University, 2019).

1. Ganache is a tool we use to simulate a local in-memory Ethereum blockchain, enabling us to perform the actions that we would carry out using the real Ethereum blockchain just without the costs associated hereto. Thus, it allows for executing commands, running tests, and ensuring that our Dapp works as intended.
2. Truffle is a developer environment that enables us to build, test, and deploy Dapps on the Ethereum blockchain. Using a suite of tools, smart contracts are deployed, and a client-side application is developed using *HTML*, *CSS*, and *JavaScript*.

3. Solidity is an object-oriented, high-level programming language that we use to develop and implement smart contracts on the Ethereum blockchain.
4. Metamask is a software that enables us to simulate a crypto wallet used to engage with the Ethereum network as an actor (Ethereum node). It gives us the opportunity for interacting with the local blockchain and its implemented smart contracts directly from the browser-based Dapp.

Example Prototype Based on Private Ethereum Blockchain

The prototype illustrates how registration points of the luggage—in this case exemplified by the check-in and flight on-loading—are recorded as blockchain transactions. The prototype is explained through a process of (1) deploying smart contracts that allows for recording luggage on the blockchain, (2) adding luggage to the blockchain from the client-side application, and (3) inspecting the block in which the transaction has been executed.

After launching and deploying smart contracts to the blockchain, the client-side application can be used to add luggage items to the blockchain. The left-hand side of Fig. 3.8 demonstrates how a piece of luggage

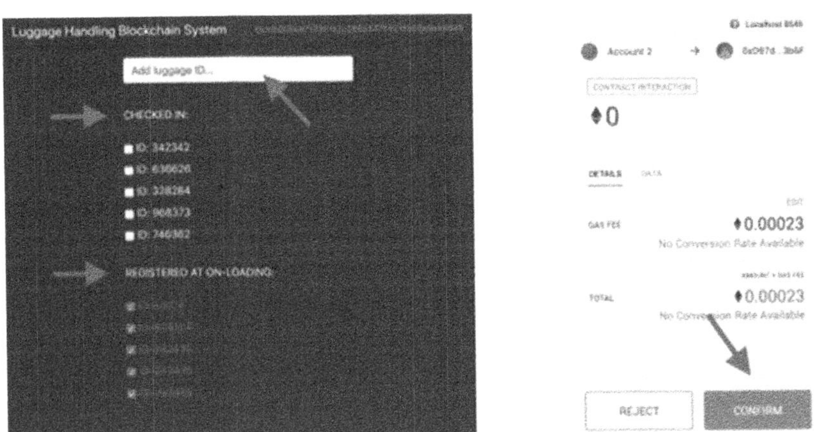

Fig. 3.8 Recording luggage pieces on the blockchain

can be added by its ID and then appear on the list of checked-in luggage. The yellow IDs represent checked-in baggage that has not yet been registered at the on-loading registration point. After baggage handlers register a piece of luggage at an on-loading point, the piece appears in green text. As depicted on the right-hand side of Fig. 3.9, a MetaMask alert appears when a piece of luggage with its ID is added. The transaction involving the registration of the piece of luggage must be confirmed (validated) by all nodes in the blockchain network with validation rights. After the transaction is validated and added to a block on the Ganache blockchain, the luggage ID is displayed under the "CHECKED IN" status. When a luggage ID is registered at the on-loading point, the status of the luggage ID changes from "CHECKED IN" to "REGISTERED".

After the transactions are carried out, in this example either by adding a luggage ID or by changing the last registration point for the luggage, the blockchain allows for accessing the block by the participating actors, thus an enabler of transaction visibility and transparency. The example in Fig. 3.9 visualizes that the local blockchain currently contains 40 blocks, each of which being represented by a transaction. However, a real blockchain may include several transactions within one block.

Finally, Ganache allows us to inspect each block and see various information. As an example, Fig. 3.10 shows the information contained in block number 80. The most valuable information is the *TH Hash*, which is the unique identifier of the transaction (TX), enabling the parties to track and trace its status.

The smart contracts developed with Solidity are migrated (deployed) to the private blockchain network as a transaction, as illustrated in Fig. 3.11. Deploying smart contracts to the Ethereum blockchain imposes

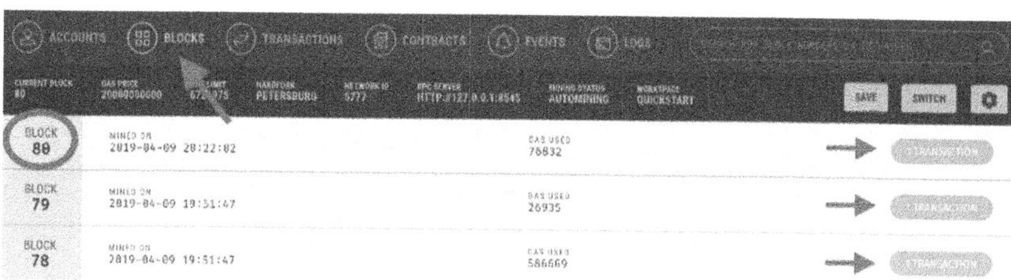

Fig. 3.9 Blocks on the blockchain

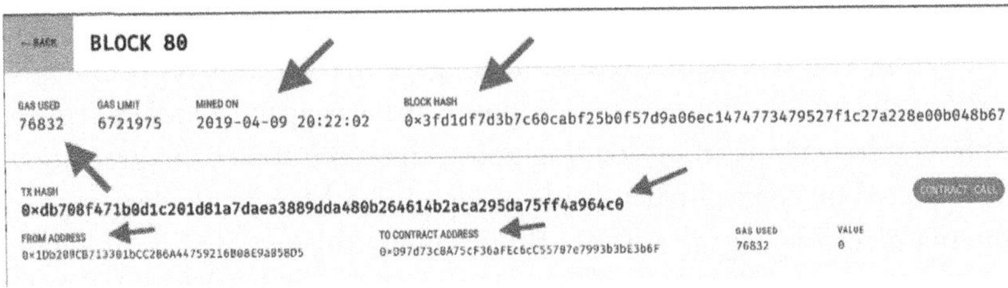

Fig. 3.10 Inspecting a block

transaction costs (i.e. computation costs) to the deployer, which is illustrated in the appendix with the final costs being 0.0167 ether (ETH),[1] a fee that is deducted from the account of the contract deployer. However, for the example prototype, it must be emphasized that the fee is fictitious and only used for validating the execution of the transaction (*TX*).

After executing the migration, it is observed in Fig. 3.12 that the fee of 0.0167 ETH is deducted from the deployer's account, while the remainders maintain a default account balance of 100 ETH.

Prototyping: Inspecting a Block

TX Hash	The unique identifier of the transaction, which can be used to track and trace the status of the TX by the involved actors. This may be used by the actors to track the status of the luggage, whether it is only registered at the check-in desk or loaded onto the flight.
Block Hash	The unique identifier of the block, which can be used to track and trace the block in which TXs are carried out.
Addresses	The block contains the address of the sender and the contract. While the former is the address of the transactor (i.e. transaction initiator), for example, the check-in desk that registers the luggage, the latter is the address of the smart contract used to define the rules for the transaction.
Mined On	*The timestamp in which the TX was recorded (mined)* on the blockchain.

```
Starting migrations...
======================
> Network name:    'development'
> Network id:      5777
> Block gas limit: 6721975


1_initial_migration.js
======================

   Replacing 'Migrations'
   ----------------------
   > transaction hash:    0x00f9bccc342434ff668747002b62b3b80afc8c594aa99a0f7189ccd9389fcf83
   > Blocks: 0            Seconds: 0
   > contract address:    0x84A81F89947c9d00e92E50B5ACF18Cc8F5B75759
   > account:             0x1Db209CB713301bCC286A44759216B08E9a858D5
   > balance:             99.822455044
   > gas used:            232981
   > gas price:           20 gwei
   > value sent:          0 ETH
   > total cost:          0.00465962 ETH


   > Saving migration to chain.
   > Saving artifacts
   -------------------------------------
   > Total cost:          0.00465962 ETH


2_deploy_contracts.js
=====================

   Deploying 'Luggage'
   -------------------
   > transaction hash:    0xa2c9b3e866ff4f964f2dd4a39505db641a46b485bef5247d7bfddae250e70915
   > Blocks: 0            Seconds: 0
   > contract address:    0xFf730eD3a12e0d133004d050239668B0DacC3982
   > account:             0x1Db209CB713301bCC286A44759216B08E9a858D5
   > balance:             99.809882964
   > gas used:            586669
   > gas price:           20 gwei
   > value sent:          0 ETH
   > total cost:          0.01173338 ETH


   > Saving migration to chain.
   > Saving artifacts
   -------------------------------------
   > Total cost:          0.01173338 ETH


Summary
=======
> Total deployments:   2
> Final cost:          0.016393 ETH
```

Fig. 3.11 Migration of smart contracts with Truffle

In this part, we conducted an evaluation of a prototype that demonstrates the process of registering a piece of baggage on a private blockchain. The primary emphasis is on the blockchain- and RFID-based solution, which was arrived at by analysing empirical data obtained from an airline industry study, relevant research obtained from selected

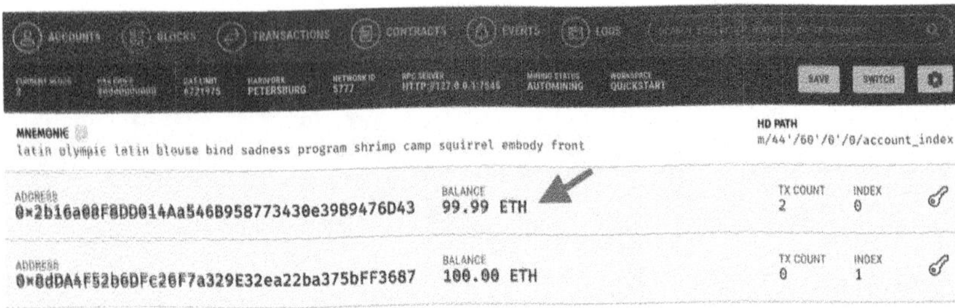

Fig. 3.12 Inspecting a block

scientific journals, and data provided by a luggage service provider. This serves as the impetus for us to derive the practical implications of the case that was investigated. The implications are derived by extrapolating interesting instances from the prototype, which show how a transaction involving baggage is recorded on a private blockchain.

Business Implications

Using the prototype evaluation results as a foundation, we discuss three business implications of a digitalized baggage handling process. Based on our theoretical assumptions and the diverse process activities described in the previous chapter, we derive the implications. Two of the implications focus on the technical value proposition of the blockchain-based solution, while the third focuses on the value-generating aspects of the baggage handling process, that is, increasing efficiency and effectiveness.

Business Implication I

With the goal of reducing the rate of mishandled luggage, creating a solution to promote transparency and cooperation should optimize the process of recognizing mishandled luggage at the airport for the assessed case. SITA (2019) highlighted the issue of mishandled luggage, and baggage handling was identified as a significant service element for passengers, who would receive vague statements for expected arrival, such as "sometime the next day" (Fitantri et al., 2017; Wyld et al., 2005, p. 384). Significantly, the papers agreed that replacing barcode technology with

RFID would reduce mishandled baggage, a change that the team leader for the airport in question approved. Idea sketching also demonstrated how the implementation of blockchain's easily scalable design may alleviate the growing pressure in the aviation industry, as well as how the technology's coupling with RFID has proven to be beneficial in the shipping industry. This formed the basis for formulating the first implication (I_1) as following:

I_1: The blockchain-based baggage management system transforms the process of identifying delayed/lost luggage by digitally provided transparency of the baggage handling process.

Business Implication II

The team leader from the baggage service provider emphasized how difficult it is to determine who is accountable for mishandled luggage. Furthermore, he acknowledged that the airline is always held accountable, regardless of who made the error. During the ideation process, it was discovered that blockchain contains programmable, smart contracts that may automatically assign responsibility and manage settlement between the parties involved. Therefore, we formulated the implication as:

I_2: The blockchain-based Smart Contracts make it easier to identify the responsible parties of mishandled luggage and simplifies the process of managing settlement between involved parties.

Business Implication III

As airlines face a squeeze on bottom-line profit margins (IATA, 2019a), the blockchain-based solution intends to reduce the costs by:

1. Increasing transparency to improve the baggage handling process.
2. Implementing smart contracts to automate the settlement process.

SITA (2019) describes the enhanced efficiencies of adopting baggage tracking, where tracking at on-loading was identified as the key to delivering tracking benefits, including cost savings. D. Mishra and A. Mishra (2010) also acknowledge the significant monetary loss resulting from mishandled luggage and elaborate on the potential cost savings that can be realized with RFID. In continuation, we express the third implication as follows:

I_3: *The blockchain-based baggage management system reduces the airlines' costs by reducing the rate of mishandled luggage and automating the settlement process.*

3.5 The Digitally Transparent Baggage Handling Solution Through Decentralized Process Management

In this chapter, we reconsider how the aviation industry can implement digital technology to improve the reliability and service levels in baggage tracking. Based on the current state of legacy solutions from the previous century, the problem of mishandled luggage may be mitigated using digital technology to increase transparency. Based on existing literature and primary data, we propose a blockchain- and RFID-based solution to the problem of lack of transparency in the baggage handling process. In addition to considering dashboards and mobile apps, this analysis provides a process perspective on the digital handling of luggage that encompasses all involved stakeholders, including customers, airports, and carrier subcontractors, by building on an evaluated prototype. The implementation of digital technology suggests a greater degree of transparency and reliability, which may lead to increased customer satisfaction because of lower mishandling rates and a reduction in the cost of compensation paid by the airlines involved.

Currently, the airline pays the full amount of compensation to the passenger because it is unclear who is liable. The increased transparency resulting from the digital transformation of baggage handling may enable the identification of the various parties' luggage responsibilities throughout the baggage handling process. Such transparency may be useful to assign blame if luggage is mishandled. For example, if a baggage handling supplier mishandles a piece of luggage, they should be assigned the most responsibility to incentivize them to continuously improve baggage handling. Consequently, smart contracts implemented as a component of the proposed blockchain can simplify the settlement between the parties by automatically delegating liability, as agreed upon by the parties. The proposed RFID implementation appears especially suited for the efficient management of larger quantities of luggage. A lower rate of mishandling may increase customer satisfaction with the entire flight experience, which is crucial as airlines compete for customer loyalty in an increasingly competitive air transport market. The use of mobile apps can also facilitate the sharing of achieved transparency with the customer, which contributes to a higher level of trust and service quality, leading to higher customer experience and satisfaction.

In addition to the insightful technical components that result from the implementation of digital technology, iterative development yields a holistic process perspective of digitized baggage handling. As the detailed descriptions of the process re-design suggest, the sequential application of the process activities reveals how the obtained data from the underlying blockchain-RFID solution can be reused to engage the distributed stakeholders. From their respective points of view, the proposed digital transformation promises computed process data to be displayed in dashboards for those involved in logistics or in mobile apps for customers. The underlying blockchain solution's trustworthiness and reliability provide a performant technical backbone for integrating and coordinating all relevant stakeholders. Even the commissioning airlines could gain access to the data and decide which stakeholders contribute to the blockchain in their various roles. In the still-growing global aviation industry, the implementation of RFID supplementary promises touch-free handling of higher volumes of baggage transport.

As a result of the validation, the proposed prototype has already proven to be useful. In terms of future implementation, the employment of the prototype would result in greater automation and the replacement of manual labour, such as existing barcode scanning. To improve the strategic implication, we would continue to iteratively design, evaluate, and adapt the solution. Based on our prototype, we can argue that our design is made up of blockchain-based instantiations, rooted in existing literature and primary data. The creation of an instantiation as a new solution to the problem of lack of transparency attests to the artefact's generation rather than appropriation. In this context, we should prioritize evaluating the artefact with a focus on novelty and utility, with the goal of reducing the magnitude of the baggage handling problem using new, innovative methods of increasing transparency. The solution's novelty is thus not only the application of blockchain to the baggage handling process in the industry but also the novelty in the organizational context of the involved airports, which have not used either RFID or blockchain in their baggage handling processes. However, the solution's organizational implementation assumes that the infrastructure is in place, which is not yet the case on a global or even local scale. With a target implementation date of June 2018, cf. IATA Resolution 753, the evaluation of a more reliable but potentially more expensive process opens the door to discussions about change management. The benefits of the digital transformation of baggage handling promise increased efficiency and effectiveness, but the costs of accelerating and increasing quality levels involve financial investments, which, in a highly decentralized setting, necessitate incentives for more stakeholders to participate (IATA, 2022b). Defining and implementing respective incentives may require additional initiatives by influential market players, such as large airlines, world-leading airports, or industry associations to make the proposed solution a reality.

References

Ahmed, T., Pedersen, T. B., & Lu, H. (2013). A Data Warehouse Solution for Analyzing RFID-Based Baggage Tracking Data. In *Proceedings - IEEE International Conference on Mobile Data Management*. https://doi.org/10.1109/MDM.2013.42

Bellamy, R., Desmond, M., Martino, J., Matchen, P., Ossher, H., Richards, J., & Swart, C. (2011). *Sketching Tools for Ideation (NIER Track)*. https://doi.org/10.1145/1985793.1985909.

Dapp University. (2019). *The Ultimate Ethereum Dapp Tutorial (How to Build a Full Stack Decentralized Application Step-By-Step)*. Retrieved from http://www.dappuniversity.com/articles/the-ultimate-ethereum-dapp-tutorial?fbclid=IwAR27fkmd-QV7yOCx5wQAodfnEI5u-F3o2fFsD9x6gJVLA7Pfe1__9tUg-zs

Djamasbi, S., Wilson, E. V., Strong, D. M., & Ruiz, C. (2016). *Designing and Testing User-Centric Systems with both User Experience and Design Science Research Principles* (pp. 1–5). Emergent Research Forum papers, Association for information systems.

Dorst, K. (2011). The Core of 'Design Thinking' and Its Application. *Design Studies*. https://doi.org/10.1016/j.destud.2011.07.006

Fitantri, A., Madhani, A. I., & Widiastuti, S. (2017). Assessment of Customer's Satisfaction on Baggage Handling Service at Soekarno-Hatta International Airport. In *Global Research on Sustainable Transport (GROST 2017)*. Atlantis Press. https://doi.org/10.2991/grost-17.2018.48

Gallagher, C. L. (2017). Sketching for Ideation: A Structured Approach for Increasing Divergent Thinking. In *Proceedings of the 2017 CHI Conference Extended Abstracts on Human Factors in Computing Systems* (pp. 106–111. CHI EA '17). ACM. https://doi.org/10.1145/3027063.3048424

Hansoti, B. N. (2010). *Business Intelligence Dashboard in Decision Making*. College of Technology.

Hevner, A., March, S. T., Park, J., & Ram, S. (2004). Design Science in Information Systems Research. *MIS Quarterly*. https://doi.org/10.2307/25148625

IATA. (2018). *IATA Forecast Predicts 8.2 Billion Air Travelers in 2037*. Retrieved from https://www.iata.org/pressroom/pr/Pages/2018-10-24-02.aspx

IATA. (2019a). *Airlines' Profitability Squeeze Lessens in Q4*. Retrieved from https://airlines.iata.org/news/airlines%5C%E2%5C%80%5C%99-profitability-squeezelessens-in-q4

IATA. (2019b). *IATA Baggage Tracking R753*. Retrieved from https://www.iata.org/whatwedo/ops-infra/baggage/Pages/baggage-tracking.aspx

IATA. (2022a). *Air Passenger Numbers to Recover in 2024*. Retrieved from https://www.iata.org/en/pressroom/2022-releases/2022-03-01-01/

IATA. (2022b). *Baggage Tracking*. Retrieved from https://www.iata.org/en/programs/ops-infra/baggage/baggage-tracking/

Mishra, D., & Mishra, A. (2010). Improving Baggage Tracking, Security and Customer Services with RFID in the Airline Industry. *Acta Polytechnica Hungarica, 7*, 139.

Mougayar, W., & Buterin, V. (2016). *What Is the Blockchain?, The Business Blockchain: Promise, Practice, and Application of the Next Internet Technology* (pp. 1–28).

Sein, M., Henfridsson, O., Purao, S., Rossi, M., & Lindgren, R. (2011). Action Design Research. *MIS Quarterly, 35*, 37–56. https://doi.org/10.2307/23043488

Shi, X., Tao, D., & Voß, S. (2011). RFID Technology and Its Application to port-Based Container Logistics. *Journal of Organizational Computing and Electronic Commerce*. https://doi.org/10.1080/10919392.2011.614202

Singh, A., Meshram, S., Gujar, T., & Wankhede, R. P. (2016). *Baggage Tracing and Handling System Using RFID and IOT for Airports* (pp. 466–470). https://doi.org/10.1109/CAST.2016.7915014

SITA. (2019). *2019 SITA Baggage IT Insights*.

Team Leader, Baggage Service Provider. (2019, March). *Semistructured interview*. Conducted 22. March 2019.

Wang, H., Zheng, Z., Xie, S., Dai, H. N., & Chen, X. (2018). Blockchain Challenges and Opportunities: A Survey. *International Journal of Web and Grid Services*. https://doi.org/10.1504/ijwgs.2018.10016848

Wyld, D. C., Jones, M. A., & Totten, J. W. (2005). Where Is My Suitcase? RFID and Airline Customer Service. *Marketing Intelligence & Planning, 23*, 382. https://doi.org/10.1108/02634500510603483

Zhang, T., Ouyang, Y., & He, Y. (2008). Traceable Air Baggage Handling System Based on RFID Tags in the Airport. *JTAER, 3*, 106–115.

4

The Five Emerging Business Models of Fintech for AI Adoption, Growth and Building Trust

Alex Zarifis and Xusen Cheng

4.1 Introduction

Fintech is widening financial inclusion and bringing extraordinary ease of use and value to consumers (Jagtiani & Lemieux, 2018). The world is in the middle of a digital transformation the likes of which have not happened since the emergence of the Internet. New technologies like Artificial Intelligence (AI) are dovetailing with proven and widely used technologies like big data and cloud computing. While AI is the obvious catalyst, the wider adoption of technologies like cloud computing, 5G,

A. Zarifis (✉)
School of Business, University of Nicosia, Nicosia, Cyprus

Cambridge Centre for Alternative Finance, University of Cambridge, Cambridge, UK
e-mail: zarifis.a@unic.ac.cy

X. Cheng
School of Information, Renmin University of China, Beijing, China
e-mail: xusen.cheng@ruc.edu.cn

A. Zarifis et al. (eds.), *Business Digital Transformation*,
https://doi.org/10.1007/978-3-031-33665-2_4

blockchain and the Internet of Things (IoT) is also important. Fintech is disrupting digital transformation, going beyond just making existing models leaner and faster (Ashta & Herrmann, 2021; Zarifis & Cheng, 2023). This change is neither top-down nor bottom-up but is being driven by many different stakeholders in many different parts of the world, making it hard to predict its final form. Innovation does not just impact the organization's business model, but the business model becomes a source of innovation (Zott & Amit, 2017). This research identifies the five prevailing approaches of digital transformation in Fintech so that the organization in finance and the other stakeholders can learn from the success stories and move forward more and grow.

The term Fintech is used quite narrowly at times to mean innovative financial companies that rely heavily on technology and automation, Fintech startups, or quite broadly to refer to any technology used in finance. While these definitions have their logic and will most likely continue to be used, a more accurate and potentially useful definition is that Fintech involves organizations that utilize the latest technologies, automation, and new processes to offer new services that are more centred on the customer's needs (Puschman & Alt, 2016).

While this widely used definition is helpful, it does not fully capture the dynamic transformation in finance that is not only generated by the traditional businesses, but also by many startups and other unexpected sources (Zarifis & Cheng, 2021). There are signs that we are in the second stage of this transformation with lessons learned on all sides and strategies refined. Incumbents often accept that they can no longer shape the market however they want, and no longer underestimate the new disrupting businesses entering finance. The new businesses entering finance, some small startups, others larger organizations from other areas outside of finance, often no longer underestimate the ability of incumbents in managing risk, shaping regulation and so on. It appears that those that like 'placing bets' on either the incumbents or the disruptors dominating will be disappointed.

While Decentralised Finance (DeFi) is a large part of Fintech it is important to make clear that it is not the only trend in Fintech and the spirit of decentralization is not the Zeitgeist of our times, as many Fintech solutions do the exact opposite, further centralizing services (Auer et al.,

2023). An example of a technology further centralizing finance would be a one-tier Central Bank Digital Currency (CBDC).

The adoption of technologies and evolution of finance will never end, but this level of disruption seems like a transitionary period that will be followed by more stability. If we take the disruption the Internet caused as a guide, the higher degree of stability will be reached in finance when (1) the new business models are clarified and (2) when those that adopt them best drive those that did not utilize them as well, out of business. A third possible scenario is consolidation across finance with organizations working together in ecosystems to offer services together. For consolidation to happen there must be clarity on the processes and business models.

Given the uncertainty in this area, and the inadequacy of simply distinguishing between incumbents and startups, identifying the broad Fintech models that are successful will give traction to move forward. Where there is uncertainty, ambiguity and turmoil, there is also risk and a need for trust. The increased use of customers' data also creates personal information privacy concerns that can challenge trust further (Zarifis et al., 2021). The issues around trust are not limited to acknowledging its importance, as there is also the question of who will build the trust with the consumer. In these broad dynamic collaborations between 'friends' and 'frenemies', building trust should not be seen just at the level of customer facing processes but at the broader business model level. Therefore, the research questions are:

What are the prevailing Fintech business models?
How do the prevailing Fintech business models build trust with the consumer?

This research used a qualitative approach in three stages, utilizing focus groups, short case studies and longer case studies with interviews to come to a degree of consensus around five models of fintech that are (a) an incumbent disaggregating and focusing on one part of the supply chain, (b) an incumbent utilizing AI in the current processes without changing their existing business model, (c) an incumbent extending their model to utilize AI and access new customers and data, (d) a startup finance disruptor only getting involved in finance and (e) a tech company disruptor adding finance to their portfolio of services. The five Fintech business models give an organization five proven routes to AI adoption and growth. Trust is not always built at the same point in the value chain or by the same type of organization. The trust building should usually happen where the customers are attracted and onboarded.

The following section presents the theoretical foundation from the literature on Fintech, trust in finance and technology and existing business models in related areas. This leads to the recommended model this research starts with (Zarifis & Cheng, 2023). The methodology explains the three qualitative methods and gives the demographic information. This is followed by the analysis, discussion and conclusion.

4.2 Theoretical Foundation

Digital Transformation with Fintech

Fintech is defined as using technology and innovation to provide new or more efficient services to individuals and organizations (Puschman & Alt, 2016). The term emerged around 2014 and gained popularity in both the industry press and academia as the role of technology increased. Fintech is driven by startups, incumbents, governments and supra-organizations like the European Union. The variety of actors in Fintech is also reflected in different degrees of centralization in Fintech, from DeFi that is very decentralized to a one-tier CBDC that is very centralized.

The progress of digital transformation with Fintech is happening in many different areas at different speeds. Some transformations, such as moving services online, have been underway for 15–20 years since e-commerce gained popularity, while others such as the AI-enabled chatbot have gained traction more recently (Zarifis et al., 2021). The digital transformation can be separated into 'front office' the relationship with the customer, 'back office' the relationship with the suppliers and partners, or 'ecosystem' with more dynamic links.

Digital transformation in the relationship with the consumer is the more visible part of this process that captures most of the attention

(Cheng et al., 2022). The use of chatbots that interact either by text or by voice is extensive. While the companies providing them can point to some numbers showing that they can handle simple cases and reduce the headcount in call centres, they are still far away from delivering the service a human can. Front-office processes that have been transformed include (1) fast onboarding without the need to submit personal information as this is taken from other sources by an Application Layer Programming (API) interphase with another organization; (2) fast response to requests 24 hours a day, 365 days a year due to automated analysis; (3) automated delivery of a service without the need to make a request, for example an insurance pay-out triggered by a smart contract and an IoT; (4) IoT, wearables such as smart watches used to collect data and adapt insurance rates; (5) 'super-apps' bringing together many services including financial services, for example Tencent's WeChat (Guo & Liu, 2021); (6) greater access to banking, finance and insurance, for example by not requiring from a new customer to visit a branch so people living far away from one can open an account and (7) understanding the customers' emotions by analysing facial expressions and the tone of voice enabling more tailored solutions.

Back-office processes that have changed significantly with Fintech are (1) analysing risk with AI and Machine Learning; (2) better fraud detection utilizing big data; (3) analysing both structured and unstructured data; (4) bringing together the necessary information for an expert to make a decision, such as the relevant regulation needed by the insurance underwriter; (5) requesting and receiving data through APIs, processing applications; and (6) more regular, automated audit. These front-office and back-office capabilities are combining to offer many new services such as crowdfunding, peer-to-peer lending platforms, mobile payments and buy-now-pay-later services.

Trust in Finance and Technology

Trust is necessary in many interactions, but its importance becomes more critical when the risk to the consumer is high. There are several dimensions of Fintech that increase the perceived risk and need for trust from the consumer's perspective. Examples of how risk in the interaction increases with Fintech are the use of chatbots in the interaction (Zarifis et al., 2021), and the use of AI in decision making (Bankins et al., 2022). The decision making of AI may not be transparent or may use criteria that may not seem relevant to the consumer, such as the speed at which they type (Bankins et al., 2022). Humans also change their approach when interacting with technology. For example, they may search for financial services on the Internet more often based on attributes, such as lowest price, rather than brands (Klaus & Zaichkowsky, 2022).

In addition to the changes in interaction and decision making, Fintech also creates some potentially negative side-effects on human behaviour. New financial services may enable impulsive and wasteful purchases and investments. This criticism is often levelled at purchases utilizing 'buy now, pay later' services like Klarna (Johnson et al., 2021). This criticism is also levelled at non-professional investors using platforms like Robinhood (Eaton et al., 2022). In addition to these negative effects a customer can easily avoid by not using these services, there are some potentially negative effects on personal information privacy that may be harder to avoid. The effortless, smooth and seamless service Fintech provides is often achieved through the sharing of customers' personal information between organizations (Zarifis et al., 2021).

When a model has matured, many processes become a habit for people, and they are not given too much thought (Polites & Karahanna, 2012). Many processes that build trust are taken for granted in a mature model. This is not the case when a new model emerges. A metaphor to illustrate this point is that if we are in a busy café, we trust that adults will not bump into us, but we are not entirely sure about children's behaviour. With the new models that rely on ecosystems that form and reform, adapting to changes in regulation for example, it should not be taken for granted that trust is being built. Some startups try to promote themselves and create a positive image and a climbing stock price, but this is like a band aid, and it does not build trust sufficiently.

Trust from the consumer towards the organization providing them a product or service requires trust in both the organizations and the institutions involved, such as the regulators, and the technology they interact with (Pavlou & Gefen, 2004). More specifically, trust in Fintech and

Insurtech has been found to be shaped by (1) the individual's psychological disposition to trust, (2) sociological factors influencing trust, (3) trust in the financial organization and (4) trust in AI and other technologies used (Zarifis & Cheng, 2022).

Business Models

General Business Models: There are several approaches to what exactly a business model is and what it should include. As with many theories this might also evolve gradually over time. Some business models cover the value chain used to deliver services or products (Eling & Lehmann, 2018). Other business models follow a similar approach but go into more detail, also covering some important processes (Zott et al., 2011). Other business models include the partners of the organizations capturing the ecosystem directly around the company (Ng et al., 2013). Sources of customers and sources of data are included in some business models, as they are central to those models' competitive or relative advantage (Zarifis & Cheng, 2023). To include a competitive advantage at the business model level it must offer a long term, resilient advantage (Morris et al., 2005). A related approach is that the business model must cover the content (what), structure (how) and governance (who), and that the priorities are novelty, lock-in, complementarities and efficiencies (Zott & Amit, 2017).

Business Models in Fintech: The literature on business models in Fintech is mostly on specific services related to a specific technology. There is less research on a taxonomy of broader business models of Fintech that identify the value chain. A taxonomy of business models attempts to identify a number of broad business models that cover all, or most Fintech organizations, as opposed to focusing on a narrower model that does not cover all of them. A broad taxonomy has been made in a subset of Fintech, the technology of insurance, Insurtech (Zarifis et al., 2019). This model identifies four general Insurtech models for getting the best out of AI. This model has been further developed into five business models that utilize AI (Zarifis & Cheng, 2023).

Previous research has shown some convergence between incumbents and disruptors but finds that they will remain distinct (Zarifis & Cheng, 2021). This is an indication that even after this transitionary period there will be distinct business models optimized for different types of Fintech, including incumbents and startups.

Research Model

The research discussed support the importance of Fintech and the importance of providing clarity on the business models that are best suited for AI adoption and growth. Many Fintech business models exist that are focused on one technology and service, but a broad taxonomy of Fintech business models optimized for AI is necessary. Such a taxonomy does exist for the related area of Insurtech. Furthermore, the higher risk and uncertainty that technology brings, particularly AI, are supported by existing literature. Therefore, trust must be included as a parameter of the Fintech business model. Research has found that trust in Insurtech and Fintech is similar (Zarifis & Cheng, 2022). Therefore, the existing taxonomy of Insurtech business models should extend to Fintech. Therefore, this research uses the existing taxonomy and explores and further develops it for Fintech.

The initial taxonomy identified four models: (a) incumbents focusing on one part of the supply chain, (b) incumbents not changing the business model, (c) incumbents expanding the business model and (d) new entrants utilizing technology to disrupt insurance (Zarifis et al., 2019). The further development of the taxonomy found support for splitting the fourth model into two. Therefore, the second version had five models: (a) focusing on one part of the supply chain, (b) utilizing AI in the current processes without changing the business model, (c) incumbent extending their model to utilize AI, (d) insurance disruptor only involved in insurance, and (e) tech company disruptor adding insurance to their portfolio of services (Zarifis & Cheng, 2023).

4.3 Methodology

Data Collection

The methodology chosen must not only develop insightful business model taxonomies, but it must ensure that the models identified are robust and hold true in these turbulent times. Therefore, an iterative qualitative approach was taken with three stages (Eisenhardt, 1989). While qualitative data collection can start without a specific focus, with a more exploratory approach, having a specific focus from the start on what kind of data will be collected is beneficial (Miles & Huberman, 1994).

Focus Groups with Experts

The first stage involved three focus groups. Focus groups are also referred to as in-depth group interviews. The first group had four participants, the second had five and the third had five also. The participants came from three fintech companies, two large and one small. The priority of this stage is to achieve a broad idea generation to capture all the perspectives on these issues and avoid any 'blind spots'. A secondary objective was to gain a deeper understanding of the issues that emerge. The focus groups were carried out online by videoconference. The focus group was not recorded to ensure participants' privacy, and so they feel more comfortable to speak freely. The topic put to the focus groups was what their experiences of Fintech are, and if they see some general patterns of what usually works and what does not. Then the five models of Fintech, based on the five Insurtech models, were put forward to them and explained. This was followed by looking at each of the five models one by one and discussing if it resonates with them, and if they think it is valid. It was then asked from the focus group what they thought the competitive advantage of each business model is. The next topic was about if they thought a different model should be added to the taxonomy. Lastly the topic put forward was the role of trust, in general, for each of the models put forward to them and in any additional models they put forward. The focus groups stopped when the topics were saturated.

From the fourteen participants six have more technology-focused roles and the remaining eight have more managerial or administrative roles. Eight are women, and six are men. Their age ranges from twenty-five to fifty-seven with the average age of thirty-seven. They all have a university bachelor's degree, and three have a master's degree.

Short Case Studies

The second stage of the iterative, qualitative research involved short case studies often referred to as case vignettes. The case studies identified and explored three companies for each proposed Fintech business model. An effort was made to cover the typical types of Fintech companies such as retail banks, investment banks, insurers and brokerage firms. The purpose for the short cases was to learn as much about the companies, and how well they fit into the proposed taxonomy. For the taxonomy to be valid, all the cases must match one of the five categories. Additionally, the cases within the same category must be similar across the criteria of that business model. The cases were chosen to cover a broad range of Fintech organizations. Five were incumbents and five were startups or disruptors. The companies chosen were active in Europe. Desk-based research reviewed these companies' websites, reports, industry press and research to create a clear picture of their business models.

Interviews with Ten Experts (Two for Each of the Five Fintech Business Models)

The third stage involved interviewing ten professionals from five companies that represent the five Fintech business models. The third iterative stage further triangulates the results but also offers a deeper understanding of each of the business models. The interview questions were semi structured. Unlike the focus groups, the interview questions were on one Fintech business model, the one the participant being interviewed is part of.

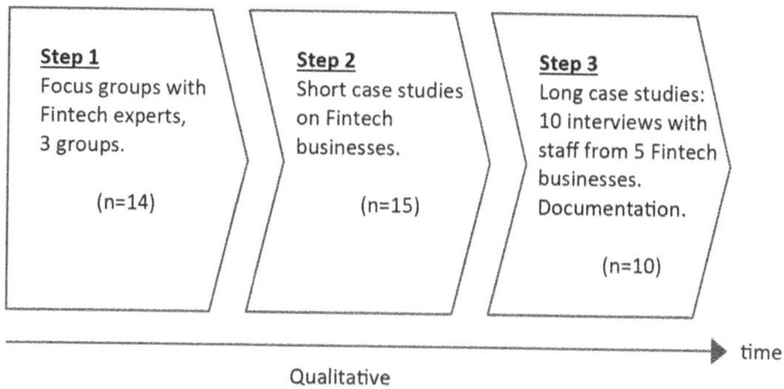

Fig. 4.1 The stages of the qualitative methodology

From the ten participants four have more technology-focused roles and the remaining six have more managerial or administrative roles. Five are women and five are men. Their age ranges from twenty-eight to fifty-four with the average age of thirty-four. They all have a university bachelor's degree, and two have a master's degree. The three stages are sumarised below (Fig. 4.1).

Data Analysis

The focus groups were conducted for two reasons, firstly to better define the problem and secondly to validate the constructs. Template analysis was used, with the five business models and the role of trust being the six initial templates. The small case studies involved analysing data from secondary sources including company reports, research from academic and other sources, and reputable industry press such as *The Financial Times* and *The Economist*. Firstly, there was a within-case analysis to evaluate if the cases that were posited to be similar are indeed similar, and then there was a between-case analysis to evaluate if the cases that were posited to be different are indeed different. Finally, the interviews used template analysis, but the templates were limited to one business model, the one that matched the company the interviewee worked for and the role of trust.

4.4 Analysis

Focus Group

Trends in Fintech: The topic put to the focus groups asked what their experiences of Fintech are and if they see some general patterns of what is working and what is not working so well. Some of the themes touched on where how banks are adapting, how branches are closing and that banks are hiring more people with skills related to technology. Another popular theme was how cryptocurrencies, stablecoins and CBDCs are going to shape Fintech. More generally the role of technology in Finance was discussed.

Five models of Fintech for AI and growth: The five models of Fintech based on the five Insurtech models were put forward to them and explained. This was followed by looking at each of the five models one by one and discussing if it resonates with them and if they believe it is valid based on their experience.

The models put forward to the participants, adapted from Insurtech, are (a) disaggregating and focusing on one part of the supply chain, (b) utilizing AI in the current processes without changing the business model, (c) finance incumbent extending their model to utilize AI and access new customers and data, (d) startup finance disruptor only getting involved in finance, and (e) tech company disruptor adding finance to their portfolio of services (Zarifis & Cheng, 2023).

The participants discussed their understanding of the five models and put forward their examples for each one. For example, in the discussion around the first proposed Fintech businesses model, examples were given of local banks that collaborate with large tech companies over payments, investment functionality and other process, reducing their part in the value chain. In most cases the competitive advantage is seen as getting access to the best technology and the most data faster than the competition.

Additional fintech business models: The next topic was if they thought a different model should be added to the taxonomy. The participants identified several business models tied to specific services such as 'retail' trading apps but not a general model that could be part of a high-level taxonomy.

Trust building: Lastly the topic put forward was the role of trust in general at each of the five models being discussed and in any additional approaches put forward by them. Most participants considered trust important both from the perspective of their role as professionals working in Fintech, as well as from their perspective as consumers of Fintech services. Several participants made the point that this should not be lost when there is business model innovation. It was mentioned in all three groups that the organization the customer engages with directly is responsible for building trust and protecting it.

Short Case Studies (Case Vignettes)

The within-case analysis evaluates if the three cases that were posited to be similar, in terms of their business model and how they utilize AI and build trust, are indeed similar. Despite the inevitable differences between different Fintech companies such as retail banks, investment banks, insurers and brokerage firms, there are similarities in relation to the part of the value chain they are active in, the competitive advantage achieved by AI and the way trust is built as illustrated in Table 4.1.

The between-case analysis evaluated if the cases that are posited to be different in terms of their business model and how they utilize AI and build trust are indeed different. Despite some similarities between the different models there were several differences supporting that they are indeed distinct models. For example, the companies that fall into the third model are indeed developing their in-house capabilities in AI extensively, unlike those that fall into the first model.

Longer Case Studies, Interviews and Documentation

The longer case studies involved two interviews from one company representing each of the five Fintech business models and desk-based research of those companies. Several of the participants emphasized the unrivalled

Table 4.1 The fifteen short cases of the five Fintech business models

Case	Fintech business model	AI competitive advantage	Trust building
1. Retail bank active in Germany. 2. Retail bank active in Germany. 3. Vehicle insurer active in Germany and several European countries.	(a) Disaggregating and focusing on one part of the supply chain.	Estimating risk, interacting with the customer twenty-four hours a day.	Reliable services, heritage.
4. Retail bank active in Germany. 5. Brokerage firm active primarily in Germany. 6. Insurer active in one region of Germany.	(b) Utilizing AI in the current processes without changing the business model.	Estimating risk, interacting with the customer twenty-four hours a day, automating some processes.	Reliable services, heritage.
7. Retail bank active in Germany. 8. Investment bank active primarily in Germany. 9. Brokerage firm (investment app) active in Germany and over ten countries.	(c) Finance incumbent extending their model to utilize AI and access new customers and data.	Estimating risk, interacting with the customer twenty-four hours a day, automating some processes, adding new highly automated services.	Reliable services, heritage, more extensive and deeper engagement with the customer.

(continued)

Table 4.1 (continued)

Case	Fintech business model	AI competitive advantage	Trust building
10. Internet bank active in Germany and over twenty other countries. 11. Internet bank active in Germany. 12. Internet insurer active in Germany.	(d) Startup finance disruptor only getting involved in finance.	Extensive automation, fast onboarding, fast payments, customized offers.	Reliable services, transparent, customizations make consumer feel close to company.
13. Tech company offering financial services in Germany and over ten other countries. 14. Tech company offering financial services in Germany. 15. Tech company offering financial services in Germany and over thirty other countries.	(e) Tech company disruptor adding finance to their portfolio of services.	Extensive automation, cross-selling, fast onboarding, fast payments, customized offers, identifying new patterns across diverse services.	Already familiar to the customer from a young age—before they need their services, reliable services, transparent, customizations make consumer feel close to company.

pace of change and the extraordinary times finance is going through. Many of interviewees made the point that there is an eagerness to move forward, combined with a hesitation to not move too quickly and make mistakes. The concern was often in both what the organization would evolve into and the process of business model innovation. Several of the interviewees stated that this change was in pursuit of a competitive advantage. All the interviewees believed trust plays an important role. Therefore, the interviews supported that the competitive advantage and trust are an integral part of the new business model.

The participants from the fourth Fintech business model, a startup finance disruptor only getting involved in finance, were very clear about what their business model is, and did not see the need to change at this point. This is very interesting as these Fintech organizations were created with a specific business model in mind and are probably the only ones out of the five models that are not in transition. It is a strength for a Fintech business when the staff know, and can explain, the Fintech's mission statement and model. The participants from the fifth model explained how by using AI, big data and A/B testing they can approach risk differently, taking on far more risk than before.

The interviewees were also concerned about how they would fit into a new business model. Their comments also illustrate how clarity on the competitive advantage pursued and the form and governance of the trust building are necessary in order to go through the process. The interviewees explained their organization's business model in their own words, but their explanation is in line with the taxonomy of five Fintech business models. While the impact on the individual working in a Fintech company going through business model transformation is not the primary focus of this research, it is worth being reminded that many, if not most, people working in a Fintech are primarily concerned with how the changes impact them as opposed to the organization's future.

Several participants also took the issues put to them one step further, reflecting on how the business model innovation would influence society in general. This is outside the scope of this research but an important issue, nevertheless.

4.5 Discussion

While it is important to have narrow business models that typically explains a specific service tied to a specific technology, such a crowdfunding or peer-to-peer lending, broader business models that identify the key processes and competitive advantages of businesses are also important. These models must be not only be insightful but also robust in turbulent times.

Contribution to Theory

There are four primary contributions to theory: (1) identifying the five Fintech models for AI adoption and growth, (2) identifying how trust is built in each of them, (3) that trust should be covered at the level of the business model, and (4) showing the similarities between Fintech and Insurtech. The five Fintech models that are based on the five Insurtech models (Zarifis & Cheng, 2023) are discussed in more detail below:

(a) Disaggregating and focusing on one part of the supply chain. This model seeks to get complementarities with partners (Zott & Amit, 2017) either through outsourcing or through an ecosystem. A financial organization utilizing this model may have less access to data and may need a way to overcome this. If it does not overcome this limited data, it will have less ability to identify trends and train Machine Learning. Using federated Machine Learning may be one of the solutions to overcome this, as this approach allows a Fintech to utilize other organizations' data without compromising privacy (Kaissis et al., 2020; Treleaven et al., 2022). Growth is achieved by attracting partners and utilizing the Fintech ecosystem better than others.
(b) Utilizing AI in the current processes without changing the business model. In this scenario a financial organization that covers the main parts of their supply chain integrates AI into their processes. Some internal capability in AI may be developed, but typically off the shelf solutions are used. In this model trust is built by the financial organization as they did before their digital transformation. Building trust

is simpler in some ways, as it is easier to maintain customers' personal information private when the processing is mostly done internally. Therefore, the organization moves forward keeping as much in-house as possible. This model will need a strong competitive advantage to overcome the challenges to scalling and achieving growth in this way.

(c) Finance incumbent extending their model to utilize AI and access new customers and data. A financial institution applying this model builds up their in-house AI capability and their ability to offer innovative services. By offering these new services they can reach new customers they would not have been able to access previously and obtain new data from those customers. Access to more data enhances their ability to utilize Machine Learning. An oversimplification of this approach would be an organization perceiving the increasing role of AI and automation as an opportunity for growth, not a threat. As AI favours large-scale operations and large-scale operations favour AI (Ashta & Herrmann, 2021), this model is a good fit for AI adoption and growth.

(d) Startup finance disruptor only getting involved in finance. These are often 'mobile-first' or at least 'born-digital' companies. They are created with a clear business model in mind with the purpose of utilizing the latest technologies, particularly AI. The model, with high automation and a low headcount, can achieve growth at a pace rarely seen in this area. These models cannot cover all the financial services and often find difficulty with the more complicated ones, such as complex loans, complex investments or complex insurance underwriting (Zarifis & Cheng, 2021).

(e) Tech company disruptor adding finance to their portfolio of services. Tech companies are in a strong position because they have a competitive advantage on AI, and they have existing customers and a vast volume of data. Previous barriers such as the need for specialized experts in the various facets of finance, and regulatory hurdles, are not what they used to be. Unlike a traditional financial organization that must build trust in their financial services, a tech-focused organization builds trust when the customers are attracted and onboarded to their other services.

The analysis supports the integral role of trust and why it should be included at the business model level. A business model should cover the governance of actions (Zott & Amit, 2017), and in the new Fintech business models, it must be clarified where in the value chain, and by who, trust is built with the consumer. Trust can be built in the traditional way by a dedicated finance company or by a tech company offering financial services.

This research contributes to a better understanding of the relationship between Fintech and Insurtech. As with previous research (Zarifis & Cheng, 2022) it finds similarities, but it also identifies some differences. The taxonomy of busines models developed and illustrated in Fig. 4.2 is similar, but not entirely the same, as the taxonomy of Insurtech it evolved out of.

Contribution to Practice

An innovative business model can increase the value for the organization, the customers and other stakeholders like suppliers and partners (Zott & Amit, 2017). Professionals working in Fintech or in a related field are looking for more clarity and direction in this transitionary period. Based on the literature review and the three stages of qualitative data collection and analysis, Fintech is going through a disruptive digital transformation. This transitionary period is happening in most parts of the world, but it may be happening at different speeds. The transition is not being driven by only one nation's economy, so it is hard to predict its development.

The five Fintech business models give an organization five proven routes to AI adoption and growth. In addition to providing a path for an organization to follow, the five models also make it easier for an organization in, or around, finance to understand what their 'friends', 'frenemies' or competitors are doing. This is helpful in a sector of the economy where success is highly dependent on choosing the best partners in the supply chain and fitting into the ecosystem better than the competition.

However, moving through a disruptive innovation in Fintech that started over five years ago and is still disrupting, with no clear sign of when this dramatic change will slow down, is not just about choosing the

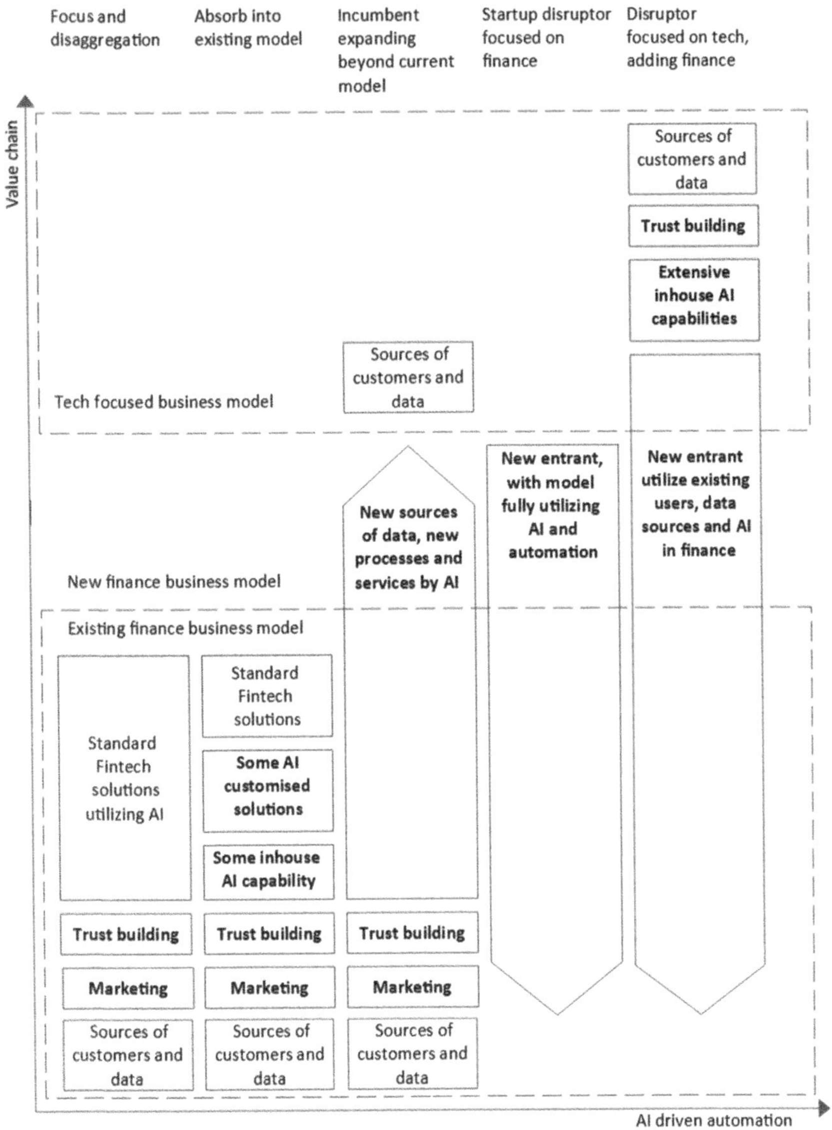

Fig. 4.2 The five Fintech business models that are optimized for AI

right business model. It is also about getting the timing right for each change that is implemented. For example, if customers are not comfortable interacting directly with AI for a claim on their insurance at this point in time, and it is implemented nevertheless, there will be pushback by the customers, and trust will be broken. While this research cannot resolve the challenge of getting the timing right on its own, it can inform these decisions. Fintech leaders can look at the taxonomy of the five Fintech business models and the dynamics of startups and tech companies entering and disrupting, and evaluate at what rate this is happening in their region.

In relation to trust, not only are Fintech managers given practical guidance on how to build it, but they are given some guidance as to where in the ecosystem it is a suitable place to build it. Trust should usually be built by the organization in the value chain that attracts and onboards the customer. Leaders of Fintech organizations should be clear where in the value chain trust is built and who is responsible, who has governance, of this.

Most governments are involved in the financial sector in various ways. Some take a more hands-on approach actively shaping the sector, while others take a more hands-off approach following the innovation in the sector. This research gives public sector managers, and leaders, a broad overview of Fintech informing their decisions. This research also has practical implications for regulators that need to understand the Fintech value chain and governance of different stages like AI development.

4.6 Conclusion

After three stages of iterative qualitative analysis this research identified five Fintech business models that are suitable for AI adoption and growth and how these models build trust. The five Fintech business models are (a) disaggregating and focusing on one part of the value chain, (b) utilizing AI in the current processes without changing the business model, (c) finance incumbent extending their model to utilize AI and access new customers and data, (d) startup finance disruptor only getting involved in finance, and (e) tech company disruptor adding finance to their portfolio of services. The five Fintech business models give an organization five proven routes to AI adoption and growth.

This research also finds support that for all Fintech models the way trust is built should be part of the business model. Trust is often not covered at the level of the business model and is left to operation managers to handle, but for the complex ad-hoc relationships in Fintech ecosystems this should be resolved before Fintech companies start trying to interlink their processes.

Trust is not always built at the same point in the value chain or by the same type of organization. The trust building is happening where the customers are attracted and onboarded. This means that while a traditional financial organization must build trust in their financial services, a tech-focused organization builds trust when the customers are attracted to other services.

Limitations and Future Research

The first limitation of this research is that the data was collected from people living in Germany and financial organizations active in Germany. The qualitative method, despite the iterative process, is based on peoples' subjective beliefs. Future research can further explore and validate the model in other countries and economic zones.

The qualitative method had a clear focus, but it did not stop participants from sharing their views on related issues. Participants were interested and, in some cases, concerned about how Fintech business model innovation affected other aspects of the economy and society in general. The broader implications of business model innovation in Fintech could be explored in future research.

References

Ashta, A., & Herrmann, H. (2021). Artificial Intelligence and Fintech: An Overview of Opportunities and Risks for Banking, Investments, and Microfinance. *Strategic Change, 30*(3), 211–222. https://doi.org/10.1002/jsc.2404

Auer, R., Haslhofer, B., Kitzler, S., Saggese, P., & Victor, F. (2023). *The Technology of Decentralized Finance (DeFi)*. www.bis.org

Bankins, S., Formosa, P., Griep, Y., & Richards, D. (2022). AI Decision Making with Dignity? Contrasting Workers' Justice Perceptions of Human and AI Decision Making in a Human Resource Management Context. *Information Systems Frontiers, 24*(3), 857–875. https://doi.org/10.1007/s10796-021-10223-8

Cheng, X., Zhang, X., Yang, B., & Fu, Y. (2022). An Investigation on Trust in AI-Enabled Collaboration: Application of AI-Driven Chatbot in Accommodation-Based Sharing Economy. *Electronic Commerce Research and Applications, 54*(May), 101164. https://doi.org/10.1016/j.elerap.2022.101164

Eaton, G. W., Green, T. C., Roseman, B. S., & Wu, Y. (2022). Retail Trader Sophistication and Stock Market Quality: Evidence from Brokerage Outages. *Journal of Financial Economics, 146*(2), 502–528. https://doi.org/10.1016/j.jfineco.2022.08.002

Eisenhardt, K. M. (1989). Building Theories from Case Study Research. *Academy of Management Review, 14*(4), 532–550. https://doi.org/10.5465/amr.1989.4308385

Eling, M., & Lehmann, M. (2018). The Impact of Digitalization on the Insurance Value Chain and the Insurability of Risks. *Geneva Papers on Risk and Insurance: Issues and Practice, 43*(3), 359–396. https://doi.org/10.1057/s41288-017-0073-0

Guo, B., & Liu, J. (2021). Internet Companies' Cultural Entrepreneurialism and Policy Interactions in China: Tencent's Case of "Neo-Culture Creativity" Strategy. *Digital Business, 1*(2), 1–8. https://doi.org/10.1016/j.digbus.2021.100015

Jagtiani, J., & Lemieux, C. (2018). Do Fintech Lenders Penetrate Areas that Are Underserved by Traditional Banks? *Journal of Economics and Business, 100*, 43–54. https://doi.org/10.1016/j.jeconbus.2018.03.001

Johnson, D., Rodwell, J., & Hendry, T. (2021). Analyzing the Impacts of Financial Services Regulation to Make the Case That Buy-Now-Pay-Later Regulation is Failing. *Sustainability (Switzerland), 13*(4), 1–20). MDPI. https://doi.org/10.3390/su13041992

Kaissis, G. A., Makowski, M. R., Rückert, D., & Braren, R. F. (2020). Secure, Privacy-Preserving and Federated Machine Learning in Medical Imaging. *Nature Machine Intelligence, 2*(6), 305–311. https://doi.org/10.1038/s42256-020-0186-1

Klaus, P., & Zaichkowsky, J. L. (2022). The Convenience of Shopping Via Voice AI: Introducing AIDM. *Journal of Retailing and Consumer Services, 65*. https://doi.org/10.1016/j.jretconser.2021.102490

Miles, M. B., & Huberman, A. M. (1994). *Qualitative Data Analysis*. Sage Publications.

Morris, M., Schindehutte, M., & Allen, J. (2005). The Entrepreneur's Business Model: Toward a Unified Perspective. *Journal of Business Research, 58*(6), 726–735. https://doi.org/10.1016/j.jbusres.2003.11.001

Ng, I. C. L., Xin, D., & Yip, N. (2013). Industrial Marketing Management Outcome-Based Contracts as New Business Model: The Role of Partnership and Value-Driven Relational Assets. *Industrial Marketing Management, 42*(5), 730–743. https://doi.org/10.1016/j.indmarman.2013.05.009

Pavlou, P., & Gefen, D. (2004). Building Effective Online Marketplaces with Institution-Based Trust. *Information Systems Research, 15*(1), 667–675. https://doi.org/10.1287/isre.1040.0015

Polites, G. L., & Karahanna, E. (2012). Shackled to the Status Quo: The Inhibiting Effects of Incumbent System Habit, Switching Costs, and Inertia on New System Acceptance. *MIS Quarterly, 36*(1), 21–42.

Puschman, T., & Alt, R. (2016). Sharing Economy. *Business & Information Systems Engineering, 58*(January), 93–99. https://doi.org/10.1016/j.nucengdes.2011.01.052

Treleaven, P., Smietanka, M., & Pithadia, H. (2022). Federated Learning: The Pioneering Distributed Machine Learning and Privacy-Preserving Data Technology. *Computer, 55*(4), 20–29. https://doi.org/10.1109/MC.2021.3052390

Zarifis, A., & Cheng, X. (2021). Evaluating the New AI and Data Driven Insurance Business Models for Incumbents and Disruptors: Is there Convergence? *Business Information Systems, July*, 199–208. https://doi.org/10.52825/bis.v1i.58

Zarifis, A., & Cheng, X. (2022). A Model of Trust in Fintech and Trust in Insurtech: How Artificial Intelligence and the Context Influence It. *Journal of Behavioral and Experimental Finance, 36*. https://doi.org/10.1016/j.jbef.2022.100739

Zarifis, A., & Cheng, X. (2023). AI Is Transforming Insurance with Five Emerging Business Models. In *Encyclopedia of Data Science and Machine Learning* (pp. 2086–2100). IGI Global. https://doi.org/10.4018/978-1-7998-9220-5.ch124

Zarifis, A., Holland, C. P., & Milne, A. (2019). Evaluating the Impact of AI on Insurance: The Four Emerging AI- and Data-Driven Business Models. *Emerald Open Research, 1*, 15. https://doi.org/10.35241/emeraldopenres.13249.1

Zarifis, A., Kawalek, P., & Azadegan, A. (2021). Evaluating If Trust and Personal Information Privacy Concerns Are Barriers to Using Health Insurance That Explicitly Utilizes AI. *Journal of Internet Commerce, 20*(1), 66–83. https://doi.org/10.1080/15332861.2020.1832817

Zott, C., & Amit, R. (2017). Business Model Innovation: How to Create Value in a Digital World. *NIM Marketing Intelligence Review, 9*(1), 18–23. https://doi.org/10.1515/gfkmir-2017-0003

Zott, C., Amit, R., & Massa, L. (2011). The Business Model: Recent Developments and Future Research. *Journal of Management, 37*(4), 1019–1042. https://doi.org/10.1177/0149206311406265

5

Digital Transformation and System Interoperability in EU Seaports: A Platform Facilitating Supply Chain in the Cruise Industry

Leonidas Efthymiou, Paraskevi Dekoulou, Yianna Orphanidou, and Eleftherios Sdoukopoulos

5.1 Introduction

Digital technology is a driving factor in contemporary businesses. It's a dynamic and transformative force, which alters all areas of organizations, including how they get organized and deliver value to customers. It facilitates adaptation, continuous improvement, new processes,

L. Efthymiou (✉) • Y. Orphanidou
School of Business, University of Nicosia, Nicosia, Cyprus
e-mail: efthymiou.l@unic.ac.cy; orphanidou.y@unic.ac.cy

P. Dekoulou
Aristotle University of Thessaloniki, University Campus, Thessaloniki, Greece
e-mail: dekoulou@jour.auth.gr

E. Sdoukopoulos
Hellenic Institute of Transport - Centre for Research and Technology Hellas, Marousi, Greece
e-mail: sdouk@certh.gr

A. Zarifis et al. (eds.), *Business Digital Transformation*,
https://doi.org/10.1007/978-3-031-33665-2_5

innovativeness, development of new products and the invention of disruptive business models (Porter & Heppelmann, 2014; Thrassou et al., 2022a). As a result, increasing digitization is rightly known as 'Digital Transformation'. However, while digital transformation is a way of progress for many businesses, not all organizations are ready to adopt its requirements and overcome its barriers (Shahi & Sinha, 2021). Existing infrastructure, knowhow and workers' skills differ from country to country. Therefore, technology diffusion takes place at different times and speeds in different parts of the world (Szabo et al., 2020).

Within this framework, the current chapter focuses on digital transformation in Greek and Cypriot seaports, along with its role in facilitating a sustainable supply chain for the cruise industry, within a broader framework of sustainable development (Efthymiou et al., 2023). The study is undertaken during a major EU-wide turn towards digitization. Part of this turn entails that seaport authorities are ought to adopt a National Maritime Singe Window (NMSW), a European Maritime Single Window (EMSW), and facilitate the interoperability between various platforms and systems. Systems like the NMSW and EMSW are digital platforms capable of receiving, processing and exchanging data among ships that arrive at or depart in seaports across the EU (Efthymiou et al., 2022a). Besides, in the context of ports, logistics and cruise supply chains, business processes are highly dependent on efficient information flows between seaport authorities and all involved organizations (Heilig et al., 2017), including cruise ships, agents and operators. Specifically, the current chapter examines the progress of the implementation of NMSW and EMSW in Greek and Cypriot ports. In addition, it examines the possible development of an e-marketplace platform, intended to support the cruise industry's supply chain while being interoperable with other systems.

The analysis draws on findings collected through face-to-face interviews and electronic questionnaires with the leadership of Shipping Deputy Ministry, Cyprus Port authority (CPA), cruise companies and other key stakeholders. Also, certain stakeholder-groups (producers, suppliers and cruise companies) were given the opportunity to test the supply-chain platform on a piloting basis, prior to participating in the survey. The chapter's structure is organized in the following manner: in the next section, the analysis offers a review of digitization, including the evolution of NMSW, EMSW and platform technology in the cruise industry. Then, a section presents the research design and methods of the study. After that, the chapter presents its findings concerning the progress of NMSW, EMSW and the pilot use of an e-marketplace platform. The final section summarizes the chapter's key points while discussing possible implications of digital transformation on the cruise industry's supply chain.

5.2 Literature Review

Digital transformation is becoming increasingly prevalent as it enables the development of new processes, products and business models (Thrassou et al., 2022b). Technologies like Artificial Intelligence (AI), Blockchain, Virtual Reality (VR), Metaverse, Augmented Reality (AR), platform-analytics and robots can now be found in various industries, including tourism (Buhalis, 2020), banking (Batiz-Lazo & Efthymiou, 2016), maritime (Sdoukopoulos et al., 2020; Kapidani et al., 2020), accounting (Batiz-Lazo et al., 2022), health-care (Garcia-Perez et al., 2022), hospitality (Efthymiou, 2018), aviation, insurance (Zarifis & Cheng, 2022), academia (Zarifis & Efthymiou, 2022; Efthymiou et al., 2022b) and learning (Epaminonda et al., 2022). Following the fast and widespread diffusion of digitization in various sectors, seaports, shipping and cruise companies couldn't be an exception.

Digital transformation in seaports concerns specific technologies, which have been deployed gradually over the last 40 years or so. According to Heilig et al. (2017), the evolution and diffusion of digital technology in seaports can be found in three main phases: (a) paperless procedures, (b) automated procedures and (c) smart procedures. In the first phase, important paper documents were transformed into electronic documents. During this phase, which took place in the 1980s, digital transformation was taking place at different levels through the deployment of isolated IT systems with basic IT functionality.

In the second phase, which took place in the 1990s and 2000s, existing Information Technology served as a foundation on which new systems were added, contributing further to process automation. The new automated systems (e.g. laser technologies for distance detection and collision prevention) provided increased safety and time efficiency (Heilig et al., 2017). Also, by the 2000s, the need to facilitate information exchange between governments and involved organizations led to the development of a National Maritime Single Window (NMSW). This time, nevertheless, digital transformation was intended to be institutionalized across all EU member states. On 20 October 2010, the 'European Parliament and of the Council' issued the 'Directive 2010/65/EU on reporting formalities for ships arriving in and/or departing from ports of the Member States and repealing Directive 2002/6/EC' (Official Journal of the European Union, 2010). Through this directive, all electronic transmissions had to become standardized through a national Single Window, which enables all involved organizations to input a specific set of information electronically, using a single point of data entry and storage. The European Parliament set a deadline for implementation by 1 June 2015, offering to Member States five years to establish a National Maritime Single Window (NMSW).

However, despite being helpful, each country's NMSW does not facilitate harmonization across EU ports. Therefore, the European Commission proposed to bring reporting requirements under one digital space through a 'European Maritime Single Window—EMSW'(Official Journal of the European Union, 2010). This development is part of the third phase of digital transformation, which began in the 2010s and is currently ongoing. The main aim of EMSW is to harmonize reporting procedures for shipping operators and ensure that data can be shared and reused efficiently through the once-only principle, where ships can report once per port-call and the same information would be reused for subsequent port-calls within the EU. The regulation was published on 25 July 2019 and entered into force on 14 August 2019 as *Regulation (EU) 2019/1239 of the European Parliament and of the Council of 20 June 2019 establishing a European Maritime Single Window environment and repealing Directive 2010/65/EU* (EU Monitor, 2019).

Digital transformation through EMSW results to improved interoperability between various systems, making it much easier to share and reuse data (Maritime Cyprus, 2019). Digitization facilitates information transfer, retention, reuse and re-dissemination. Also, EMSW promotes cooperation between customs and business communities, enables traders to trade with a single administrative authority and support the smooth movement of goods through secure international supply chains (Koliousis & Katsoulakos, 2015).

The capabilities offered in the third phase of digital transformation enable us to explore further the development and application of an e-marketplace platform, capable of supporting a supply chain in the Cruise Industry in Greece and Cyprus. More specifically, we explore the progress of the implementation of EMSW in Greece and Cyprus and whether the interoperability of systems could enable the development of an e-marketplace platform that brings together small producers, local suppliers and international cruise companies, as part of sustainable supply chains.

5.3 Research Design and Methods

Two different studies have been conducted for the purposes of this chapter. The first study was qualitative and included face-to-face interviews with different stakeholders. The purpose was to explore the progress of the implementation of NMSW and EMSW in Greek and Cypriot seaports. The interviews were conducted with government officials from the Shipping Deputy Ministry, Port Managers, cruise-company representatives, local producers, suppliers, Information Technology and Communication companies, International Ship Management companies, International Cruise and Infrastructure Consultants, and representatives of DP World (operator of the largest port in Cyprus). During face-to-face interviews, we also had the opportunity to observe how different platforms operate. For example, in one of our visits, the Cyprus Port Authority's (CPA) representative offered a tour of NMSW by sharing his computer screen with us. To align with established ethical standards on anonymity, all participants' names are kept confidential.

The second study was quantitative, aiming to collect findings concerning the evaluation of the e-marketplace platform. Prior to circulating the questionnaire, responders were asked to test the platform (e-marketplace).

The Platform was put into trial operation at the beginning of 2021, and a pilot implementation was carried out for the ports of Heraklion, Chania, Rhodes, Mytilene, Chios, Santorini, Larnaca and Limassol.

The total population from which the primary data of this research was drawn is composed of the two main categories of users involved: (a) suppliers/producers of local products and (b) cruise companies/agencies. Primary data were collected with the aid of a structured self-completion questionnaire. The questionnaire was created with the help of the Google Forms web tool and distributed electronically. The completion of the questionnaire was anonymous and was delivered only to respondents being registered on the Platform.

The questionnaire was distributed to:

- One hundred seventy-nine companies, members of the Cyprus Chamber of Commerce and Industry. These enterprises were invited to register on the Platform and to take part in the pilot application. These are enterprises active in the primary and secondary sector—dairies, mills, wineries, producers of sausages, traditional sweets and bakeries
- Two cruise companies in Cyprus
- Members of the Cyprus Sustainable Tourism Association (local producers and passengers)

The evaluation of the Platform in Greece, which followed the pilot implementation stage, was developed in two levels. At the first level, producers and suppliers of local traditional products registered on the Platform. At the second level, they responded to the evaluation questionnaire. The questionnaire was created with the use of the Google Forms online tool, was not anonymous and was distributed to the 71 businesses that had registered on the Platform to take part in the pilot. Convenience sampling method was selected, and 38 questionnaires were collected. The businesses that participated in the survey are active in the primary and secondary processing sectors—mills, cheese dairies, wineries, distilleries, beekeepers, producers of local sweets and local traditional products—and the trade of their products.

5.4 Findings

Study 1: Implementation of NMSW, EMSW and Links to the Cruise Supply Chain

The findings of the first study suggest that the National Maritime Single Window was established fully in most EU countries, including Cyprus, in line with the Directive 2010/65/EU. However, the system in Greece has only been implemented partially. The delay has to do with a number of factors, such as the numerous Greek islands and ports, often with limited availability of human resources. Also, our findings suggest that different stakeholder-groups are trained on how to use it, such as the private shipping agents who interact with the NMSW system directly via the Cyprus Port Authority (CPA).

At the same time, authorities in each EU member state (e.g. Ministries of Shipping) work in a coordinated way to implement the European Maritime Single Window (EMSW). The deadline for implementation is 15 August 2025. Representatives of CPA and the Shipping Deputy Ministry of Cyprus explained that much of the work has already been done. Although its full implementation is going to take some years, many of the processes have already been established, employees have attended relevant training and much of the infrastructure is already in place. According to officials in CPA's IT Department, several meetings took place with the other 26 member states, where they decided what exactly the EMSW should include. The system will be standardized for all ports across the EU. The components and forms used will be the same across the entire network, and no changes will be allowed on the platform by individual member states.

When we asked about the possible contribution of EMSW to the supply chain, the immediate response was *No. EMSW will neither be related to, nor enhance the cruise supply chain. The system will be so standardized that leaves no space for modifications relating to the supply chain.* As we understand by such statements, due to its standardized structure, EMSW will have no direct impact on the cruise supply chain. However, some of its benefits, which concern time efficiency and information transfer in real time across EU ports, are likely to enhance cooperation between customs and business communities, facilitate smooth movement of goods and minimize the complexity of inter-stakeholder relationships (Interview 5 in a Ship Management Company, Control Room Manager). Also, due to the interoperability of systems, EMSW can work in parallel with existing systems, such as the NMSW and SafeSeaNet, to enhance the utilization of information in the cruise supply chain. In other words, while EMSW will not contribute directly, it adds to the development of a digital environment, in which other systems and stakeholders coexist.

Moreover, departing by the benefits stemming by the EMSW environment, we attempted to identify the intention of stakeholders in using an e-marketplace platform through a second study. Below we present the survey's findings.

Study 2: Stakeholders' Opinion About the Development of a Platform-Based e-Marketplace

The findings in this section were collected through a survey, by responders who tested the actual e-marketplace platform. In Cyprus, the majority of participants in the evaluation process (60%) state that they are satisfied with the Platform, while 20% are very satisfied. Similarly, in Greece, the vast majority of respondents (82%) from the three regions expressed an overall satisfaction with the Platform, with 53% stating that they are satisfied and 29% very satisfied. A comparative assessment of the responses from the three regions shows a common positive view of the participants.

Platform Strengths

Concerning the Platform's strengths, companies in Cyprus indicated the ease of registering a new user, with which the majority of respondents said they were satisfied (55%) or very satisfied (25%), as well as the ease of access, which gained the satisfaction of all respondents (90%). Almost all participants (90%) in the evaluation process expressed their

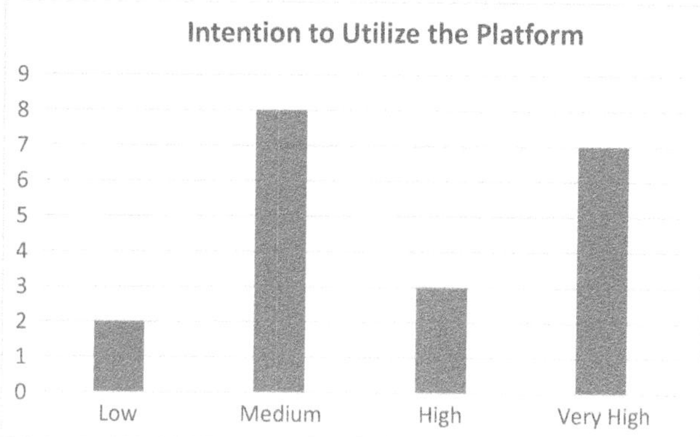

Graph 5.1 Intention to use the Platform in Cyprus

satisfaction with the usability of the Platform, while the majority of them positively evaluated the loading speed (Graph 5.1) and the way products are presented, and described the Platform as elegant and user-friendly. One element of the Platform that, according to the participants, is subject to significant improvement is the support through the submission of queries.

Similarly, businesses in Greece pointed out the ease of user registration as the strongest point of the platform, followed by the platform's aesthetics and friendliness and the speed of loading. One element of the platform that, according to the participants, is subject to significant improvement is its usability and ease of access to it.

Use of the Platform by PDO Organizations and Products

One of the most important findings of the survey is the view expressed by respondents in Cyprus that the Platform is quite (40%) to very (35%) likely to be used by organizations related to the cruise industry (Graph 5.2).

In Greece, regarding the likelihood of the Platform being used by local producers/suppliers, a generally positive attitude emerges, with 21% responding that it is very likely and 58% responding that it is very or

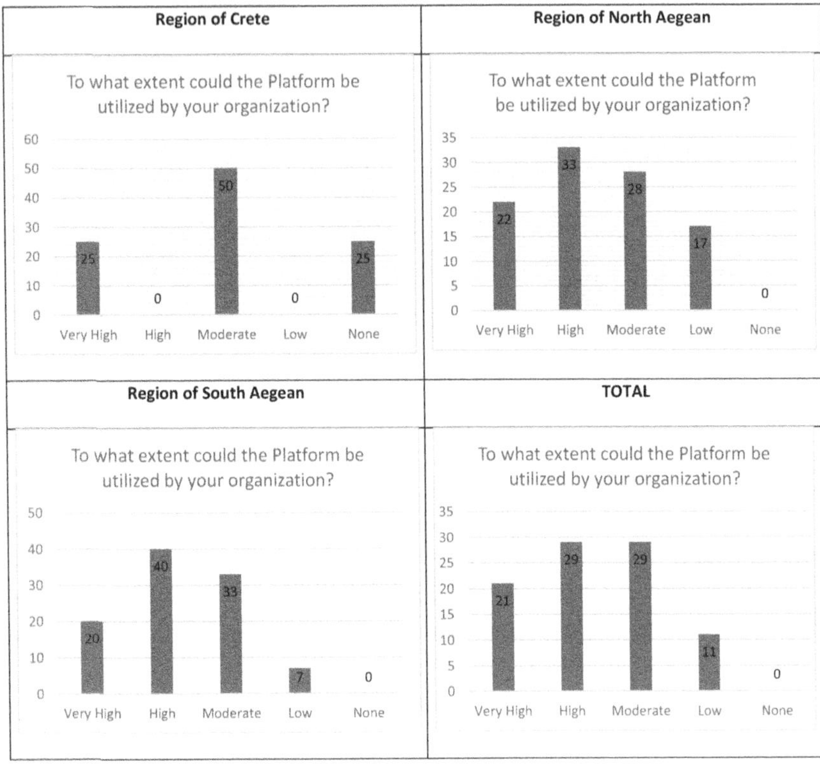

Graph 5.2 Intention to utilize the Platform in Greece

likely that the platform will be used by organizations related to the cruise industry (Graph 5.2).

In both Cyprus (60%) and Greece (59%) the majority of respondents expect that the new products available through the Platform will meet the market needs for PDO (protected designation of origin) products. Regarding the possibility to carry out economic transactions through the Platform, in Cyprus, a sufficient number of evaluation participants expressed their distrust, which may be due to the lack of sufficient information on how the Platform is managed. On the contrary, in Greece, the majority of participants (64%) in the evaluation expressed a positive attitude towards the possibility of conducting financial transactions through the Platform if the Platform operates smoothly and under certain conditions to secure transactions. Noteworthy, however, is the percentage of participants (32%) who expressed reservations about the Platform's ability to support financial transactions.

5.5 Competitive Advantages of the Platform (Graph 5.3)

Exploring the potential competitive advantages of the Platform, participants both in Cyprus and in Greece acknowledge its important role as a source of information and consider it an important marketing tool. The Platform's contribution to the development of new sales channels and the promotion of innovation has been regarded as less important. In Cyprus, half of the respondents state that the Platform could improve

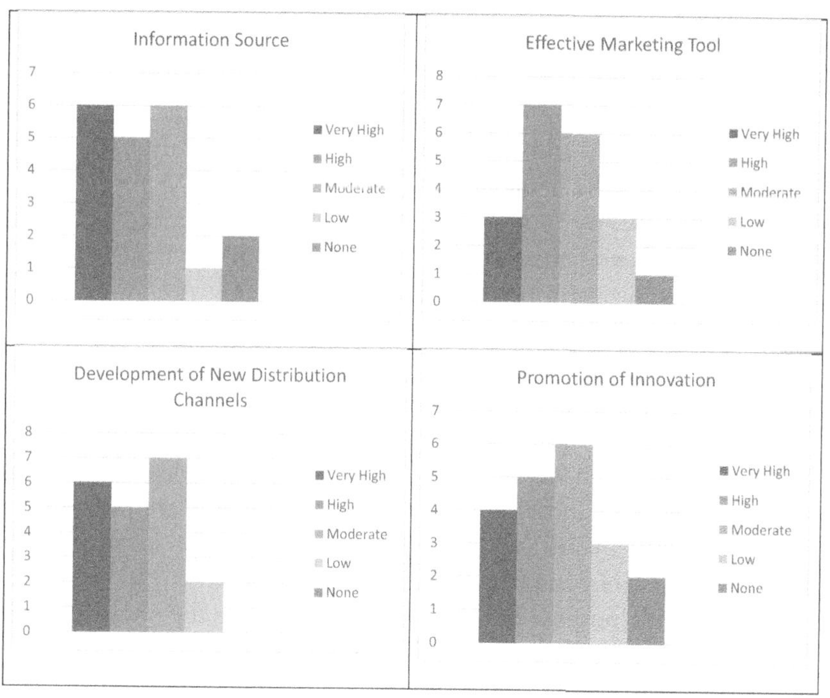

Graph 5.3 Platform's competitive advantage points (firms in Cyprus)

employability, while 45 of them highlight the possibility of local products being offered through interconnection with other ports. In Greece, the vast majority of respondents stress that the Platform could significantly enhance employability, while 70% of them consider possible the provision of local products through other ports.

5.6 Discussion and Conclusion

Our findings reconfirm that digital transformation is subject to localized conditions and takes place in different places at different times. The example of National Maritime Single Window (NMSW) is quite indicative. While Cyprus has implemented the 2010/65/EU directive in all ports, other EU member states are yet to complete its deployment. This finding resembles with previous studies, suggesting that some technologies are implemented easier and more frequently, depending on different factors, such as each country's available resources, specialization, existing technology, expertise and workers' skills (Szabo et al., 2020).

Moreover, digital transformation these days is also about institutionalized standardization and efficiency. For example, the EU2019/1239 directive concerns the implementation of the European Maritime Single Window (EMSW) by 15 August 2025, across all EU member states. The system will be standardized in all EU ports, and no changes will be allowed on the platform by individual member states. According to our participants, standardization is the only way towards materialization.

Another finding concerns the interoperability of EMSW and e-marketplace platforms. While EMSW is not expected to contribute directly to an enhanced supply chain for the cruise industry, there are a number of indirect benefits. Time efficiency, fast turnover, information transfer amongst EU ports and reuse of that information are amongst the benefits, creating an environment where supply chains can improve along with enhanced interconnectivity among stakeholders.

Then, another purpose of this study was to explore the possible development of a platform-based e-marketplace, aiming to elicit the involvement of various stakeholders in the cruise supply chain in Greek and Cypriot ports. More specifically, the idea was to examine whether different stakeholders are willing to become users of a platform that links end-users directly with local producers through trustworthy and secured transactions while promoting tourism authenticity with the provision of local products. According to the responders and participants, the Platform is an innovative tool for the supply chain in Greek and Cypriot ports. It strengthens interoperability with other systems while enhancing the dissemination of information between stakeholders. Also, the Platform can significantly strengthen local economies, offering opportunities for local producers in both Greece and Cyprus to promote their products in the cruise sector without mediation.

In terms of Authenticity, the promotion of certified local products, which promise guaranteed quality while promoting their traditional profile, can contribute significantly to the enhancement of tourists' experience. Also, new products can be made available that are labelled as PDO (Protected Designation of Origin). In other words, it can be a means of promoting and exhibiting local products.

The evaluation survey of the NAYS e-marketplace platform in both Cyprus and Greece shows the remarkable overall satisfaction of the respondents from the operation of the Platform. However, while in Greece the majority of the respondents underlined that the Platform can significantly facilitate the sale and distribution of products through interconnection with other ports, in Cyprus more than half of the respondents expressed their distrust regarding the ability of the Platform to facilitate the sale and distribution of products through interoperability with other ports. This reveals that the Cypriot market is not yet ready to interchange through the Platform. Also, it goes back to the main point discussed in this section, suggesting the digital transformation is also subject to local conditions. Furthermore, participants suggested that the Platform needs to be centrally managed and marketed to the cruise market. If done properly, the Platform can boost employment.

Finally, the current study makes a significant contribution to literature as it is driven by the voice of leading stakeholders to explore the digitization of the cruise industry and its impact on its supply chain. It's not a study that generalizes its findings. Rather, it provides a micro-snapshot of how two countries influence and are influenced by digital transformation. Also, the digital transformation presented in this study concerns both institutionalized and private initiatives, which can both contribute towards efficiency in a digitized supply chain for the cruise industry. The study's findings can be useful to ports in the Mediterranean region and other member states. Future research can examine EMSW's progress of implementation and how new technologies contribute further to inclusion and interoperability.

References

Batiz-Lazo, B., & Efthymiou, L. (2016). Introduction: The 360 Degrees of Cashlessness. In B. Batiz-Lazo & L. Efthymiou (Eds.), *The Book of Payments: Historical and Contemporary Views on the Cashless Economy* (pp. 1–10). Palgrave Macmillan.

Batiz-Lazo, B., Efthymiou, L., & Davies, K. (2022). The Spread of Artificial Intelligence and Its Impact on Employment: Evidence from the Banking and Accounting Sectors. In A. Thrassou, D. Vrontis, L. Efthymiou, Y. Weber, S. M. R. Shams, & E. Tsoukatos (Eds.), *Business Advancement through Technology Volume II. Palgrave Studies in Cross-disciplinary Business Research, In Association with EuroMed Academy of Business*. Palgrave Macmillan. https://doi.org/10.1007/978-3-031-07765-4_7

Buhalis, D. (2020). Technology in Tourism-from Information Communication Technologies to eTourism and Smart Tourism Towards Ambient Intelligence Tourism: A Perspective Article. *Tourism Review, 75*(1), 267.

Efthymiou, L. (2018). Worker Body-Art in Upper-Market Hotels: Neither Accepted, nor Prohibited. *International Journal of Hospitality Management, 74*, 99–108.

Efthymiou, L., Dekoulou, E., Orphanidou, Y., Sdoukopoulos, E., Perra, V., Boile, M., & Bras, I. (2022a). Crisis, Adaptation and Sustainability: Digital System Interoperability in the Cruise Industry. In D. Vrontis, A. Thrassou, Y. Weber, S. M. R. Shams, E. Tsoukatos, & L. Efthymiou (Eds.), *Business Under Crisis, Volume III. Palgrave Studies in Cross-disciplinary Business Research, In Association with EuroMed Academy of Business*. Palgrave Macmillan. https://doi.org/10.1007/978-3-030-76583-5_5

Efthymiou, L., Ktoridou, D., Epaminonda, E., & Michailidis, M. (2022b). *The Relationship of Strategy and Technology in Education: Bidirectional Pedagogical Considerations*. 2022 IEEE Global Engineering Education Conference (EDUCON), 2022, pp. 2099–2103. https://doi.org/10.1109/EDUCON52537.2022.9766467

Efthymiou, L., Kulshrestha, A., & Kulshrestha, S. (2023). A Study on Sustainability and ESG in the Service Sector in India: Benefits, Challenges, and Future Implications. *Adm. Sci. 13*, 165. https://doi.org/10.3390/admsci13070165

Epaminonda, E., Efthymiou, L., & Doukanari, E. (2022). *Linking Digital Transformation to Learning Strategies and Pedagogy*. 2022 IEEE Global Engineering Education Conference (EDUCON), 2022, pp. 2088–2092. https://doi.org/10.1109/EDUCON52537.2022.9766614

EU Monitor. (2019). COM(2018)278 - European Maritime Single Window environment. Online at: https://www.eumonitor.eu/9353000/1/j9vvik7m1c3gyxp/vl0h7d6zqbz6. Accessed 11-September-2019.

Garcia-Perez, A., Cegarra-Navarro, J. G., Sallos, M. P., Martinez-Caro, E., & Chinnaswamy, A. (2022). Resilience in Healthcare Systems: Cyber Security and Digital Transformation. *Technovation*, 102583. ISSN 0166-4972. https://doi.org/10.1016/j.technovation.2022.102583

Heilig, L., Schwarze, S., & Voß, S. (2017). *An Analysis of Digital Transformation in the History and Future of Modern Ports*. Proceedings of the 50th Hawaii International Conference on System Sciences. https://doi.org/10.24251/HICSS.2017.160

Kapidani, N., Tijan, E., Jović, M., Kočan, E. (2020). National Maritime Single Window – Cost-Benefit Analysis of Montenegro Case Study. *PROMET*. Available from: https://traffic.fpz.hr/index.php/PROMTT/article/view/3422. Accessed 11 Nov 2020

Koliousis, I., & Katsoulakos, T. (2015). Maritime Single Windows: Lessons learned from the eMAR Project. In Ehlers et al. (Eds.), *Maritime-Port Technology and Development*. Taylor & Francis Group. ISBN 978-1-138-02726-8.

Maritime Cyprus. (2019). *EU – Modernizing ship reporting systems (European Maritime Single Window environment)*. 07-01-2019. Online at: https://maritimecyprus.com/2019/01/07/eu-modernizing-ship-reporting-systems-european-maritime-single-window-environment/. Accessed 22 Aug 2019.

Official Journal of the European Union. (2010). *Directives: 'Directive 2010/65/EU on reporting formalities for ships arriving in and/or departing from ports of the Member States and repealing Directive 2002/6/EC'*. 29 October 2010. Online at: https://eur-lex.europa.eu/LexUriServ/LexUriServ.do?uri=OJ:L:2010:283:0001:0010:EN:PDF. Accessed 12 Aug 2019.

Porter, M. E., & Heppelmann, J. E. (2014). How Smart, Connected Products Are Transforming Competition. *Harvard Business Review, 92*, 64–88.

Sdoukopoulos, E., Perra, V. M., Boile, M., Efthymiou, L., Dekoulou, E., & Orphanidou, Y. (2020). *Connecting Cruise Lines with Local Supply Chains for Enhancing Customer Experience: A Platform Application in Greece, #113*. Paper Presented at CSUM 2020, 17–19 June 2020, Greece. http://csum.civ.uth.gr/wp-content/uploads/2020/05/VirtualCSUM2020_programme.pdf

Shahi, C., & Sinha, M. (2021). Digital Transformation: Challenges Faced by Organizations and Their Potential Solutions. *International Journal of Innovation Science, 13*(1), 17–33. https://doi.org/10.1108/IJIS-09-2020-0157

Szabo, R. Z., Vuksanović Herceg, I., Hanák, R., Hortovanyi, L., Romanová, A., Mocan, M., & Djuričin, D. (2020). Industry 4.0 Implementation in B2B Companies: Cross-Country Empirical Evidence on Digital Transformation in the CEE Region. *Sustainability, 12*(22), 9538. https://doi.org/10.3390/su12229538

Thrassou, A., Vrontis, D., Efthymiou, L., & Uzunboylu, N. (2022a). An Overview of Business Advancement Through Technology: Markets and Marketing in Transition. In A. Thrassou, D. Vrontis, L. Efthymiou, Y. Weber, S. M. R. Shams, & E. Tsoukatos (Eds.), *Business Advancement through Technology Volume I. Palgrave Studies in Cross-disciplinary Business Research, In Association with EuroMed Academy of Business*. Palgrave Macmillan. https://doi.org/10.1007/978-3-031-07769-2_1

Thrassou, A., Vrontis, D., Efthymiou, L., & Uzunboylu, N. (2022b). An Overview of Business Advancement Through Technology: The Changing Landscape of Work and Employment. In A. Thrassou, D. Vrontis, L. Efthymiou, Y. Weber, S. M. R. Shams, & E. Tsoukatos (Eds.), *Business Advancement through Technology Volume II. Palgrave Studies in Cross-disciplinary Business Research, In Association with EuroMed Academy of Business*. Palgrave Macmillan. https://doi.org/10.1007/978-3-031-07765-4_1

Zarifis, A., & Cheng, X. (2022). A model of trust in Fintech and trust in Insurtech: How Artificial Intelligence and the context influence it, *Journal of Behavioral and Experimental Finance*, 36, 100739, ISSN 2214–6350, https://doi.org/10.1016/j.jbef.2022.100739

Zarifis, A., & Efthymiou, L. (2022). *The Four Business Models for AI Adoption in Education: Giving Leaders a Destination for the Digital Transformation Journey*. 2022 IEEE Global Engineering Education Conference (EDUCON), pp. 1868–1872. https://doi.org/10.1109/EDUCON52537.2022.9766687

6

The Six Ways to Build Trust and Reduce Privacy Concern in a Central Bank Digital Currency (CBDC)

Alex Zarifis and Xusen Cheng

6.1 Introduction

Central Bank Digital Currencies (CBDCs) have been implemented by only a handful of countries, but they are being explored by many more (Kosse & Mattei, 2022). CBDCs are digital currencies issued and backed by a central bank. Consumer trust can encourage or discoura ge the adoption of this currency, which is also a payment system and a technology. This research attempts to understand consumer trust in CBDCs so that the development and adoption stages are more effective and satisfying for all the stakeholders.

A. Zarifis (✉)
School of Business, University of Nicosia, Nicosia, Cyprus

Cambridge Centre for Alternative Finance, University of Cambridge, Cambridge, UK
e-mail: zarifis.a@unic.ac.cy

X. Cheng
School of Information, Renmin University of China, Beijing, China
e-mail: xusen.cheng@ruc.edu.cn

A. Zarifis et al. (eds.), *Business Digital Transformation*,
https://doi.org/10.1007/978-3-031-33665-2_6

The digital transformation sweeping through many sectors of the economy and facets of people's lives is also disrupting money and payment systems. Governments want a currency and payment solution that is more efficient and intelligent, and consumers want to make transactions faster and cheaper (Abramova et al., 2021). Consumers have shown an interest in the functionality provided by cryptocurrencies, but the recurring problems with cryptoassets, such as the FTX collapse, suggest that a more centralized and regulated cryptocurrency solution should be provided by governments to offer similar functionality with less risk. If this is not achieved however, history shows that when consumers do not want a currency or payment system, they chose alternatives such as other countries' currencies, cryptoassets, Decentralized Finance (DeFi), or the grey economy (Grassi et al., 2022). Therefore, as with many solutions involving technology, it is more effective to design something appealing to the consumer than push a flawed solution onto them, either with promotions, regulations, or laws. It may seem like a simple choice to implement CBDCs, but however, it is far from simple. The cautious, slow progress of some central banks through many pilot implementations is probably warranted (Xu, 2022). Unlike some technologies like the metaverse that can be repeatedly pitched to the consumer year after year until they are successfully adopted, a failed implementation of a CBDC would have far-reaching consequences. This cautious approach, however, must not take longer than necessary, and the optimum solutions for CBDCs, including trust, must be reached. Recent events showed that governments around the world want to make a variety of interventions as fast as possible, such as giving citizens of a whole country some additional money to deal with high inflation (Walker & Sexton, 2022). Many consumers lives seem to be going from one disruption to the other recently (Gielens, 2022), with the word 'permacrisis' being selected as the word of the year by Collins Dictionary (Shariatmadari, 2022). The uncertainty many consumers face, and will probably face for some time to come, means having their trust should not be taken as a given. Research into CBDCs recognizes that more needs to be done to understand this phenomenon and, in particular, the role the technology plays from the consumer's perspective (Bhaskar et al., 2022). Consumer trust is an important factor in technology adoption (Lankton et al., 2015). Therefore, the two related research questions are:

What are the methods to build consumer trust in a CBDC?
Does trust in a CBDC encourage its adoption by a consumer?

There are a variety of CBDC solutions. The primary distinctions are between wholesale and retail CBDCs, and one or two-tier CBDCs (Auer & Böhme, 2020). For this research we are considering the one-tier CBDC solution. This is for two reasons. Firstly because of its popularity within early movers like the Chinese CBDC, formally known as the electronic Chinese Yuan or the e-CNY (Xu, 2022). The second reason is because it is a simpler implementation, with fewer factors influencing the consumer's perspective, and therefore easier to create a representative model and validate it.

This research found support for a model with six factors influencing trust in a CBDC and found that trust in the CBDC did indeed encourage its adoption. The six factors that influence trust in a CBDC identified in this research are the following: (1) Trust in the government and the central bank issuing a CBDC, (2) expressed guarantees for the user of a CBDC, (3) positive reputation of existing CBDCs implemented in other countries, (4) automation and reduced human involvement achieved by a CBDC technology, (5) trust-building functionality of a CBDC, and (6) privacy features of the CBDC wallet app and back-end processes such as anonymity.

The following literature review of CBDCs and trust gives a sufficient foundation for the research model, that is presented in the third section. This is followed by the methodology section, where the quantitative approach using Structural Equation Modelling (SEM) is outlined. After that comes the analysis and results, the discussion of the findings, and finally the conclusion, which includes suggestions for future research.

6.2 Theoretical Foundation

This review first explores the various models and implementations of CBDCs before moving on to trust in the related areas of currencies, payments, and technology. While the literature of trust in CBDCs does not sufficiently cover this topic, the extensive literature of trust in the constituent parts of a CBDC (currency, payment system, and technology) gives this research a sufficient theoretical foundation to build on.

Central Bank Digital Currencies (CBDCs)

CBDCs are different to other cryptocurrencies like Bitcoin as they are issued by a country's central bank and cannot be mined. Therefore, they are very centralized and not decentralized at all. The use of cash is declining over time in most countries, and the idea to offer a purely digital currency and payment system is not new (Tee & Ong, 2016). As is often the case with new technologies, the timing can make the difference between successful adoption by consumers or failure. The confluence of cryptoasset popularity, DeFi popularity, the digital transformation in many sectors of the economy and several other factors have convinced many countries that the right time is now (Luu et al., 2022; Lee et al., 2021).

There are several variations of CBDCs. The most important variations are between (a) retail and wholesale and (b) one and two tiers (Auer & Böhme, 2020): (a) A CBDC can either be retail or wholesale. A retail CBDC is used by individuals for their savings and to make purchases. A wholesale CBDC is primarily used by financial institutions for their reserves and large payments. (b) The operations of a CBDC can either be over one or two tiers. If it operates over one tier, a central bank provides an electronic wallet to the individual to use it. The Chinese e-CNY operates in this way (Xu, 2022). A CBDC that operates with two tiers essentially replicates the current design where a currency is issued by a central bank but private banks hold individuals' savings and process their payments. It is possible to have both systems in parallel, a hybrid CBDC, so the user has a choice.

CBDC advantages: There are several advantages to CBDCs. Firstly, as it is entirely digital it is more efficient than the current solution of paper money, both within and between borders (Bossone & Ardic, 2021). In a one-tier system there is also disintermediation which further increases efficiency (Ahn & Chen, 2022). Secondly, transactions can be tracked which should reduce crime, particularly money laundering and fraud. Thirdly, by offering a CBDC a government reduces the appeal of risky cryptocurrencies and stablecoins. From the user's perspective, opening an account is easier as their government already has the necessary personal details. It should also make having a bank account easier for citizens that live in remote areas as they do not need to travel to a physical bank.

CBDC risks: CBDCs may introduce some risks that must be analysed and understood before an implementation. The three main ones are as follows: (a) Inevitably, a greater reliance on technology makes cybersecurity risks more dangerous. The vulnerabilities can be with the infrastructure providers, the operators of the CBDC and the users (Banxico, 2021). (b) A problematic implementation may lead to low adoption or even reduce trust and confidence in CBDCs. (c) The ease of use of CBDCs may lead to competition between several CBDCs. If a user can easily access several CBDCs they will compare them based on how well they keep their value, as with current currencies. However, unlike current currencies the functionality of the digital wallet may also play a role and become a relative advantage.

Trust in Currencies, Payments, and Technology

Despite trust typically being based on principles from psychology and sociology that remain relatively consistent, it often has significant differences in a new context where the relationship between the trustor and the trustee is different. For the digital Euro, early signs suggest that image and credibility influence trust (Tronnier et al., 2022). The trustor, in this context a citizen, must trust a government to back the monetary value of the cash they have. In many countries this used to be backed by gold, meaning a citizen in theory could receive gold to the monetary value of the cash they had. This then evolved, leaving gold out of the equation, but the citizen could still hold cash in the form of physical notes if they wanted to. CBDCs once again change this relationship leaving any physical proof out of the equation. This is a fundamental change, and hence 'digital' is in the name of this new form of currency and payment system. While in many countries cash has been on the way out for some time

(Tee & Ong, 2016), its role in the relationship with the user, and its role in building trust with the user, should not be underestimated. The new relationship between the trustor (citizen) and trustee (government and central bank) replaces previous physical assurances, with technology. Therefore, trust in the technology is important. Previous research has shown that trust in technology is different to trust in people (Lankton et al., 2015).

In addition to technology, in the relationship between the trustor (citizen) and trustee (government and central bank), there are still people that play a role in the process on the side of the trustee. However, there is a limited direct interaction between the citizen and the people that make up the government and the central bank, and a limited or no personal relationship. Therefore, in this relationship, as with other similar ones, it is better to look at trust in the institutions (Pavlou & Gefen, 2004). The literature therefore suggests that the citizen's trust in a CBDC may be based firstly on trust in institutions and secondly trust in technology. Institutional trust is defined as the consumer's perception that third-party organizations (not the one purchasing or making a sale) can effectively support the exchange (Pavlou & Gefen, 2004).

The term institutional trust has been used since the 1980s to describe the ability of institutions to build trust (Zucker, 1986). For CBDCs institutional trust will depend on the specific risks people and societies face, and which institutions are in an ideal position to build trust back up to the necessary level. These institutions are not just a third party that the consumer is familiar with. There is 'trust transference' between the third party and the trustee. This trust transference is covered by literature on network trust (McEvily et al., 2003), but it is not the only way institutions build trust. The primary way an organization builds institutional trust is by fulfilling a related role to the transaction effectively.

For example, for someone purchasing insurance the institutions that regulate the internet and insurance, are in a position to build trust.

Trust in technology plays a role in the consumer trusting a CBDC because the reduced contact with humans, is replaced with an increased interaction with technology. For example, if a user relies on a CBDC for their payments and they cannot access their electronic wallet due to problems with the Internet connection, or the shop they are trying to pay does not receive the payment, their trust will be reduced. Trust in a technology can be based on different criteria to trust in a person (Lankton et al., 2015). Trust in a system can be influenced by functionality, helpfulness, and reliability (Lankton et al., 2015).

6.3 Research Model

Trust has been separated into several different categories by previous research. Two of the most popular distinctions are (1) into people-centric trust and technology-centric trust (Lankton et al., 2015) and (2) institutional trust and technology-focused trust (Pavlou & Gefen, 2004). In a similar way, this research puts forward a model that separates trust in CBDCs into (1) trust in institutions implementing CBDCs and (2) trust in a specific CBDC technology. The four hypotheses related to the influence of trust associated to the institutions involved in CBDCs are presented first, followed by three hypotheses related to the technology used by CBDCs. The eighth and final hypothesis tests whether trust positively influences the intention to use a CBDC.

Trust Built by Institutions Implementing CBDCs

If institutions directly involved in the implementation of a CBDC such as the government and the central bank are trusted, this will increase trust in the CBDC. The exact role of a government and a central bank may not be the same in all cases, but in the cases implemented so far and the main ones proposed, both have a role. For example, an EU and UK implementation involves different responsibilities for the respective governments and central banks, but in both cases both institutions are involved (Morgan, 2022; Mooij, 2022). Typically, a government will pass certain related laws, and the central bank will implement and run the operations of a CBDC. Some countries' central banks, or equivalent, have more independence from the government, but in most cases, there is close cooperation. For a historical decision such as implementing a CBDC there is no evidence to this day of governments not working closely with their central banks. Therefore, the first hypothesis is:

H1: Trust in the government and the central bank issuing a CBDC will increase trust in the CBDC.

A guarantee is a formal assurance in writing that something will happen. Guarantees have a history of being used to reassure users of technology or consumers of financial services, and they are often beneficial (Martínez-López et al., 2020). Specific guarantees offered to the user of a CBDC will increase trust in the CBDC. The guarantees can be on any aspect of the CBDC including the currency retaining its value or it being able to complete all the forms of payment necessary. Therefore, the second hypothesis is:

H2: Expressed guarantees for the user of a CBDC will increase trust in the CBDC.

Personal information privacy concern is caused when consumers must share sensitive personal information to receive a product or service (Yun et al., 2019). New privacy concerns can emerge each additional time this personal information must be shared with a new organization (Dinev et al., 2013). Evidence of this is the extent to which consumers will provide false personal information to avoid revealing their genuine personal information (Miltgen & Jeff Smith, 2019). As the government already holds personal information of the consumer, this might increase trust. Therefore, the third hypothesis is:

H3: Personal data handled when operating a CBDC by a government, that already holds personal information of the user, will increase trust in the CBDC.

While the trust in the organizations implementing the technology is clearly important, it is not sufficient on its own. This technology, as most technologies, has been implemented for some time before the consumer is considering adopting it. During this time a reputation has been built. Reputation has been proven to influence trust in a variety of contexts involving technology (Einwiller, 2003), including trust in financial services (Dupont & Karpoff, 2020). Therefore, it is hypothesized that:

H4: The positive reputation of existing CBDCs implemented in other countries will increase trust in the CBDC.

Trust Built by the Specific CBDC Technology Implemented

The process of using a CBDC is digital and over the Internet, so the technology, including blockchain, handles the necessary processes (Bossone & Ardic, 2021). This automation reduces human involvement and corruption (Ahn & Chen, 2022). As human involvement is reduced, so is the need to trust humans. Therefore, it is hypothesized that:

H5: The automation and reduced human involvement achieved by a CBDC technology increases trust.

A service can include trust-building functionality such as third-party certification, and policies that protect the consumer (Chang et al., 2013). For example, in the European Union like many other parts of the world, there are policies protecting the consumer's bank savings, up to a certain point (Chiaramonte et al., 2020). Similarly, the technology of a CBDC and the policies around it can have specific trust-building features. These can include a well-designed interphase and two-factor authentication to give the user a strong sense that they are in control of their money (Reese et al., 2019). Therefore, it is hypothesized that:

H6: The trust-building functionality of a CBDC wallet app will increase trust in the CBDC.

Despite the large volume of data provided by a typical consumer so that they can receive the products and services they want, this does not happen without some privacy concerns (Gu et al., 2022). CBDCs have already generated some privacy concerns (Pocher & Veneris, 2022) despite not being widely available yet for most people. Additional privacy features of the CBDC wallet app and back-end processes, such as anonymity, can reduce personal information privacy concern (Dinev et al., 2013). Therefore, it is hypothesized that:

H7: Privacy features of the CBDC wallet app and back-end processes such as anonymity will increase trust in the CBDC.

The previous seven hypotheses identified the institutional and technological ways trust is built. The eighth and final hypothesis attempts to verify that consumer trust in a CBDC does, indeed, encourage the use of CBDCs. The originality and contribution of this research lies primarily in the previous seven hypotheses, but the final hypothesis is necessary to confirm that trust plays a role in this context as it does in many other similar contexts (Lankton et al., 2015; McKnight & Chervany, 2002). Therefore, the final hypothesis is:

H8: Trust in a CBDC will increase the willingness to use a CBDC.

The initial research model on how trust in a CBDC is built in seven ways, and how trust in CBDCs increased the willingness to use them, is illustrated in Fig. 6.1.

6.4 Method

Data Collection

The data for the quantitative analysis was collected by online survey hosted on the SoSci Survey tool (www.soscisurvey.de). The survey items are based on measures validated in similar contexts and use a seven-point Likert-type scale. The classic Likert-type scale started from 1, strongly disagree, up to 7, strongly agree. Each latent variable was measured by three measured variables, as illustrated in Table 6.1. The survey was designed to take less than ten minutes to complete. These ten minutes included the time needed to read the instructions, complete the demographic questions and those related to the model.

The minimum sample size necessary was calculated based on the guidelines for SmartPLS (Hair et al., 2021). Based on the maximum number of arrows pointing to a latent variable being seven, the minimum sample size is 228, for a statistical power of 80% (Hair et al., 2021). The

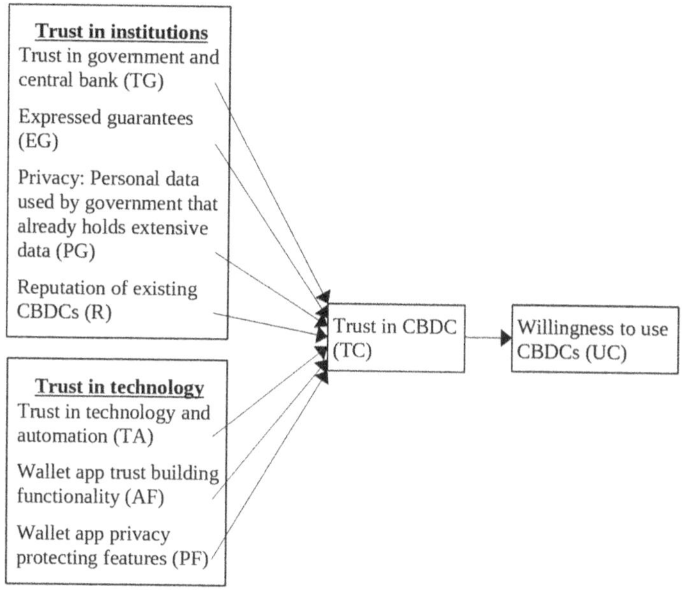

Fig. 6.1 Initial research model on how trust in a CBDC is built in seven ways

minimum number was exceeded as after 429 were collected, 388 were considered to be valid. Using a higher number than the minimum increases the precision of the estimations (Hair et al., 2021). Of the 429 surveys collected, 41 raised a red flag and did not pass the survey quality checks. Firstly, there was a question at the start asking the participant to select a definition of what a CBDC is, to test if they had sufficient knowledge to give useful answers. Additionally, there was a question that was asked twice with a different wording to check if conflicting answers were given. Surveys were also rejected for other typical reasons such as being incomplete, completed too fast known as 'speeder flag', and for the same response being selected for all the questions known as 'straight-lining flag'. The demographic analysis of the 388 valid surveys completed, presented in Table 6.2, show a good balance between genders, age groups, education levels, and incomes.

Table 6.1 Latent variables and their measures

Latent variables	Measures	Source of construct measures adapted
Trust in government and central bank (TG)	TG1, TG2, TG3	Grimmelikhuijsen and Knies (2017)
Expressed guarantees (EG)	EG1, EG2, EG3	Martínez-López et al. (2020)
Privacy: Personal data used by government that already holds extensive data (PG)	PG1, PG2, PG3	Dinev et al. (2013), and Yun et al. (2019)
Reputation of existing CBDCs (R)	R1, R2, R3	Einwiller (2003)
Trust in technology and automation (TA)	TA1, TA2, TA3	Lankton et al. (2015), McKnight and Chervany (2002)
Wallet app trust-building functionality (AF)	AF1, AF2, AF3	Pavlou (2002)
Wallet app privacy-protecting features (PF)	PF1, PF2, PF3	Dinev et al. (2013)
Trust in CBDC (TC)	TC1, TC2, TC3	Lankton et al. (2015), McKnight and Chervany (2002)
Intention to use CBDC (UC)	UC1, UC2, UC3	Venkatesh et al. (2003)

Data Analysis Technique

The quantitative method evaluated the model developed using Structural Equation Modelling (SEM) with the variance-based Partial Least Squares (PLS) approach. This is an Ordinary Least Squares regression method. An initial model was tested and improved so that a model with strong empirical and theoretical support is generated. The SmartPLS 4.0 software was used to explore and evaluate the model. The PLS algorithm was set to run for 3000 iterations. Because the model has a degree of complexity with three tiers of latent variables, the analysis first evaluated the measurement model, followed by the evaluation of the structural model. The reflective measurement model evaluates the relationship between the measured variables and their respective latent variables, while the structural model evaluates the relationship between the latent variables themselves (Hair et al., 2021). It is necessary to verify that the measured variables do indeed represent the latent variables, before moving on to exploring the relationship between the latent variables.

Table 6.2 Demographic information of the survey sample group

Measure	Category	Frequency
Gender	Female	222
	Male	166
Age	Younger than 18	0
	18–24	147
	25–44	126
	45–64	84
	64 or older	31
Education level	No high school education	4
	High school graduate	193
	University bachelor degree	154
	University master or doctoral degree	37
Income (in Euro per month)	No regular income	48
	400–1200	57
	1201–3000	147
	3001–5000	110
	More than 5000	26

6.5 Analysis and Results

Measurement Model

Before the relationships between the latent variables can be tested, the relationship between each latent variable and its respective measured variables must be tested to see if it meets the necessary criteria (Hair et al., 2021). The first thing to be evaluated are the measured variables' factor loadings. These are above the minimum required level of 0.7 with the lowest being 0.864. The Average Variance Expected (AVE) should be above 0.5, and this requirement is met by all of them as the lowest is 0.807. Therefore, both the factor loadings and AVE meet the requirements and show a sufficient level of convergent validity. The Composite Reliability (CR) is above 0.7 for all the variables with the lowest value being 0.883. This indicates that there is adequate internal consistency and individual construct reliability, between the latent variable and the measured variables. The discriminant validity, presented in Table 6.3 evaluated using the Fornell-Larcker criterion, shows that the measured variables have a stronger relationship with their own latent variable

Table 6.3 Results of the measurement model analysis

Variables		Loadings	CR	AVE	Discriminant validity (Fornell-Larcker criterion)								
					TG	EG	PG	R	TA	AF	PF	TC	UC
TG	TG1	0.949	0.948	0.905	0.951								
	TG2	0.953											
	TG3	0.952											
EG	EG1	0.899	0.913	0.851	0.893	0.923							
	EG2	0.954											
	EG3	0.914											
PG	PG1	0.920	0.887	0.814	0.900	0.848	0.902						
	PG2	0.896											
	PG3	0.891											
R	R1	0.926	0.883	0.807	0.812	0.862	0.794	0.898					
	R2	0.904											
	R3	0.864											
TA	TA1	0.934	0.916	0.853	0.875	0.834	0.872	0.808	0.924				
	TA2	0.918											
	TA3	0.919											
AF	AF1	0.893	0.889	0.818	0.713	0.754	0.708	0.748	0.679	0.905			
	AF2	0.898											
	AF3	0.922											
PF	PF1	0.928	0.899	0.828	0.647	0.703	0.642	0.733	0.640	0.883	0.910		
	PF2	0.921											
	PF3	0.880											
TC	TC1	0.916	0.867	0.789	0.857	0.875	0.835	0.857	0.855	0.844	0.823	0.904	
	TC2	0.869											
	TC3	0.880											
UC	UC1	0.897	0.882	0.807	0.803	0.821	0.770	0.822	0.792	0.796	0.783	0.888	0.899
	UC2	0.915											
	UC3	0.884											

compared to any of the other variables. Based on the analysis discussed above and present in Table 6.3, the measurement model is supported, and the analysis can move on to the structural model.

Structural Model

The structural model, also referred to as the inner model, evaluates the relationship between the latent variables, also known as constructs (Hair et al., 2021). As with the measurement model, several criteria must be met. The coefficient of determination R2 for the endogenous latent variable TC is 0.898, and for the second endogenous variable UC is 0.817. Both are above 0.67 and can be considered 'substantial' (Chin, 1998). The effect size ($f2$) for the paths TG-TC (0.020), EG-TC (0.035), R-TC (0.025), TA-TC (0.107), AF-TC (0.048), PF-TC (0.111) are weak but significant. TC-UC (4.460) is strong. The effect size of the path PG-TC (0.000) can be considered insignificant. Effect sizes are typically interpreted in the following way: insignificant under 0.02, weak between 0.02 and 0.15, moderate between 0.15 to 0.35 and strong above 0.35 (Chin, 1998). PLS-SEM is not focused on model fit, and there is a debate as to whether the estimations of fit it produces should be reported (Hair et al., 2021). However, as an additional indication, with the reservations noted, the Standardized Root-Mean Residual (SRMR) for a saturated model is 0.051. Values below 0.08 indicate a good model fit (Hu & Bentler, 1999). The structural model was further explored with the bootstrapping method set to 5000 samples, and the results were similar, as illustrated in Table 6.4. We see that there is support for all the relationships apart from PG-TC.

There are three typical approaches to SEM analysis. The first is to test a model and the second is to compare alternative models. The third approach, which is followed here, is to generate a model. This is achieved by first proposing an initial model and then making adjustments to improve the statistical support for it. Given the insufficient support for the relationship PG-TC, this variable was removed, and the PLS algorithm and Bootstrapping tests were repeated. The final supported model with one variable omitted is still logical and supported by the literature.

Table 6.4 Results of the initial structural model

Path	Sample mean	Standard deviation	T statistics	*p*-value
TG-TC	0.127	0.052	2.436	0.015
EG-TC	0.160	0.044	3.606	0.001
PG-TC	0.012	0.051	0.318	0.750
R-TC	0.113	0.039	2.869	0.004
TA-TC	0.246	0.044	5.510	0.001
AF-TC	0.164	0.047	3.546	0.001
PF-TC	0.236	0.040	5.850	0.001
TC-UC	0.904	0.012	72.768	0.001

The effect size ($f2$) for the paths TG-TC (0.026), EG-TC (0.036), R-TC (0.026), TA-TC (0.126), AF-TC (0.050), PF-TC (0.111) are weak but significant. TC-UC remains strong as it is not affected by removing the variable PG. Therefore, removing the variable PG has increased the effect sizes of the remaining variables and thus improved the model. The model fit did not change significantly as the SRMR for a saturated model remains at 0.051. The SRMR for the estimated model had an insignificant change from 0.053 to 0.052. As mentioned earlier, values below 0.08 indicate a good model fit (Hu & Bentler, 1999). The structural model was further explored with the bootstrapping method set to 5000 samples, and the results were similar as illustrated in Table 6.5.

6.6 Findings

Several countries have plans to implement CBDCs, while many others are exploring this option (Xu, 2022; Banxico, 2021). The starting point of this research was reviewing the literature and identifying both the potential benefits of CBDCs and the importance of consumer trust in its adoption. An initial model recommended seven ways trust in a CBDC is built. This was evaluated and further developed using Structural Equation Modelling (SEM). The fourth hypothesis, which is the only one not supported, states: 'Personal data handled when operating a CBDC by a government, that already holds personal information of the user, will increase trust in the CBDC'. It appears that users of a CBDC do not see it as an advantage that their personal information is shared with an organization

Table 6.5 Results of the final structural model

Path	Sample mean	Standard deviation	T statistics	*p*-value
TG-TC	0.127	0.052	2.436	0.015
EG-TC	0.160	0.044	3.606	0.001
R-TC	0.113	0.039	2.869	0.004
TA-TC	0.246	0.044	5.510	0.001
AF-TC	0.164	0.047	3.546	0.001
PF-TC	0.236	0.040	5.850	0.001
TC-UC	0.904	0.012	72.768	0.001

that already has extensive information on them. The final model, with six ways trust in a CBDC is built, is supported by the data and literature and is illustrated in Fig. 6.2.

Theoretical Contribution

This research makes three primary theoretical contributions: (1) The first contribution is the model of trust in CBDCs that identifies six ways to build trust in a CBDC. (2) The second contribution is that the model supports the importance of consumer trust in the adoption of a CBDC. (3) Thirdly, this research links the literature on trust to CBDCs and highlights the benefits of exiting literature to understanding CBDCs and overcoming their challenges to adoption.

From the six approaches to building trust, the first three apply to trust in the institutions involved, while the final three apply to trust in the technology used. The first three that apply to trust in the institutions involved are as follows: (1) Trust in government and central bank, (2) expressed guarantees for the user, and (3) the positive reputation of existing CBDCs active elsewhere. The final three that apply to trust in the technology used are thus: (4) The automation and reduced human involvement achieved by a CBDC technology, (5) the trust-building functionality of a CBDC wallet app, and (6) privacy features of the CBDC wallet app and back-end processes such as anonymity.

These six methods to build trust in CBDCs now extend the literature they were based on to CBDCs. The literature on institutional trust (Pavlou & Gefen, 2004), the benefits of guarantees to building trust

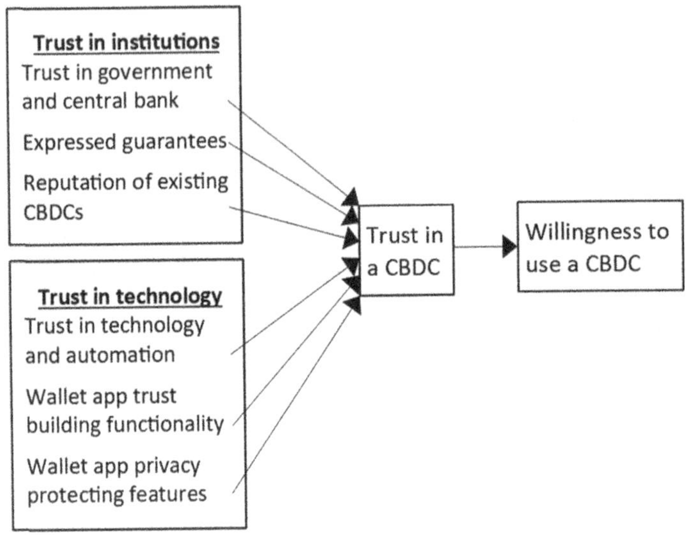

Fig. 6.2 Final, supported research model on how trust in a CBDC is built in six ways

(Martínez-López et al., 2020), and the role of reputation in building trust (Dupont & Karpoff, 2020) are extended to CBDCs. Similarly, the literature of the three more technology-focused variables is extended to CBDCs. These are automation and AI (Ahn & Chen, 2022), trust-building functionality in technology (Chang et al., 2013), and privacy features in a technology (Dinev et al., 2013).

Practical Contribution

This research has practical implications for the various stakeholders involved in implementing and operating a CBDC but also the stakeholders in the ecosystem using a CBDC. The stakeholders involved in delivering and operating CBDCs such as governments, central banks, regulators, retail banks, and technology providers can apply the six trust-building approaches so that the consumer trusts a CBDC sufficiently and adopts them. The many organizations that are not directly involved in operating the CBDC, but are affected by it, such as retailers can also build trust with some of the six methods. The six methods may not apply to all the stakeholders, and a stakeholder may not be able to implement all six, but they can identify those that do apply.

6.7 Conclusion, Limitations, and Future Research

CBDCs are an important part of the new Fintech solutions disrupting finance, but also more generally society. This research evaluated a model on how trust in a CBDC is built. Data was collected by survey and analysed with PLS-SEM. This research verified the importance of trust in CBDC adoption and identified six ways to build trust in CBDCs. These are (1) trust in government and central bank issuing the CBDC, (2) expressed guarantees for the user, (3) the positive reputation of existing CBDCs active elsewhere, (4) the automation and reduced human involvement achieved by a CBDC technology, (5) the trust-building functionality of a CBDC wallet app, and (6) privacy features of the CBDC wallet app and back-end processes such as anonymity. The first three trust-building methods relate to trust in the institutions involved, while the final three relate to trust in the technology used. Trust in the technology is like the walls of a new building, and institutional trust is like the buttresses that support it.

This research has practical implications for the various stakeholders involved in implementing and operating a CBDC but also the stakeholders in the ecosystem using CBDCs. The stakeholders involved in delivering and operating CBDCs such as governments, central banks, regulators, retail banks, and technology providers can apply the six trust-building approaches so that the consumer trusts a CBDC and adopts it.

The limitations of this research open new paths for future research. The use of CBDCs is still at a nascent stage. Firstly, while the few existing and many planned implementations give us a sufficiently stable foundation to build on, the findings should be taken in the context of a technology in the early stages of adoption. Secondly, the sample was from one country, Germany, so the findings can be tested in other countries and regions of the world. Thirdly, in the future, new measures can be taken to build trust in CBDCs, so this space should be reviewed regularly. Finally, this research recommends that Fintech is not only treated as an interdisciplinary topic, as it rightly is until now, but also as a distinct field of research that needs specialized research that captures its idiosyncrasies. The full impact of Fintech may not be captured just by repurposing theory from adjacent fields like finance and information systems.

References

Abramova, S., Böhme, R., Elsinger, H., Stix, H., & Summer, M. (2021). *WORKING PAPER 241: What Can CBDC Designers Learn from Asking Potential Users? Results from a Survey of Austrian Residents*. Oesterreichische Nationalbank.

Ahn, M. J., & Chen, Y. C. (2022). Digital Transformation Toward AI-Augmented Public Administration: The Perception of Government Employees and the Willingness to Use AI in Government. *Government Information Quarterly, 39*(2), 101664. https://doi.org/10.1016/j.giq.2021.101664. Elsevier Inc.

Auer, R., & Böhme, R. (2020). The Technology of Retail Central Bank Digital Currency. *BIS Quarterly Review*, 85–100.

Banxico. (2021). *Estrategia de Pagos Del Banco de México*, https://www.banxico.org.mx/sistemas-de-pago/d/%7BA9287AEE-664E-324B-9599-4FF89B6D7791%7D.pdf

Bhaskar, R., Hunjra, A. I., Bansal, S., & Pandey, D. K. (2022). Central Bank Digital Currencies: Agendas for Future Research. *Research in International Business and Finance, 62*(December), 101737. https://doi.org/10.1016/j.ribaf.2022.101737. Elsevier Ltd.

Bossone, B., & Ardic, O. (2021). *Central Bank Digital Currencies for Cross-Border Payments*. World Bank. https://doi.org/10.1596/36764

Chang, M. K., Cheung, W., & Tang, M. (2013). Building Trust Online: Interactions Among Trust Building Mechanisms. *Information and Management, 50*(7), 439–445. https://doi.org/10.1016/j.im.2013.06.003. Elsevier B.V.

Chiaramonte, L., Girardone, C., Migliavacca, M., & Poli, F. (2020). Deposit Insurance Schemes and Bank Stability in Europe: How Much Does Design Matter? *European Journal of Finance, 26*(7–8), 589–615. https://doi.org/10.1080/1351847X.2019.1607763. Routledge.

Chin, W. W. (1998). The partial least squares approach to structural equation modelling. In Marcoulides G. A. (Ed.), In *Modern Methods for Business Research* (Issue JANUARY 1998, pp. 295–336). Lawrence Erlbaum Associates.

Dinev, T., Heng, X., Smith, J. H., & Hart, P. (2013). Information Privacy and Correlates: An Empirical Attempt to Bridge and Distinguish Privacy-Related Concepts. *European Journal of Information Systems, 22*(3), 295–316. https://doi.org/10.1057/ejis.2012.23. Nature Publishing Group.

Dupont, Q., & Karpoff, J. M. (2020). The Trust Triangle: Laws, Reputation, and Culture in Empirical Finance Research. *Journal of Business Ethics, 163*(2), 217–238. https://doi.org/10.1007/s10551-019-04229-1. Springer.

Einwiller, S. (2003). When Reputation Engenders Trust: An Empirical Investigation in Business-to-Consumer Electronic Commerce. *Electronic Markets, 13*(3), 196–209. https://doi.org/10.1080/1019678032000092246

Gielens, K. (2022). From One Disruption to the Next: How to Navigate Chaos? *Journal of Retailing*. https://doi.org/10.1016/j.jretai.2022.09.001. Elsevier Ltd.

Grassi, L., Lanfranchi, D., Faes, A., & Renga, F. M. (2022). Do We Still Need Financial Intermediation? The Case of Decentralized Finance – DeFi. *Qualitative Research in Accounting and Management, 19*(3), 323–347. https://doi.org/10.1108/QRAM-03-2021-0051. Emerald Group Holdings Ltd.

Grimmelikhuijsen, S., & Knies, E. (2017). Validating a Scale for Citizen Trust in Government Organizations. *International Review of Administrative Sciences, 83*(3), 583–601. https://doi.org/10.1177/0020852315585950. SAGE Publications Ltd.

Gu, J., Tian, J., & Yunjie Calvin, X. (2022). Private or Not? The Categorical Differences in Mobile Users' Privacy Decision-Making. *Electronic Commerce Research and Applications, 52*(January), 101122. https://doi.org/10.1016/j.elerap.2022.101122. Elsevier B.V.

Hair, J., Hult, T., Ringle, C., & Sarstedt, M. (2021). *A Primer on Partial Least Squares Structural Equation Modeling (PLS-SEM)* (3rd ed.). Sage Publishing.

Hu, L. T., & Bentler, P. M. (1999). Cutoff Criteria for Fit Indexes in Covariance Structure Analysis: Conventional Criteria Versus New Alternatives. *Structural Equation Modeling, 6*(1), 1–55. https://doi.org/10.1080/10705519909540118

Kosse, A., & Mattei, I. (2022). Gaining Momentum – Results of the 2021 BIS Survey on Central Bank Digital Currencies. *BIS Papers*.

Lankton, N., McKnight, H., & Tripp, J. (2015). Technology, Humanness, and Trust: Rethinking Trust in Technology. *Journal of the Association for Information Technology, 16*(10), 880–918.

Lee, D. K., Chuen, L. Y., & Wang, Y. (2021). A Global Perspective on Central Bank Digital Currency. *China Economic Journal, 14*(1), 52–66. https://doi.org/10.1080/17538963.2020.1870279. Routledge.

Luu, H. N., Do, D., Pham, T., Ho, V. X., & Dinh, Q. A. (2022). Cultural Values and the Adoption of Central Bank Digital Currency. *Applied Economics Letters*. https://doi.org/10.1080/13504851.2022.2089342. Routledge.

Martínez-López, F. J., Li, Y., Liu, H., & Feng, C. (2020). Do Safe Buy Buttons and Integrated Path-to-Purchase on Social Platforms Improve Users' Shopping-Related Responses? *Electronic Commerce Research and Applications, 39*(January). https://doi.org/10.1016/j.elerap.2019.100913. Elsevier B.V.

McEvily, B., Perrone, V., & Zaheer, A. (2003). Trust as an Organizing Principle. *Organizational Science, 14*(1), 91–103.

McKnight, H., & Chervany, N. L. (2002). What Trust Means in E-Commerce Customer Relationships: An Interdisciplinary Conceptual Typology. *International Journal of Electronic Commerce, 6*(2), 35–59.

Miltgen, C. L., & Jeff Smith, H. (2019). Falsifying and Withholding: Exploring Individuals' Contextual Privacy-Related Decision-Making. *Information and Management, 56*(5), 696–717. https://doi.org/10.1016/j.im.2018.11.004. Elsevier B.V.

Mooij, A. M. (2022). A Digital Euro for Everyone: Can the European System of Central Banks Introduce General Purpose CBDC as Part of Its Economic Mandate? *Journal of Banking Regulation*. https://doi.org/10.1057/s41261-021-00186-w. Palgrave Macmillan.

Morgan, J. (2022). Systemic Stablecoin and the Defensive Case for Central Bank Digital Currency: A Critique of the Bank of England's Framing. *Research in International Business and Finance, 62*(December). https://doi.org/10.1016/j.ribaf.2022.101716. Elsevier Ltd.

Pavlou, P. A. (2002). Institution-Based Trust in Interorganizational Exchange Relationships: The Role of Online B2B Marketplaces on Trust Formation. *The Journal of Strategic Information Systems, 11*(3–4), 215–243. https://doi.org/10.1016/S0963-8687(02)00017-3

Pavlou, P. A., & Gefen, D. (2004). Building Effective Online Marketplaces with Institution-Based Trust. *Information Systems Research, 15*(1), 667–675. https://doi.org/10.1287/isre.1040.0015

Pocher, N., & Veneris, A. (2022). Privacy and Transparency in CBDCs: A Regulation-by-Design AML/CFT Scheme. *IEEE Transactions on Network and Service Management, 19*(2), 1776–1788. https://doi.org/10.1109/TNSM.2021.3136984. IEEE.

Reese, K., Smith, T., Dutson, J., Armknecht, J., Cameron, J., & Seamons, K. (2019). A Usability Study of Five Two-Factor Authentication Methods. In *Proceedings of the Fifteenth Symposium on Usable Privacy and Security* (pp. 1–15). https://www.usenix.org/conference/soups2019/presentation/reese

Shariatmadari, D. (2022). A Year of 'Permacrisis'. *Collins Dictionary Blog*, https://blog.collinsdictionary.com/language-lovers/a-year-of-permacrisis/

Tee, H. H., & Ong, H. B. (2016). Cashless Payment and Economic Growth. *Financial Innovation, 2*(1). https://doi.org/10.1186/s40854-016-0023-z. SpringerOpen.

Tronnier, F., Harborth, D., & Hamm, P. (2022). Investigating Privacy Concerns and Trust in the Digital Euro in Germany. *Electronic Commerce Research and Applications, 53*(April). https://doi.org/10.1016/j.elerap.2022.101158

Venkatesh, V., Morris, M. G., Davis, G. B., & Davis, F. D. (2003). User Acceptance of Information Technology: Toward a Unified View. *MIS Quarterly, 27*(3), 425–478.

Walker, R., & Sexton, A. (2022). *FAQ's on the Cost of Living Payment*. https://www2.deloitte.com/nz/en/pages/tax-alerts/articles/cost-of-living-payment-FAQs.html

Xu, J. (2022). Developments and Implications of Central Bank Digital Currency: The Case of China e-CNY. *Asian Economic Policy Review*. https://doi.org/10.1111/aepr.12396. John Wiley and Sons Inc.

Yun, H., Lee, G., & Kim, D. J. (2019). A Chronological Review of Empirical Research on Personal Information Privacy Concerns: An Analysis of Contexts and Research Constructs. *Information and Management, 56*(4), 570–601. https://doi.org/10.1016/j.im.2018.10.001. Elsevier B.V.

Zucker, L. G. (1986). Production of Trust: Institutional Sources of Economic Structure. *Research in Organizational Behavior, 8*, 53–111.

7

Insight and Control Over Personal Data: A View from Sweden

Theodor Andersson

7.1 Introduction

In July 2020, the Swedish Public Employment Service, the Swedish eHealth Agency, the Agency for Digital Government (DIGG) and the Swedish Tax Agency were collectively tasked with showing how an individual's ability to have insight and control over data that have been stored about them by the public sector—and, in the long term, also data about the individual that are stored in the private sector—can be enhanced[1] (Andersson et al., 2021).

The assignment was given in response to a growing interest in the possibility of increasing citizen engagement, and understanding, of the value and potential use of personal data as a tool of empowerment and better, more individualised public digital services. Although the assignment's

[1] https://www.regeringen.se/regeringsuppdrag/2020/09/uppdrag-att-mojliggora-losningar-for-individen-till-kontroll-och-insyn-av-data-om-individen/

T. Andersson (✉)
Agency for Digital Government (DIGG), Sundsvall, Sweden

A. Zarifis et al. (eds.), *Business Digital Transformation*,
https://doi.org/10.1007/978-3-031-33665-2_7

resulting recommendations were not acted on by the then government, it did lead to a number of insights into the potential benefits and obstacles to such a development that will be highlighted in this chapter. Several legal challenges were identified that need to be investigated further before ideas about an ecosystem for increased individual insight and control can become a reality. The main insight, however, that will be further developed herein, circles around a potential conflict between an individual's entitlement to insight and control on the one hand, and the prerequisites and incentives for authorities to realise such insight and control on the other. Information, including personal information, is the lifeblood of digital transformation. Digital transformations cannot be successful without citizens being satisfied that their personal information is protected. Firstly, it is important, however, to place this topic into a European context and then say something about the specifics of the Swedish public sector's decentralised model.

The European Context

The EU Data Strategy (Commission, 2020) established that it is in line with the General Data Protection Regulation (GDPR) to allow users to be able to influence their own data and to give them the possibility of asserting their rights with regard to the use of the data they generate. The GDPR actually goes further, stating that individuals in the EU must be able to exercise their right to insight and control over their personal information, which creates new obligations for everyone processing personal data.[2]

Personal data is commonly viewed as the most valuable resource fuelling the new data economy. The voluntary (or involuntary) sharing of this data is what enables the algorithms of the largest social media and other platform-providing companies to personalise content, drive engagement and monetise behaviour and the demand for customised services. In general, the vast majority of people have accepted this trade-off.

[2] Communication from the Commission to the European Parliament, the Council, the European Economic and Social Committee and the Committee of the Regions, A European strategy for data, Brussels, 19.2.2020 COM (2020) p.10.

Personal data has become the subject of transactions within the social contract, much like taxes. The main issue with such transactions is that the deliverables of the transactions must perpetuate trust in the system and its actors, both public and private, in order for the trade-off to be viewed as benign to the well-being of the individual as well as of society as a whole.

A main problem for the EU and its citizens has been the lack of homegrown significant companies operating within the digital platform economy (Smit et al., 2022). Both the monetary gains of this economy and the insights into behavioural patterns and individual preferences used to further develop and improve the services of these companies do not remain within the jurisdictions of the European citizens using the services and neither does their personal data.

Whether driven by private sector ingenuity and market forces like in the US or by a coordinated long-term market plan with political goals like in the People's Republic of China (PRC), the fact remains that the EU has failed to create a competitive inner market for personal data-driven companies and services. This has several consequences regarding the development and implementation of new technologies as well as for the retention and attraction of much-needed skilled labour in the innovation and advances technology sectors of Europe.

For Europe to succeed in securing an internal data market it has decided to create a third alternative to the US and PRC examples. This alternative needs to be competitive without acting too protectionist, it needs to pursue value-driven policies that differentiate it but doesn't alienate non-European companies, and it needs to offer unique premises for attracting talent that differs from existing business models but nevertheless make use of the same technologies and so on. The EU data strategy gives answers to many of the questions of how the EU intends to manage this.

Strict data protection regulations like the GDPR are considered ethically justified but can also be seen as a tool for ensuring trust on the part of the general public towards sharing personal data within the EU. Trust, security and empowerment of the individual can be said to be the main ingredients of this differentiation strategy. EU-funding will be provided to member states until 2027 for developing infrastructure, data-sharing tools, architecture and control mechanisms for robust data-sharing ecosystems and artificial intelligence. Data-sharing tools must be able to handle consent, applications for managing personal information (including completely decentralised solutions built on, e.g. blockchain technology), and cooperatives or trusts for personal data that serve as neutral intermediaries in the personal data economy.[3]

Standardising interfaces for accessing data in real time and making it obligatory to use machine-readable formats for data from certain products and services are considered to be essential prerequisites. The EU-Commission will support the establishment of nine common European data spaces, including a common European data space for public administration. Measures taken for the public administration data space focus on legal data and that from public procurement.[4]

Reading the finer detail of the European data strategy will give you a good idea of the vision but not much in the way of how to practically achieve it on the ground. The right to have insight into who holds your personal data, why and for what it is used seems logical and just, but how this insight is to be accessed remains in question. The same applies to matters relating to exercising control over the data, which in practical terms means opting out of data sharing with private as well as public entities. It also includes a right to initiate public errands from a position of being able to follow the handling of an errand, direct the flow of information between government agencies in service of your errand being handled efficiently, as well as being able to identify and act when and where you believe a mistake or wrongful decision has been made regarding the outcome of your errand.

Sweden is here an anomaly in not just Europe but amongst its northern European and Scandinavian neighbours as well as its public governance model is extremely decentralised with government agencies and municipalities alike enjoying the right (or bearing the burden) of being able to decide on its own which IT-solutions to develop, procure or license for the handling of data. Hitherto this right has not been

---

[3] Communication from the Commission to the European Parliament, the Council, the European Economic and Social Committee and the Committee of the Regions, A European strategy for data, Brussels, 19.2.2020 COM (2020) p.11.

[4] http://dataspaces.info/common-european-data-spaces/#page-content

accompanied by any demand for interoperable systems that can communicate with each other or for standards in the labelling and further managing of data. This means that a country where the first archive was established in 1618 to hold government and court records[5] has not been able to systematically share data between municipalities within a region, between regions, between government agencies or even, in some cases, between departments of the same agency.

Within the European context, EU-regulation such as the eIDAS-regulation[6] is mandating the sharing of some personal data and data files (e.g. exam records or health data) between member states. This poses a great challenge to a nation with a decentralised governance system such as Sweden although strides are being made to solve these challenges within affected sectors. The problem is however that a solution is needed that is independent of which type of personal data that is in question for any single EU-regulation. One solution is to simply give each citizen control over their own personal data and provide tools for retrieving data from one source and pass it on to another.

Seen as a common challenge for all EU member states, efforts are under way to strengthen the European interoperability framework for public services that aim to ensure that the collection and processing of data from different sources is done in a standardised and interoperable manner.[7]

Personal Data Spaces

Further measures for strengthening trust in the use of data in Europe are needed. Trust increases with empowering citizens with their own personal data. Individuals can be allowed to have an influence over their data by means of tools and methods that allow for detailed decisions to be made regarding what is done with the information via what the European Commission calls "personal data spaces". An individual's entitlement to data portability is supported by Article 20 of the General Data Protection Regulation and would provide people with greater control over who is

[5] https://riksarkivet.se/history

[6] https://digital-strategy.ec.europa.eu/en/policies/eidas-regulation

[7] https://joinup.ec.europa.eu/collection/interoperable-europe/interoperable-europe

able to access and use machine-generated data. This development is predicted to be able to provide significant benefits for private individuals, such as better personal finances, reduced environmental impact, simplified access to public and private services and improved health. Standardising interfaces for accessing data in real time and making it obligatory to use machine-readable formats for data from certain products and services are considered essential prerequisites for this.

The legal basis for sharing data in a citizen-centric way is being investigated with the purpose of clarifying rules, responsibilities and possibilities. The EU's ultimate objective is to take advantage of the benefits of improved and increased data use, where data that includes personal information is secure, but can nevertheless be used for promoting growth and generating value in an ecologically sustainable manner.

At the time of the assignment, the Data Governance Act (DGA) had not yet entered into force.[8] The DGA seeks to increase trust in data sharing, strengthen mechanisms to increase data availability and overcome technical obstacles to the reuse of data. It will also support the set-up and development of common European data spaces.

It aims to increase data availability by addressing four different points:

- Making public sector data available for reuse in situations where such data is subject to the rights of others
- Data sharing amongst businesses
- Allowing personal data to be used with the help of a "personal data-sharing intermediary", who is supposed to help individuals exercise their rights under the GDPR
- Allowing data sharing and use for purposes of general interest ("data altruism")

Personal data-sharing intermediaries are not yet established, and it is not clear how current public agency efforts to create a legal, robust and secure infrastructure for the sharing of data relate to the establishment of

[8] The Data Governance entered into force on 23 June 2022 and, following a 15-month grace period, will be applicable from September 2023.

a new market segment where these intermediaries are intended to act as a trusted partner to citizens, companies and public agencies.

7.2 European Building Blocks

A more immediate area of interest for exploring giving increased insight and control to citizens over their personal data was the common European building blocks. In order to support the digital internal market, the Connecting Europe Facility (CEF) programme funds an arrangement of generic reusable digital service infrastructures (DSI), also known as common European Building Blocks.[9] The building blocks offer basic functions that can be reused in all European projects in order to facilitate the delivery of digital public services across borders and sectors. The objective of the building blocks is to ensure interoperability between IT systems so that private individuals, businesses and administrations can benefit from seamless digital public services wherever they are in Europe. By means of a certification review mechanism, users ought to retain their control.

This can be interpreted as meaning that the certification goes via the user, whilst previous assessments have indicated that it is a question of an exchange between authorities. According to Swedish law, the discrepancy is crucial in order to determine the need of regulatory measures regarding, for example, Swedish privacy legislation or registry laws.

7.3 Blockchains and Self-Sovereign Identity

Since 2018, the EU has been carrying out exploratory development efforts for self-sovereign identity (SSI) and blockchain-based solutions via the European Blockchain Partnership (EBP) initiative, which has 29 participating countries.[10] Through EBP, the European Blockchain Services Infrastructure (EBSI) is being developed, with the vision of

---

[9] https://ec.europa.eu/cefdigital/wiki/display/CEFDIGITAL/What%2Bis%2Ba%2BBuilding%2BBlock

[10] https://digital-strategy.ec.europa.eu/en/news/european-countries-join-blockchain-partnership

utilising blockchains for cross-border digital services as part of European public administration.

Within the scope of EBSI, work is under way on the European Self-Sovereign Identity Framework (ESSIF), which, amongst other things, focuses on cross-border information exchange via SSI using specific standards. These efforts are considered to increase in importance as additional fields of application are investigated for these technical solutions, especially with regard to the enabling of an individual's increased insight and control over their personal data.

For any nation in the EU looking to address problems of inefficiency in public administration and non-personalised public digital services, it is increasingly important to track developments and roll-outs of EU-regulation as to avoid creating architectural solutions that will have to be amended in the short term to either meet demands of pan-European interoperability or due to new resources being made available that would save a lot of public expenditure on developing own solutions.

The Single Digital Gateway (SDG) regulation is one such regulation to be considered when developing national systems for sharing personal data and making use of data that has already been collected, in order for the EU to be able to realise the full potential for the internal market. The SDG involves providing 20 cross-border e-administration services that require public administration to reuse data already provided by citizens and businesses (the Once-Only Principle—OOP). In order to achieve this, standardised data sets, semantics and an infrastructure for cross-border data exchange are needed.

7.4 A Swedish Context

eSam is a member-driven programme for cooperation between 34 Swedish government agencies formed in 2015. The purpose of this cross-agency cooperation is to take advantage of the possibilities of digitisation to make it easier for private individuals and companies to utilise digital public services and for public agencies to use common resources in a more efficient way. In 2018 eSam published a report "An agency's user area – a further development",[11] which sought to further the conceptualisation of citizens' user areas (the equivalent of a log-in "my page" area at a public agency's website). The concept sought to develop common user areas where different agencies can be reached from the same home page. The idea is that a single agency should be seen as the owner of the area, whilst various authorities provide content and access to the area. The common user area is a portal service where users authenticate themselves, and once inside the common user area, they can interact with a single common area for various agency services.

The way the common user area is run and managed needs to be consistent with applicable laws, and, according to the report, a number of questions arose regarding who is responsible for what with regard to the area. In addition, questions arose regarding which agency should examine a request for an official document, be responsible for the confidentiality of information stored in the area, and be responsible for data protection and information security. Common areas can generate ambiguities with regard to responsibility between agencies, but also between agencies and an individual using the area who needs to know who to turn to if they wish to exercise their rights according to applicable law. eSam notes that long-term sustainability is promoted when each agency has legal control over its own information assets and is solely responsible for functions that they provide for others which makes common user areas a non-viable solution as it can provide more insight but not necessarily more control for the individual wishing to have agency over the flow of data to and from the user area.

Open Data and Data Sharing

In an international context, Sweden is often considered a digitally advanced nation with a digitally mature population, a digitalised public sector and a disproportionally high number of so-called unicorn companies per capita within the tech-sector. However, this image has in recent years been tarnished by low rankings in certain international indexes

[11] https://www.esamverka.se/download/18.4472a99d1784abb64fe55a6e/1617090755211/V%C3%A4gledning%20eget%20ut

measuring digital transformation of, amongst other things, the public sector.

The OECD Digital Government Index (DGI) is such a ranking tool, often cited by internal critics of the pace of digitalisation in the Swedish public sector. The evaluation is based on how different countries have performed according to dimensions that a completely digital public administration should exhibit. The United Kingdom, Japan and Denmark are highlighted as examples of countries that have been most successful by means of a holistic approach in their respective digitalisation strategies. The index consists of recurring proposals for improved and clearer governance, the importance of the right skills within public administration and the benefits of including the users of digital services in design processes.

No direct connection is made to the subject of increased insight and control for individuals over personal data and how this should affect a country's ranking in the DGI. The open and transparent public sector dimension does not highlight increased insight into personal data as a factor; instead, the focus is on published open data and requirements for standards and interoperability that this entails. It is mainly in this dimension that Sweden has suffered a blow to its image as a digitally advanced country, although considerable work has been done since the latest ranking.

In the evaluation of the data-driven public sector dimension, the result is affected by whether citizens and businesses have access to, the possibility of granting approval for and the entitlement to refuse data sharing with the public sector and third parties.[12] How this has been achieved according to the way that actual and perceived legal obstacles have been handled on the basis of the GDPR, national legislation or praxis is not analysed. Neither is any comparison made regarding national governance models and the potential these give for achieving the desired results in a specific manner valued by this index. In some ways, national strategies that seek to centralise the management, storage and sharing of data and that give broad mandates to a national coordinator to govern a common digitalisation policy among public authorities are rewarded. As

[12] Digital Government Index: 2019 results, p. 20 4de9f5bb-en.pdf (oecd-ilibrary.org).

mentioned earlier, this is in stark contrast to the Swedish model of governance.

The authorities in the Nordic countries have a long tradition of collecting data about individuals, but there are challenges for authorities to develop their management strategies in a digital ecosystem where innovation and data economy are watchwords. Sweden, Finland and Norway have had ambitious goals of being world leaders in developing eGovernment, and Denmark has been especially noted for restructuring its public administration in order to seek to incorporate sustainable development as encouraged by the EU.

The data registers used by the Nordic countries are unique not only in that they have existed for such a long time but also because they have a legal mandate that allows various authorities to collect and maintain information about the population. Citizens lack an ability to opt out because the systems comprise a key part of the way that the welfare system itself works. In order to keep the system working in accordance with the increasing expectations that citizens have for public services, there is a risk that it be assumed that all eligible citizens understand the consequences, costs, benefits and risks of sharing personal data (or not doing so). Without this assumption, the basis upon which more and more collected data is expected to be used for more effective public services based on data that are shared by consent becomes a problem.

The way that efficiency, legal security, focus on citizens and harmonisation with supra national initiatives are ensured is something characteristic of not only the Nordic countries but is also a distinguishing mark for all countries when combined with other circumstances, such as the country's digital maturity, the prevailing model of governance and whether it is a country with a relatively large or small population.

7.5 Finland and MyData

Finland is often mentioned as a frontrunner with regard to data portability, not least due to the fact that the MyData principles (Various, 2017), which have become widespread internationally and are mentioned in the

EU Data Strategy,[13] originate in the Finnish Open Knowledge Festival, and the fact that the MyData Global headquarters are located in Finland. In its data strategy, the European Commission has stated that great value can be achieved by allowing individuals to have increased control over their data.

Consideration for consumer influence is part of the reason for the provisions on access to and reuse of data in the Payment Services Directive. Similar to what is advocated by the MyData movement and others, the view of the Commission is that tools and methods allowing people to make detailed decisions about what is done with their data will provide significant advantages to individuals, including financial benefits.[14]

The MyData Example

MyData Global is an interesting organisation that, amongst other things, aims to strengthen the empowerment of individuals in relation to data about themselves, improve people's ability to make well-informed decisions and work more consciously and effectively with organisations that create or use an individual's personal data. In Sweden, the term MinaData is used to describe MyData.

MyData Global has developed the following principles for designing user-centric data ecosystems:

- Individuals must have a complete understanding of and insight into policies, agreements and how their data is used.
- Individuals must have the power to give, refuse or withdraw their consent to the sharing of data.
- Individuals in focus when services need data from each other.
- Individuals must be able to safely manage their personal information in the manner they prefer.

---

[13] Communication from the commission to the European parliament, the council, the European economic and social committee and the committee of the regions—A European strategy for data p.10.

[14] Communication from the commission to the European parliament, the council, the European economic and social committee and the committee of the regions—A European strategy for data p.12.

- Data portability between services and storage areas must be promoted.
- Interoperability must be promoted so that all personal information is transferable and reusable without individuals losing control.

Finland has distinguished itself by, amongst other things, interconnecting certain digital public services and by collecting information on digital public services in one location (see Soumi.fi below). This allows citizens to experience more seamless flows between different authorities when carrying out errands related to handling life-events that demand interacting with public services. The objective is to increasingly enable authorities to act proactively in individual cases in order to generate welfare for individuals and society in general. An example would be by making use of various sources of data to create an individualised health profile.

Finland saw early that providing more individualised digital public services would have to make use of new technologies. The national strategy for handling life-event management was therefore a part of Aurora, the national artificial intelligence (AI) programme.[15] The Aurora network is an AI-based virtual assistant that guides citizens to public services based on their user data and personal circumstances. The aim is to allow for an individual to complete an errand that demands contacts with multiple government agencies through a single point of entry.

7.6 Is It All About Life-Event Management?

The example from Finland touches on an important realisation about the uses for individuals in having more insight and control over their data. For some this is an ideological standpoint, but often the use-cases have shown limited interest and engagement from citizens regarding handling one's own data.

There are several examples of bottom-up initiatives, often inspired by the MyData principles, where start-ups and innovative economic associations create various pilot projects in test environments and within regulatory sandboxes. In France, MesInfos is France's equivalent of MyData,

[15] https://vm.fi/en/auroraai-en

and the governing principle is that if someone else can use your data, you should be able to do so as well. Experiments have been carried out since 2013 in test environments between private individuals and companies. Customer data were provided to the individual customers of participating companies within a dedicated space with a personal cloud storage provider. Results from such tests showed an initial increase in trust for the companied making customer data available. As more companies and organisations added their data to the personal cloud, focus shifted to visualisation tools and making the data manageable and meaningful. The final report of one such large project showed how important the interface is for customer retention since only about 10% used the service after 150 days.[16]

In 2016, the EU adopted the General Data Protection Regulation (GDPR), and focus shifted towards adhering to the regulation rather than exploring more innovative methods for giving individuals control over their personal data. This may be especially true of the public sector, which nevertheless has had some novel projects although within narrow use-cases. For government-initiated projects around access and control over personal data, political will in combination with an opportunity and desire to fund projects can generate commitment from several different parties. To generate commitment and political goodwill, the targeted group the project aims to help or the problem to which a solution is being sought have to be of an apolitical nature, that is, something both sides of the political spectrum can agree on.

In the US, the so-called "Blue Button" was just such a case where veteran health provided an area for political cooperation that neither side wished to be perceived as being opposed to. Veterans could not download their personal health information and share it with doctors or other persons of interest. Veterans or not, people have the same challenge of being able to quickly access their records, regardless of what health plan they have, what doctor they see or where they receive their care. The solution was to allow veterans who have identity verified access to a central site called My HealtheVet, to click a "Blue Button" on the website and thus

[16] http://mesinfos.fing.org/wp-content/uploads/2018/12/MesInfos-2016-2018-final-research--report.pdf

download their health information to their own home computer or portable memory device. They were then free to share that information with other providers, caregivers or family members safely, securely and privately.[17]

Such a solution may seem simplistic in comparison to the EU's vision for the eIDAS-regulation on how personal information is to be retrieved and shared but nevertheless set an example for solving data-sharing problems that afflict vulnerable groups that can be up-scaled to the broader population. Health-related data is a primary example of an area where data-sharing between public and private healthcare actors as well as the individual citizen can be life-saving. It can not only provide better and timely care on an individual basis, but consensus around what data is shared, with whom and for what purpose could also enable a greater use of personal data for research into the development of new medicines and care methodology. Health data spaces, supporting individuals to take control of their own health data, are thus a priority for the EU, and the European Health Data Space[18] is the first common EU data space in a specific area to emerge from the European strategy for data. Due to the sensitivity of the data involved, progress in this area that builds further on the GDPR, the proposed Data Governance Act, the draft Data Act and the Network and Information Systems Directive will likely accelerate the development of other data spaces with less sensitive data.

The involvement of the public sector is viewed as necessary in order to create trust in data-sharing systems as well as security and robustness in the necessary digital infrastructure (Zarifis et al., 2022). There is in general a need for venues in which public and private entities can jointly produce solutions based on clearly identified needs amongst citizens. In order to motivate the allocation of public funds to such projects, life-events that are particularly complex to navigate for citizens and/or frequently occurring are selected for a proof-of-concept solution.

Public agencies, private companies, citizens and trade and industry organisations need a common understanding of what is meant by data portability and how existing structures, business models and policies are

[17] https://obamawhitehouse.archives.gov/open/innovations/BlueButton

[18] https://health.ec.europa.eu/ehealth-digital-health-and-care/european-health-data-space_en

affected by giving individuals insight and control into personal data. Some of the data is held by public administration, while consumer and behavioural data are typically kept by businesses and other organisations. The transition is complex, and the need of test environments and expertise in designing digital environments is therefore of paramount importance.

Clear incentives need to be created for all parties in the value chain to use shared data. Individuals need to understand how data can be used and what benefit this can bring for them, such as new services that create value; otherwise, solutions for providing increased insight and control will only result in inactivity and disengagement (as in the MesInfos pilots) and potentially a reduction rather than an increase of shared data. This places high demands on the design and interfaces that affect the user experience, and the generation of commitment to continued use of the services that suppliers in different areas of insight and control can offer.

Likewise, companies need to see new possibilities and business models due to their customers controlling more of the interaction between them. Otherwise, they will not take part in initiatives that attempt to explore the opportunities for increased innovation and value creation. There is also a clear link between the interest of trade and industry to explore new possibilities and the opportunity to fund participation in an experiment or government initiative by means of funds earmarked for projects within the company's social responsibility strategy. That is, in cases where potential profits cannot be used to engage businesses, there may be an interest in participating if the participation itself can generate goodwill amongst the public and contribute positively to brand development for a certain company or organisation.

These prerequisites lend themselves to life-event management projects within the public sector as there exists within such projects incentives for public-private cooperation with citizen needs in focus. There exist methodologies for analysing customer journeys and interactions with available services and, in many cases, inhouse expertise in designing digital services from a humancentric perspective. Furthermore, life-event management projects in the public sector have a special attention on legality issues as well as criteria for security measures and the robustness of the system, not at least in the EU, where several already mentioned regulations affecting data-sharing rights and practices are close to being adopted and passed into European law.

Suomi.fi: Information and Services for Your Life-Events

Suomi.fi[19] is an online citizen-portal in Finland that collects together other services and instructions for citizens and businesses organised by life-events. Individuals can use the website to request authorisation and check their personal data and which public agencies have what data on them. An individual can thus use Suomi.fi to see data that are saved in registers belonging to certain agencies. Each data processor decides what information is shown, and each register has instructions regarding how an individual can correct or request corrections to inaccurate information.

Likewise, and similar to the Blue button example from the US, Finish citizens can see their own health data and prescriptions online,[20] where patients are also able to give or withdraw consent regarding who else can see the patients' health information. Self-generated data from approved healthcare applications can be saved in the data warehouse for a person's own information including current weight, steps and daily activity. All use of the Kanta-services is recorded in a log, which provides insight into which healthcare organisations have processed a person's data. However, patients are not able to control whether their health data may be used in research or not.

7.7 User-Centric Data Ecosystems

In the Swedish government assignment for exploring possibilities for increased individual control and insight into personal data held by public agencies, certain characteristics for user-centric data ecosystems were identified that are fundamentally important to include. Amongst other things, the data ecosystem must:

---

[19] https://www.suomi.fi/frontpage

[20] https://www.kanta.fi/en/citizens

- Meet the needs of individuals regarding control and insight
- Enable individuals to personally store information in their own chosen place in the ecosystem
- Have an entity responsible for the ecosystem
- Have a functioning infrastructure that bridges interoperability issues as a basis for data sharing
- Have a clear framework for roles, responsibility, approaches and authorisation for the various features of the ecosystem

Health Journals

As in Finland and other countries, Sweden too provides the possibility to digitally access health records online. The service is called "patient records online" (journalen på nätet) and is accessed via a secure log-in via 1177.se, which is the national portal for health-related matters. Individuals over 16 years of age can access all or parts of their patient records via a service provided by Inera AB,[21] a Swedish limited company jointly owned by Sweden's regions and municipalities and tasked with creating the conditions for digitising welfare by providing the owners with common digital infrastructure and architecture.

The details shown vary between regions, and joining the service is voluntary. No region shows all of the information contained in the patient records to private individuals. Each healthcare provider also chooses what information from their system should be made visible to the individual, which results in variation even within regions.

Individuals have direct access to details in their patient records, but there is currently no way for them to download or forward information to other parties. Additionally, individuals also have the ability to seal, that is, remove the possibility of direct access to all or parts of the journal. Individuals can do this themselves or request the healthcare services to do it for them. Sealing can also be initiated by the healthcare services if it is assessed that the information is harmful to the individual, healthcare staff or third parties.

[21] https://www.inera.se/om-inera/ineras-uppdrag/

Pensions

Similarly, everyone who has earned towards a pension in Sweden can log in to My Pension (minPension) to see their entire pension and pension projections. The service is run and funded half by the government and half by the pension providers themselves.

The Swedish Pensions Agency is assigned to provide pension savers an overview of their entire pension with projections based on the needs of the individual. Everyone who earns a pension in Sweden is provided a general picture of their pensions, a projection for future pensions, and information about what affects pensions. Data is retrieved from the government as well as the insurance industry and is a good example of collaboration between the private and public sectors providing citizens with greater insight into the information upon which future pensions are based.

Digital Post

The Swedish Agency for Digital Government (Digg) is responsible for the infrastructure for digital post from public entities called My Messages (Mina meddelanden). Digg is also one of four entities that provide a digital post box service. Joining My Messages means that a person agrees to receive digital post from public entities that have also joined the service or that will join it in the future. It is possible for an individual to decide if they do not wish to receive digital post from specific senders.

The Address Forwarding Register (FaR) is the basis of the infrastructure for digital post. The register contains information about everyone who is in some way connected to the infrastructure. This includes recipients, public entities who are sending post, distributors and post box operators. When the recipient acquires a digital post box, they are registered in FaR, and a profile is created. The profile that is created during registration contains the recipient's Swedish personal identity number and the individual's choice of post box operator. The profile also contains information about how the recipient wishes to receive messages. Messages that are stored in a digital post box cannot be requested as official documents because the digital post box should be considered as the post box holder's personal user area.

These are examples of how access to data is perceived to be important for increasing the agency of citizens in dealing with life-events and staying informed about errands that can affect their well-being and financial status. However, many parts of the data-sharing ecosystem are based on voluntary adoption by public agencies, and there is as yet no standardised mandatory guide to how data should be managed and shared. Where access to personal data is granted it is often a form of one-way communication or mirroring of what data is kept. The insight part of the equation is prioritised, in other words, while the control part is lagging. There is no possibility, for example, to answer digital post digitally (although certain invoices sent digitally allow the recipient to pay the invoice directly linking the invoice to a digital payment system authorised with eID). There is no way to send information about, for example, your health from your journal to a chosen recipient from within the journal online service and so on.

Health for Me: A Failed Attempt at More

Health for me (Hälsa för mig) was a government initiative started in 2012 by the Swedish eHealth Agency. The service would contain a user area at the Swedish eHealth Agency for storing information, a "health account" that would make it possible for individuals to collect, get an overview of and share their health information. The personal health account would be free of charge, and the aim of the initiative was to strengthen the involvement of individuals in their own health and to give them the right and ability to exercise control over their own health data. The personal health account would give private individuals in Sweden the possibility to save, manage and share their health data throughout their lives.

The initiative would consist of a platform upon which businesses and organisations could build innovative health-related services for private individuals in the form of applications. People would be able to use their personal health accounts to decide for themselves what information would be saved and shared with other parties and to ensure the accuracy and quality of the information. Information from the health account would only be made available to others after a user had granted their consent by means of a consent feature built into the service. If an application were to be linked to the health account and the individual had given consent to his or her information being shared, the recipient of that personal data (i.e. the application provider) would be responsible for the continued use of the information in the application.

In its agreement with application providers, the Swedish eHealth Agency aimed to set requirements that personal information could be used only in accordance with the current data protection legislation and that consent would be required each time information was to be disclosed.

Using the infrastructure that the Swedish eHealth Agency was supposed to provide, an API-based ecosystem would have been created so that both public and private organisations would be able to offer services over which the individual would have control and be in the centre of.

Following a judicial review, the Swedish Data Inspection Board,[22] and later the Administrative Court,[23] did not approve the Swedish eHealth Agency's interpretation of the legal bases for carrying out the assignment.

In its review, the Swedish Data Inspection Board found that the health account did not meet the requirements of the data protection legislation and therefore issued a number of injunctions. The Swedish eHealth Agency appealed against the decision to the Administrative Court of Stockholm, which in turn rejected the appeal.

In its ruling, the Administrative Court of Stockholm assessed that controllership of the health account fell on the Swedish eHealth Agency, since it was the entity that determined the outer framework for processing personal data and, in the long term, the purposes and means of processing operations. The court found that this was not a case of a so-called user area (e.g. My Pages, My Profile) as offered by some agencies as digital storage for individual user data. The Administrative Court also found that, although individual users of the service would retrieve information

[22] Supervision according to the Personal Data Act (1998:204) – the Swedish eHealth Agency's Hälsa För Mig service, 2017-04-21, Reg. No.: 2276-2016.

[23] Administrative Court of Stockholm, judgement of 2018-05-24, Case No. 11458-17.

and share data, it was only the Swedish eHealth Agency and its personal data processors that would manage data collection as a whole. According to the Administrative Court, the fact that registered users would have considerable influence over the service and that information was to be retrieved from other data controllers did not reduce or limit the accountability of the Swedish eHealth Agency for the data contained within the data-sharing ecosystem or for how it was used. Neither did the fact that data subjects would have given their consent to having their information processed mean an end to the responsibility of the data controller, as asymmetries in power between the individual user on one side and the public agencies and private companies involved in the data-sharing process were deemed too large, making the consent null and void in matters of legal responsibility.

Following the verdict of the Administrative Court, the Swedish eHealth Agency assessed that legal support for the health account was insufficient, so the authority chose not to appeal against the judgement, abandoning the project days before its official launch.

7.8 Conclusion

Individual services as described above are good examples that can be considered ecosystems based on collaboration between the private and public sectors.

Digital post, the online pension service and the digital health journals all focus on improving an individual's ability to have insight. The fourth example "Health for me" aimed to go further than merely giving insight by also providing individuals with control over their information and the possibility of sharing data with other parties, be they public or private entities. The project showed that there are considerable challenges, especially legal ones, in providing individuals with control over their information, not least in relation to public agencies.

The services shown are largely sector-specific solutions, but there are experiences from all of the above services, where issues concerning collaboration between the public and private sectors, business interests, funding, legal questions, development and administration are all of interest for further efforts in developing individual solutions for insight and control. The question is if the current mode of thinking about an individual's access to data will enable us to design and develop data-sharing ecosystems that are fully in line with national and European laws. Perhaps, a paradigm shift is necessary whereby each individual is granted ownership of their personal data in order to fully realise the potential of more informed and engaged citizens, using their personal data for common solutions to common problems facing entire societies such as health pandemics, ageing populations, inefficient government and eroding trust in public institutions.

This option, as set out in the MyData principles, shifts a large portion of responsibility for sharing but also for protecting data onto the individual. Therefore, a digitally mature population is needed to support such a shift, but the population also needs to be trusted to act in their own self-interest and the best interest of society at large, and this is an unexplored area from the perspective of data-ownership. In the past few years, terms such as data-unions or data altruism have gained some attention, people working together or in solitude to ensure that their personal data is used wisely and for the benefit of other people through scientific research and for the more targeted, individually adopted and proactive digital services. How to handle your personal data, what the relationship between you and your data is, how it can affect your future and how it influences the relationship between you and the wider community are perhaps suitable subjects to teach our children in school before a national system is adopted that is based on the competence of each citizen to understand such relations.

As the Swedish Agency for Data Protection (IMY) states; "*in order to be able to use consent as a legal basis, the power relationship must be equal. Keep in mind that the power relationship is often unequal in the relationship between authorities and citizens, and between employers and employees. If there is an unequal power relationship, you cannot rely on consent*".[24]

If consent is not sufficient it is hard to imagine a system for data sharing, where the individual is empowered by other means, to have greater

[24] https://www.imy.se/en/organisations/data-protection/this-applies-accordning-to-gdpr/lawful-grounds-for-personal-data-processing/—quoted from the Swedish language site.

agency over their personal data, while ownership of the data still resides with public or private entities. At the same time, it is hard to imagine a system of data-sharing based on individual ownership of personal data and where consent is binding that will function to provide corporate interests with the data they need for their current business models and public agencies with the data they need to design better digital public services. The risk is that the complexity, each individual is expected to handle with regard to decisions over data-sharing and the resulting consequences of sharing, not sharing, opting out and so on, will overwhelm the individual and result in a passive, non-directional handling of personal data by the individual owner.

While there are no easy answers to these questions, education on the empowerment of the individual through the usage of one's own personal data is one necessary component. Another is creating and communicating a shared vision for the kind of society each nation is wanting to pursue and how the role of the individual within that society's social contract is likely to change as a result of further empowerment in relation to the public and private sectors. This vision must also serve to answer the questions of what the prioritised challenges (global and local) that a change in data-management and ownership over personal data is likely to contribute solution to and how.

Lastly, the capabilities of each individual and indeed willingness to participate in this ongoing digital transformation that makes up the Fourth Industrial Revolution or Industry 4.0 era must also be considered. Perhaps the well-known statement that *the greatness of a nation can be judged by how it treats its weakest members* needs an update for this era. The treatment and quality of life of those not able *or willing* to participate in this digital transformation are what we first must agree on before any further empowerment of the able and willing can be explored so as to not needlessly endanger the socioeconomical sustainability of our current models for using personal data for digital services, however flawed or inefficient the current system may be.

References

Andersson, T., Sjösten, J., Ahlqvist, H., & Saleh, B. (2021). *Commission to Enable Solutions for Individuals to be Able to Have Insight and Control Over Data Kept About Them*. The Swedish Agency for Digital Government. Retrieved from https://www.digg.se/analys-och-uppfoljning/publikationer/publikationer/2021-06-01-uppdrag-att-mojliggora-losningar-for-individen-till-kontroll-och-insyn-av-data-om-individen

European Commission. (2020, February 19). Communication from the Commission to the European Parliament, the Council, the European Economic and Social Committee and the Committee of the Regions. A European Strategy for Data. Retrieved from https://eur-lex.europa.eu/

Smit, S., et al. (2022). *Securing Europe's Competitiveness*. McKinsey Global Institute.

Various. (2017). *Declaration of MyData Principles*. MyData Organisation. Retrieved from https://www.mydata.org/participate/declaration/

Zarifis, A., Cheng, X., Jayawickrama, U., & Corsi, S. (2022). Can Global, Extended and Repeated Ransomware Attacks Overcome the User's Status Quo Bias and Cause a Switch of System? *International Journal of Information Systems in the Service Sector (IJISSS), 14*(1), 1–16. Retrieved from https://doi.org/10.4018/IJISSS.289219

8

Digital Transformation in the Indian Service Sector: Benefits, Challenges and Future Implications

Ambika Kulshrestha, Sandeep Kulshrestha, Leonidas Efthymiou, and Despo Ktoridou

8.1 Introduction

Currently, India has the fastest growing service sector in the world, contributing over 60% to the country's Gross Domestic Product (Deloitte, 2022). The growth of the service sector is facilitated by government-led initiatives, aiming to encourage cooperation among firms and start-ups in the field of Information Technology (IT), media, banking, transportation, energy, logistics and education. However, amidst the increasing diffusion of technology (Thrassou et al., 2022a, b), it's important to examine how digitization influences the service sector, including its challenges and long-term prospects. Therefore, the current chapter explores how service-sector organizations in India have transitioned towards digitalization, the

A. Kulshrestha (✉) • S. Kulshrestha
Rectangle Consulting, Hyderabad, India
e-mail: sandeep@rectangleconsulting.com

L. Efthymiou • D. Ktoridou
School of Business, University of Nicosia, Nicosia, Cyprus
e-mail: efthymiou.l@unic.ac.cy; ktoridou.d@unic.ac.cy

A. Zarifis et al. (eds.), *Business Digital Transformation*,
https://doi.org/10.1007/978-3-031-33665-2_8

implications they had to face owing to technology adoption and the strategies they implemented towards adaptation.

The analysis draws on findings collected through a survey among managers in the service sector. The survey responders belong to middle, senior and top management levels—all of them empowered with decision-making authority. The responders work in IT Enabled Services, Information Technology, Financial Services, Business Consulting, and e-Commerce firms.

It is worth mentioning two distinctive points about this chapter. First, two of the chapter's co-authors are business consultants in India. Therefore, they have direct access to businesses and managers, who have then provided us with the contact details of other managers, as part of the snowball sampling approach. The second point is that most of the literature review relies on sources focusing on the Indian context, to enable a more accurate conceptualization prior to conducting primary research.

The remaining chapter is structured as follows: the next section presents a review of the literature. Then, the analysis presents the research design and methods of the study. The findings are presented in the subsequent chapter prior to summarizing the main points in the conclusion.

8.2 Review of Literature

Contemporary digitization concerns cross-boundary digital technologies such as the Internet of Things (IoT) (Nadkarni & Prügl, 2020; Ng & Wakenshaw, 2017), 3D printing (Rayna & Striukova, 2016), Artificial Intelligence (Zarifis & Efthymiou, 2022), learning platforms (Ktoridou et al., 2022) and big data analytics (Dremel et al., 2017). Such technologies have induced transformations, which are way ahead of simply optimizing internal operational processes and thus creating radical changes to business models (Rayna & Striukova, 2016), organizational strategy (Bharadwaj et al., 2013), corporate culture (Dremel et al., 2017) and industry re-structuring (Kohli & Johnson, 2011). But what exactly is digitization, and how did we reach this point?

Digital transformation is about changes arising from digital technologies and the automation of processes facilitated by Information

Technology (Hess et al., 2016). In the digitization process, analogue information is encoded into strings of zeros and ones, resulting in a digital format. This conversion enables systems to store, process and transit data (Efthymiou et al., 2023; Loebbecke & Picot, 2015). The conversion process of digitization, nevertheless, focuses upon converting only the internal and external documentation processes, whereas value creation activities do not undergo any change (Verhoef et al., 2021).

However, when we refer to digitization across an industry or sector, we mean that organizations utilize technologies that change existing business processes (Li et al., 2017). For example, the creation of communication channels allows customers to have ease in connectivity with firms, thus changing the conventional customer-firm interactions by using online and mobile technologies (Ramaswamy & Ozcan, 2016). In this process, digitization has three key components: process, organization and technology (Talamo & Bonanomi, 2020). Also, while some technologies improve certain aspects of the job, some inventions are so innovative that are capable of developing new business models (Pagani & Pardo, 2017; Ktoridou, 2013).

Brief History of Digital Transformation

In the early 1990s and 2000s, digitizing business processes, products and services was introduced with many organizations commencing their journey towards digital transformation. However, the entire change process towards technology paced up in the 2010s, when smartphones and social media came into being (Bhattarai, 2020; Christou et al., 2015). Digital transformation was made possible through the development of infrastructure. The current hybrid environment is the result of mainframes to servers to networks to cloud hosting. A 2GB server changed their infrastructure when it began hosting the World Wide Web in 1991, and every business needing internet needed access to a server (Red Hat, 2018).

Infrastructure was also about applications. Servers became the popular infrastructural tool, and applications began disrupting the market. Monolithic applications were first: one application had one server. N-tier architecture of some monoliths breaks functional pieces of architecture thus allowing one server to handle more than one application. A client server method process was used to pool requests in two tiers running on client systems (tier 1) connecting back to servers (tier 2). Evolution in application architecture was preceded by market disruption of server and gave rise to applications prevailing in business (Red Hat, 2018). In the past an entire mainframe was required to run complex mathematical calculations, and the mainframe was larger in size, took more than 350 square feet of space and was more expensive compared to machines of the current era. Agile development processes were possible due to multitier processing, although development and operations teams yet worked separately with the teams needing different workflows and environments.

Benefits and Challenges of Digital Transformation

Nadkarni and Prügl (2020) provide points of difference between product and process disruptiveness. The former includes new product classes, substitutions or primary improvements in the products, while the latter is about process substitutions and innovations radically improving industry-specific dimensions. Disruptive technologies, nevertheless, impose challenges on employees. For example, Ambrosio et al. (2020) claim that labour markets and business regulations force employees to delay the adoption of digital technology. Also, employees are likely to experience technostress and digital stress, which blur the boundaries of work-life balance (Trenerry et al., 2021).

According to Fareri et al. (2020), the onus of learning new digital skills and getting accustomed to newer technologies is directly placed on employees by their employers. They also claim that the employee's refusal to adapt to changes is a primary barrier to upskilling. On the other hand, around 52% of employees blame their organizations for focusing only on maximizing their returns on investments, thereby trying to align their talent towards it, and hence they vehemently get critical of their employers, pointing out that the training programmes do not help them in enhancing and gaining new digital skills. In addition, technology is often responsible for demeaning interpersonal relationships between top management and middle managers, at they get severely affected during the digital transformation process (Nadkarni & Prügl, 2020).

Furthermore, Aeppel (2015) state that over the last 30 years the revolution that occurred in the field of digital technology has taken away many middle skill jobs. In the same vein, Rotman (2013) argues that jobs of typical workers have been replaced by machines thus adversely affecting their financial sustenance. On the other hand, the jobs for computer programmers and web designers have increased (Aeppel, 2015). Also, many organizations, machinery, shipments, infrastructure, devices and employees are being equipped with networked sensors to enable monitoring of the environment, guidance and informed decision-making (Cascio & Montealegre, 2016)—a process that is also known as Internet of Things (IOT). Such technologies facilitate control over the flow of operations and help avoid disruptions by taking immediate steps to deploy preventive strategies as and when issues occur.

Moving further ahead with their narrative, Cascio and Montealegre (2016) state that systems enabling employees to track their work status aid in enhancing their productive levels help them in managing their timelines as per tasks in hand and assist them in achieving their goals efficiently. Yet, tracking technology often lacks the capabilities that effective managers portray. This occurs because machines cannot comprehend high levels of emotional ambiguity and lack the capability to motivate people at all levels of the organization. Also, while tracking technologies may be helpful, this kind of monitoring may also increase employees' stress levels as they feel that they are being controlled at all times (Castanheira & Chambel, 2010; Efthymiou, 2010). About wearable computing devices like smartphones, Vanderkam (2015) state that there is a deficit in the attention span of the people since they are half present and half absent, with them checking their phones an average of 150 times a day. This may result in major issues in work-life balance owing to lack of boundaries of time.

Moreover, Delaney and D'Agostino (2015) provide two examples of employees' resistance to new technologies. Employees at the ALMAC Clinical Technologies, Souderton, PA, resisted a new testing tool (HP Quality Centre), which was needed to improvise their system testing ability. A similar example concerns employees in the New Jersey Division of

Gaming Enforcement (NJDGE), which adopted a Business Intelligence tool. Again, the adoption of technology was resisted by employees since they thought it took them much time to learn and would provide minimum efficiency. They preferred their regular routine of conducting their investigations rather than optimizing the new system. In both examples, employees were forced into using the new system by their management.

Furthermore, technology does not only challenge labour. Disruptions can also occur in processes, due to process substitutions or innovations (Nadkarni & Prügl, 2020). An example is provided by Vial (2019), suggesting that banking using mobile applications for transactions is preferred by Asian consumers. This has created a pressure on DBS bank to offer such new services to their customers to remain competitive.

Despite the challenges there have been examples where organizations have benefitted owing to technology. A digital simulation of a Product Life Cycle Management (PLM) system was created by a leading automotive company, enabling its teams to work and identify complex collaboration processes. The system also aimed at improving the teams' cohesiveness thus speeding up the release of features (Defossez et al., 2020). Likewise, Tabrizi et al. (2019) provide an example of the department of planning and development of Santa Clara County in California. The department's customer portal was enriched so that customers could track their application progress from one part to the other. The organization also managed to configure staff software that could automatically identify applications that were stalled. Also, in the banking and accounting sectors, Artificial Intelligence is utilized for recruitment, selection and hiring purposes (Batiz-Lazo et al., 2022).

Such examples reveal that digital transformation is capable of transforming a wide range of processes and functions within firms. The list of course is by no means exhaustive. However, our review reveals that people, processes, functions and business models do get affected owing to adoption of digital technologies. At the same time, technology diffusion is sometimes beneficial and sometimes challenging. Within this framework, the goal of this chapter is to examine digitization in organizations in the Indian service sector and the trajectory that they have adopted to sustain its positive effects and mitigate the negative ones.

8.3 Methodology

To explore the impact of digitization on service-sector organizations in India, a primary research has been conducted through questionnaires. The survey responders belong to middle, senior and top management levels. All of them were empowered with decision-making capabilities in their respective organizations. The data which is collected is descriptive since it describes the way the organizations have managed to cope up with technological adoptions by using strategies, thereby trying to manage its adversities and imbibe the positive effects.

The questionnaire comprised multiple-choice questions. Questions could be answered without intervention or influence by researchers. The questions were directly related to the topic thus ensuring face validity. Also, content validity is ensured since the data collected and tested is focused upon the technologies adopted by organizations, the impact it has had and the strategies that have been adopted to manage the impact.

Based on the objective of the study, the population size is limited to two parameters:

1. The services sector
2. India

The sampling frame included the above two parameters in a precise way. Also, owing to the research methods applied, non-probability sampling technique is used with a sampling mix of convenient, snowball and purposive sampling methods. Below, the analysis presents the specifics of each method.

Survey

The aim of the survey is to explore (a) the impact of digitization on people, processes, business models and culture in organizations in the services sector, and (b) the adaptive strategies towards adopting and managing digitization. Hence, it is imperative to analyse, initially, whether a relationship exists between the two variables ('Areas in organizations' and 'technology/digitalization'). For this purpose, the responses received through the survey are analysed using quantitative data analysis techniques. Hypothesis is formulated using the Chi-Square test to find out the result. The research hypotheses to be studied in this chapter are:

H1: Technology/digitalization has impacted people.
H2: Technology/digitalization has impacted processes.
H3: Technology/digitalization has impacted business model.
H4: Technology/digitalization has impacted the culture.

The hypotheses are designed to investigate the level of impact due to technology/digitalization on the various areas in the organizations, in the service sector after they commenced using it. These hypotheses, if true, would prove that technology/digitalization did impact the areas.

The questionnaire was created on 'Google Forms'. A convenient sampling has been used by forwarding the questionnaire's link online to all those directly associated with and working in the services sector. The questionnaire was emailed through WhatsApp and LinkedIn. Hence, purposive sampling is used to ensure all those working in the services sector including their organizations get an equal opportunity to get selected for responding to the survey to gain maximum data on various technologies adopted and used by the respective organizations. Also, the snowball sampling was used so that the first responders could forward the survey link to their contacts who work in the service sector, and they in turn forward it to their contacts. The names of the responders and their respective organizations are unknown to the authors since the survey is anonymous.

The survey consists of a mix of multiple-choice questions and questions that require long answers. Some of the multiple-choice questions are based on specific variables like the hierarchical level in the organization, the domain/vertical the responder works in and organizational variables like size, success level of the digitalization process adopted and whether the technological impact was as per set standards/there were deviations. The long questions included the years of existence of the organization in the market, digital technology adopted with its name, functional unit where it was adopted, areas/departments impacted by technology, influence of technology on different stakeholders, deviations due to technology adoption from set standards and strategies adopted to manage the deviations. Chi-Square test was used to test and analyse the data received regarding the impact of technology/digitalization. The selection of the areas impacted was done based on a review of the literature in the field of digitization.

At the time of writing these lines, the number of responders who had already responded to the survey was 22. Although the collection of findings is still in progress, the current analysis draws on the findings collected by the sample of 22 responders, whereas additional findings will be utilized in future research.

8.4 Findings

The findings presented in this section reveal the direct impact of Digital Transformation on employees' managerial and everyday processes in the Indian service sector.

To start with, out of the 22 survey responders, 9 work in IT Enabled Services, 6 in Information Technology, 5 in Financial Services, 8 in Business Consulting and 4 in e-Commerce. Out of the total sample of responders, 7 belong to organizations having a size between 0 and 50, 21 belong to organizations having a size between 51 and 500 and 4 belong to organizations having a size which is over 500. Table 8.1 presents the responders' level on the managerial hierarchy.

All 22 survey responders mentioned that their organizations were impacted by digitalization, in regard to the firm's processes, business models, culture and people. The details are presented in Table 8.2.

Table 8.1 Managerial level of responders

Hierarchical level	Survey responders
Junior management	4
Middle management	8
Senior management	4
Top management	6

Table 8.2 The areas impacted by digitalization

	Positive		Negative	
In areas	By respondents			
	Number	%	Number	%
Processes	11	50	6	27.27
Business model	11	50	9	40.91
Culture	8	36.36	3	13.64
People	9	40.91	2	9.09

Note: The responses are grouped since there is more than one area where the responders experienced the impact

As shown in Table 8.2, 11 out of 22 responders in middle and senior management in IT Enabled Services, Financial Services, and IT firms felt that digitalization had a positive impact on the processes in their organizations. Individual accountability improved due to the reports of work done provided by technology system software, like 'Zoom' based on 'Chrome OS Linux' and 'Google Meet' based on 'WebRTC' technologies. Also, video meetings could be recorded, assisting in minutes development and drafting of the subsequent agendas. In the case of 'Slack' based on 'Java' and 'Kotlin' technologies, workspace analytics dashboard could also be utilized, as discussed earlier in the literature (e.g. Rayna & Striukova, 2016; Hess et al., 2016). Such findings reveal the direct effect of Digital Transformation, and how it facilitated positively some of employees' everyday processes.

Also, six responders in junior and middle management levels, in IT-Enabled and e-Commerce, felt that they faced a negative impact. Three of them are still struggling with 'Salesforce IOT Cloud platform' and 'XMPP' software on WhatsApp. Especially in WhatsApp three of the responders mentioned that they had to deal with several connection issues. Six responders claimed that using 'Microsoft Teams' based on 'Azure' makes the work process more complicated and results to increased stress level. Such findings resonate with some of the studies we discussed earlier in the literature review (e.g. Trenerry et al., 2021). In addition, it is worth adding that technology is often introduced unexpectedly, under the pressure of crises and critical events (Vrontis et al., 2022; Thrassou et al., 2022c, d).

Moreover, 11 of the responders in senior and top management positions, in Financial Services and IT Enabled Services, felt that digitalization had a positive impact on the business model. This is because their customers had better experiences; they could attract talent; and their margins increased through the application of CRM software, such as 'Salesforce' and 'Zoho Analytics' based on 'Google Analytics', 'HTML 5', and 'jQuery'. This finding resembles the findings of Rayna and Striukova (2016), who analysed how CRM software enhances margins. On the other hand, nine of the responders who experienced a positive impact also felt that it had a negative impact due to security breaches, whereas technology was expensive, thus impacting their margins negatively.

Eight responders in the middle and senior management in Business Consulting, e-Commerce and IT Enabled Services felt culture was affected positively by digitalization since collaboration between teams throughout the organization was enhanced. Also, technology makes it easier to communicate key performance indicators (KPIs). Accurate data can be collected with the use of software like Zendesk based on 'Google Analytics', 'HTML 5' and 'jQuery' for better customer services, as previously discussed by Rayna and Striukova (2016) and Dremel et al. (2017).

Three responders who had responded positively about digitization felt that there are occasions of negative impact due to lack of privacy, especially for employees working from home. Also, once again the responders had to deal with increased stress levels, as explained previously by Castanheira and Chambel (2010). Nine responders felt that people in the organization were affected positively by digitalization: chief executives and senior management leaders in IT Enabled Services and Financial Services felt that using software like 'Zoom', 'Google Meet' and 'Microsoft Teams' based on 'Azure' enabled them to keep track of meetings and verify productivity levels, as discussed in a previous study by Bharadwaj et al. (2013). On the other hand, two responders from middle and junior management in IT Enabled firms were affected negatively as existing and newly hired employees found it difficult to adapt to newly installed systems, such as the 'Salesforce' IOT cloud platform. In this situation, existing employees could not help newly hired employees, as technology was new to both categories of employees. One responder mentioned that employees feel they work hard on the new software, but the fruits of their labour are taken by the organization leaving them without a pay hike or motivation (Rotman, 2013). What is interesting, overall, is how executives and senior management expressed themselves positively about technology, whereas middle and junior management felt a negative impact, due to their different roles, performed at different levels.

Overall considering the impact on 'Areas', the positives outweigh the negatives; hence, it can be easily deduced that technology was as per the expectations of many responders. This is presented in Table 8.3. However, considering the impact on each individual 'Area', as presented in Table 8.2 in conjunction with Table 8.3, it is deciphered that digitalization had neither a good nor a bad impact on the organizations.

As presented in Table 8.3, one responder felt that the success of the digitalization process exceeded their expectations. Nine felt it was as per their expectations, four felt it was average and thirteen believed it was neither good nor bad. Based on the survey responses, further analysis is done using the Chi-Square test, as mentioned in section "Pearson's Chi-Square" and presented in Table 8.4.

Table 8.3 Success level of digitalization process adopted

	Respondents	
	Number	%
Exceeded expectations	1	9.09
According to expectations	9	40.91
Average	4	13.64
Neither good nor bad	13	59.09

Note: The responses are grouped since there is more than one alternative selected by the responders

Table 8.4 Chi-Square test

Areas	Chi-Square value	*df*	*p* Value	Result
People	8.91	1	3.84	Significant
Processes	5.778	1	3.84	Significant
Business model	2.2	1	3.84	Insignificant
Culture	4.54	1	3.84	Significant

Pearson's Chi-Square

For the Chi-Square test, categorical discrete variables are used, which are the number of responders in the survey who have specifically selected the areas impacted by digitization in their respective organizations. Experimental design is used because cause is digitalization and effect is the impact in various areas. Also, the reason for using experimental design is to understand the result of using technology or digitalizing the entire organization, and it turns out to be an experiment that organizations could have undertaken to learn what could happen after adopting technology. Whether they would succeed or fail.

To identify the impact of digitalization on these organizations, while calculating the Chi-Square test, the number of people who pointed out the positive impact on the relevant areas, as mentioned in Table 8.2, is considered together with those who pointed out the negative impact in the same areas.

As presented in Table 8.4, there is a relationship between digitalization and processes (Chi-Square = 5.778). There is no relationship between digitalization and business model (Chi-Square = 2.2). There is a relationship between digitalization and culture (Chi-Square = 4.54) and people (Chi-Square = 8.91).

The Chi-Square test is used by the authors since the variables to be tested are categorical and discrete, and they need to be tested to identify whether they are associated with each other or not, thus trying to draw an inference, thereby using inferential statistics. The results of the test reveal the following.

The 'Areas in Organization: Processes, People, Culture' have a Chi-Square value which is more than the p value thus indicating that these variables are statistically significant. Also, it means that the hypothesis can be accepted since the independent variable 'Technology/Digitalization' and the dependent variable 'Areas in Organization' have an association with each other, thereby concluding that the use of technology by the respective organizations has had an impact on the above-mentioned 'Areas', which have been enumerated in the Sect. 8.4.

The 'Area in Organization: Business Model' has a Chi-Square value which is less than the p value thus indicating that this variable is statistically insignificant. Also, it means that the hypothesis can be rejected since the independent variable 'Technology/Digitalization' and the dependent variable 'Areas in Organization' have no association with each other thereby concluding that the use of technology by the respective organizations had an insignificant impact on the above-mentioned 'Area' and which has been enumerated in the Sect. 8.4.

From the paragraph above it can be observed that the Chi-Square test presents the relationship as it exists/does not exist between the categorical variables 'Areas in Organizations' and 'Technology/Digitalization', through its results. Hence it is evident from Table 8.4 that there does exist a relationship between 'Processes, People and Culture' which comprise the 'Areas in Organizations' and 'Technology/Digitalization'. On the other hand, there is no relationship between 'Business Model' which also comprises the 'Areas in Organizations' and 'Technology/Digitalization'.

To prove that a relationship does exist between variables (independent and dependent), the observed values (discrete and categorial variables: number of responses positive/negative for the 'Areas in Organizations') have been compared with the expected values derived through the process of using the Chi-Square test. The observed values are compared with the expected values after providing a sufficient scope for 'Degrees of Freedom', which is used in inferential statistics to help derive the conclusion, specifically in this case, as depicted in Table 8.4 ($df = 1$), the level of effect the independent variable 'Technology/Digitalization' has had on the dependent variable 'Areas in Organization'. The calculated values of Chi-Square as per Table 8.4 are compared with the p value [(3.84) with 0.05 as the level of significance as per standard normal distribution], as per the Chi-Square distribution table, aligned with specific degrees of freedom ($df = 1$).

In the case of 'Area: Business Model' having a Chi-Square, which is less than 3.84, there is no association between the independent variable 'Technology/Digitalization' and the dependent variable 'Business Model' thus rejecting the hypothesis that 'Technology/Digitalization' has impacted the 'Area: Business Model'. And the reverse is applicable in the case of 'Areas: Processes, People and Culture', where the Chi-Square is more than the p value of 3.84. It indicates that there is an association between the independent variable 'Technology/Digitalization' and the dependent variable 'Areas in Organization', thus accepting the hypothesis that 'Technology/Digitalization' has impacted the 'Areas: Processes, People and Culture'.

Thus, based on the explanation in the above paragraphs it can be deduced that the Chi-Square test has aided in identifying the gaps between the observed data based on the 'Survey' samples and the expected data as per the Chi-Square test model. The test enables an analysis of the reasons/causes of the gaps, which can be observed in the Sect. 8.4. The differences/gaps emerging by the Chi-Square test have revealed that the hypotheses are 'True' or 'False' and 'Why' did they comply/not comply with the hypothesis set.

The authors used Chi-Square test of independence to analyse the data collected because it was able to determine whether the observed values were in line with the expected results, thereby testing the hypothesis set by them. The observed data that was analysed is from a random sample where survey questions were used to draw the sample. The two variables (independent and dependent) are categorical variables.

It can also be deduced that since the sample size is not large enough, the test showed a significant result for the 'Areas: Processes, People, Culture'. Had the sample size been large enough, the probability of these areas being insignificant or the 'Area: Business Model' having a significant relationship with the independent variable 'Technology/Digitalization' cannot be ruled out.

Finally, the survey responses are a small sample that is representative of the entire population. This is because the entire population would comprise all employees at all levels in all organizations across the service sector in the country. Although small, the sample size represents employees at all levels, in various organizations in the service sector. Also, in each organization, there is a probability of at least one employee, in at least one level having responded to the survey questions. And since the population parameter is unknown here, inferential statistics is used, which will take the sampling error into account, although there is an increased probability of there being a difference between the population parameter and the sample statistic. The probability of sampling error is increased in the case of the survey because non-probability sampling techniques are used. All the organizations in this sector in the country did not receive equal chance of getting chosen in the sample. Over this aspect, the authors had no control since snowball sampling method is used. Under Snowball sampling, randomly people who received the link to the survey questionnaire have managed to respond to the questions, and hence, random responders have been able to answer the questions. This process has given rise to two issues: (1) all the organizations in the service sector have not received an opportunity to take part in research; hence there is a gap between the population parameter and the sample statistic, which is covered under the sampling error; and (2) there is a gap between the data received by the authors and the actual data as it would be, but it is unknown to the authors. Hence the authors will have to form their conclusions be drawing on the limited data received.

8.5 Discussion and Conclusion

The service sector in India began to develop dynamically from the second half of the twentieth century. Today this sector contributes over 60% to GDP and 70% to employment (Deloitte, 2022). The service-sector firms examined in the study included a sample of IT Enabled Services, Information Technology, Financial Services, Business Consulting and e-Commerce. Our findings revealed the direct effect of Digital Transformation on organizations and how it influenced positively or negatively their processes, employees, culture and business model.

The findings of the survey were scattered between positive and negative perceptions. In all categories, there were managers who experience digitization positively in certain areas managers who experience digitization negatively in other areas, and same managers who expressed themselves both positively and negatively for different technologies. Overall, the positives outweigh the negatives; hence it can be easily deduced that technology was as per the expectations of many responders (see Table 8.3). However, considering the impact on each individual 'Area' (as presented in Table 8.2 in conjunction with Table 8.3), it is deciphered that digitalization had neither good nor bad impact on organizations.

Moreover, responders referred to both benefits and challenges. For example, some responders linked digitization to improved accountability, time efficiency, higher profit margins, better collaboration between teams, talent management, enhanced communication of KPIs, data collection, better customer reservice and an overall positive impact on organizational culture. At the same time, some responders referred to challenges, which largely concern the work becoming more complex, resulting to increased stress, security breaches, lack of privacy and high costs of technology acquisition.

Also, those who experienced a positive impact by digitization are mostly chief executives and managers in senior positions, whereas those who experienced a negative impact were managers in middle and junior positions. This is because, on the one hand, senior management and chief executives are satisfied since technology enables them to monitor work, exercise control over employees, keep track of meetings and verify productivity levels. On the other hand, middle and junior managers had to overview the application of new technologies, train existing and new employees on those technologies, work extra hours without being compensated, deal with employees' increased stress levels, and deal with the resistance that is often associated with employees' reaction to change and stress.

Such findings reveal that technology is experienced differently by people in different roles, with different kinds of authority and at different levels of the managerial hierarchy. Thus, the current study generates a number of implications for organizations. It seems that executive and top management should do more to involve lower-level managers in the decision-making processes of selecting and purchasing different technologies. In addition, the likely benefits of each technology should be communicated to the entire workforce in advance, so that all employees understand the advantages of committing themselves to new technologies. At the same time, challenges and difficulties expressed by first-line managers and employees should not be neglected. Moreover, different types of training should be offered to existing and new employees, whereas the time invested on learning new technologies may somehow be compensated. All these actions will contribute to bridging the gap between positive experiences at top managerial levels and negative experiences at lower managerial levels and make digital transformation more sustainable in the long term.

References

Aeppel, T. (2015, February 24). What Clever Robots Mean for Jobs: Experts Rethink Belief that Tech Always Lifts Employment as Machines Take on Skills Once Thought Uniquely Human. *The Wall Street Journal.* Online at http://www.wsj.com/articles/what-clever-robots-mean-for-jobs-1424835002. Accessed 21 Dec 2022.

Ambrosio, F., Ruckert, D., & Weiss, C. (2020). *Who Is Prepared for the New Digital Age? Evidence from the EIB Investment Survey [online].* European Investment Bank, 2019. [cit. 2021-14-06]. Available at: https://1url.cz/jKHgO

Batiz-Lazo, B., Efthymiou, L., & Davies, K. (2022). The Spread of Artificial Intelligence and Its Impact on Employment: Evidence from the Banking and Accounting Sectors. In A. Thrassou, D. Vrontis, L. Efthymiou, Y. Weber, S. M. R. Shams, & E. Tsoukatos (Eds.), *Business Advancement Through Technology Volume II. Palgrave Studies in Cross-Disciplinary Business Research, In Association with EuroMed Academy of Business.* Palgrave Macmillan. https://doi.org/10.1007/978-3-031-07765-4_7

Bharadwaj, A., El Sawy, O. A., Pavlou, P., & Venkatraman, N. (2013). Digital Business Strategy: Toward a Next Generation of Insights. *MIS Quarterly, 37,* 471–482.

Bhattarai, D. (2020). *A Detailed Summary of Digital Transformation from McKinsey.* Online at https://www.lftechnology.com/blog/digital-transformation/digital-transformation-mckinsey/. Accessed 18 Dec 2022.

Cascio, W. F., & Montealegre, R. (2016). How Technology Is Changing Work and Organizations. *Annual Review of Organizational Psychology and Organizational Behavior, 3*(1), 349–375. https://doi.org/10.1146/annurev-orgpsych-041015-062352

Castanheira, F., & Chambel, M. J. (2010). Reducing Burnout in Call Centers Through HR Practices. *Human Resource Management, 49,* 1047–1065.

Christou, C. S., Ktoridou, D., Papatheocharous, A., & Domenach, F. (2015). Cypriot Firms, Social Media & User-Generated Content Platforms. In *2015 International Conference on Interactive Mobile Communication Technologies and Learning (IMCL), 2015* (pp. 378–382). https://doi.org/10.1109/IMCTL.2015.7359623

Defossez, K., McMillan, M., & Vuppala, H. (2020). *Managing Large Technology Programs in the Digital Era.* Online at https://www.mckinsey.com/business-functions/mckinsey-digital/our-insights/managing-large-technology-programs-in-the-digital-era. Accessed 12 Dec 2022.

Delaney, R., & D'Agostino, R. (2015). *The Challenges of Integrating New Technology into an Organization.* Mathematics and Computer Science Capstones. 25, http://digitalcommons.lasalle.edu/mathcompcapstones/25

Deloitte. (2022). *India Services Sector: A Multi-trillion Dollar Opportunity for Global Symbiotic Growth.* Online at: https://www2.deloitte.com/in/en/pages/industries/articles/india-services-sector.html. Accessed 21 Dec 2022.

Dremel, C., Wulf, J., Herterich, M. M., Waizmann, J. C., & Brenner, W. (2017). How AUDI AG Established Big Data Analytics in Its Digital Transformation. *MIS Quarterly Executive, 16*(2), 81–100.

Efthymiou, L. (2010). *Workplace Control and Resistance from Below: An Ethnographic Study in a Cypriot Luxury Hotel.* University of Leicester. PhD Thesis. https://hdl.handle.net/2381/9742

Efthymiou, L., Kulshrestha, A., & Kulshrestha, S. (2023). A Study on Sustainability and ESG in the Service Sector in India: Benefits, Challenges, and Future Implications. *Adm. Sci. 13*, 165. https://doi.org/10.3390/admsci13070165

Fareri, S., Fantoni, G., Chiarello, F., Coli, E., & Binda, A. (2020). Estimating Industry 4.0 Impact on Job Profiles and Skills Using Text Mining. *Computers in Industry, 118*(103222), 1–19.

Hess, T., Benlian, A., Matt, C., & Wiesböck, F. (2016). Options for Formulating a Digital Transformation Strategy. *MIS Quarterly Executive, 15*(2), 123–139.

Kohli, R., & Johnson, S. (2011). Digital Transformation in Latecomer Industries: CIO and CEO Leadership Lessons from Encana Oil and Gas (USA) Inc. *MIS Quarterly Executive, 10*(4), 141–156.

Ktoridou, D. (2013). Cultivating Entrepreneurial Thinking Through a Management of Innovation and Technology Course: Evidence from the University of Nicosia. In A. Szopa et al. (Eds.), *Academic Entrepreneurship and Technological Innovation: A Business Management Perspective* (pp. 114–133). IGI Global. https://doi.org/10.4018/978-1-4666-2116-9.ch006

Ktoridou, D., Doukanari, E., Epaminonda, E., & Efthymiou, L. (2022). Developing Digital Transformation Management Graduate Education. In *2022 IEEE Global Engineering Education Conference (EDUCON), 2022* (pp. 2093–2098). IEEE Computer Society. https://doi.org/10.1109/EDUCON52537.2022.9766592

Li, L., Su, F., Zhang, W., & Mao, J. Y. (2017). Digital Transformation by SME Entrepreneurs: A Capability Perspective. *Information Systems Journal, 28*(6), 1129–1157.

Loebbecke, C., & Picot, A. (2015). Reflections on Societal and Business Model Transformation Arising from Digitization and Big Data Analytics: A Research Agenda. *Journal of Strategic Information Systems, 24*(3), 149–157.

Nadkarni, S., & Prügl, R. (2020). Digital Transformation: A Review, Synthesis and Opportunities for Future Research. *Management Review Quarterly*. https://doi.org/10.1007/s11301-020-00185-7

Ng, I. C., & Wakenshaw, S. Y. (2017). The Internet-of-Things: Review and Research Directions. *International Journal of Research in Marketing, 34*(1), 3–21.

Pagani, M., & Pardo, C. (2017). The Impact of Digital Technology on Relationships in a Business Network. *Industrial Marketing Management, 67*, 185–119.

Ramaswamy, V., & Ozcan, K. (2016). Brand Value Co-creation in a Digitalized World: An Integrative Framework and Research Implications. *International Journal of Research in Marketing, 33*(1), 93–106.

Rayna, T., & Striukova, L. (2016). From Rapid Prototyping to Home Fabrication: How 3D Printing Is Changing Business Model Innovation. *Technological Forecasting and Social Change, 102*, 214–224.

Red Hat. (2018). *What Is Digital Transformation?* Online at https://www.redhat.com/en/topics/digital-transformation/what-is-digital-transformation. Accessed 22 July 2022.

Rotman, D. (2013, June 12). How Technology Is Destroying Jobs. *MIT Technology Review*. http://www.technologyreview.com/featuredstory/515926/how-technology-is-destroying-jobs/.

Tabrizi, B., Lam, E., Girard, K., & Irvin, V. (2019). The New World of Work. *Harvard Business Review*. Online at https://hbr.org/2019/03/digital-transformation-is-not-about-technology. Accessed 15 Nov 2022.

Talamo, C., & Bonanomi, M. M. (2020). The Impact of Digitalization on Processes and Organizational Structures of Architecture and Engineering Firms. In B. Daniotti, M. Gianinetto, & S. Della Torre (Eds.), *Digital Transformation of the Design, Construction and Management Processes of the Built Environment. Research for Development*. Springer. https://doi.org/10.1007/978-3-030-33570-0_16

Thrassou, A., Vrontis, D., Efthymiou, L., & Uzunboylu, N. (2022a). An Overview of Business Advancement Through Technology: Markets and

Marketing in Transition. In A. Thrassou, D. Vrontis, L. Efthymiou, Y. Weber, S. M. R. Shams, & E. Tsoukatos (Eds.), *Business Advancement Through Technology Volume I. Palgrave Studies in Cross-Disciplinary Business Research, In Association with EuroMed Academy of Business*. Palgrave Macmillan. https://doi.org/10.1007/978-3-031-07769-2_1

Thrassou, A., Vrontis, D., Efthymiou, L., & Uzunboylu, N. (2022b). An Overview of Business Advancement Through Technology: The Changing Landscape of Work and Employment. In A. Thrassou, D. Vrontis, L. Efthymiou, Y. Weber, S. M. R. Shams, & E. Tsoukatos (Eds.), *Business Advancement Through Technology Volume II. Palgrave Studies in Cross-Disciplinary Business Research, In Association with EuroMed Academy of Business*. Palgrave Macmillan. https://doi.org/10.1007/978-3-031-07765-4_1

Thrassou, A., Efthymiou, L., Vrontis, D., Weber, Y., Shams, S. M. R., & Tsoukatos, E. (2022c). Editorial Introduction: Crisis in Context. In D. Vrontis, A. Thrassou, Y. Weber, S. M. R. Shams, E. Tsoukatos, & L. Efthymiou (Eds.), *Business Under Crisis Volume I. Palgrave Studies in Cross-Disciplinary Business Research, In Association with EuroMed Academy of Business*. Palgrave Macmillan. https://doi.org/10.1007/978-3-030-76567-5_1

Thrassou, A., Vrontis, V., Efthymiou, L., Weber, Y., Shams, S. M. R., & Tsoukatos, E. (2022d). *Business Advancement Through Technology Volume I: Markets and Marketing in Transition*. Palgrave Macmillan. https://doi.org/10.1007/978-3-031-07769-2

Trenerry, B., Chng, S., Wang, Y., Suhaila, Z. S., Lim, S. S., Lu, H. Y., & Oh, P. H. (2021). Preparing Workplaces for Digital Transformation: An Integrative Review and Framework of Multi-level Factors. *Frontiers in Psychology, 12*. https://doi.org/10.3389/fpsyg.2021.620766

Vanderkam, L. (2015, March). Work/Life Integration is the New Normal. *Fortune*, p. 139.

Verhoef, P. C., Broekhuizen, T., Bart, Y., Bhattacharya, A., Dong, J. Q., Fabian, N., & Haenlein, M. (2021). Digital Transformation: A Multidisciplinary Reflection and Research Agenda. *Journal of Business Research, 122*, 889–901. https://doi.org/10.1016/j.jbusres.2019.09.022. ISSN 0148-2963.

Vial, G. (2019). Understanding Digital Transformation: A Review and a Research Agenda. *The Journal of Strategic Information Systems, 28*(2), 118–144. https://doi.org/10.1016/j.jsis.2019.01.003. ISSN 0963-8687.

Vrontis, D., Thrassou, A., Efthymiou, L., Uzunboylu, N., Weber, Y., Shams, R. S. M., & Tsoukatos, E. (2022). Editorial Introduction: Business Under Crisis: Avenues for Innovation, Entrepreneurship and Sustainability. In

D. Vrontis, A. Thrassou, Y. Weber, S. M. R. Shams, E. Tsoukatos, & L. Efthymiou (Eds.), *Business Under Crisis Volume III. Palgrave Studies in Cross-Disciplinary Business Research, In Association with EuroMed Academy of Business*. Palgrave Macmillan. https://doi.org/10.1007/978-3-030-76583-5_1

Zarifis, A., & Efthymiou, L. (2022). The Four Business Models for AI Adoption in Education: Giving Leaders a Destination for the Digital Transformation Journey. In *2022 IEEE Global Engineering Education Conference (EDUCON), 2022* (pp. 1868–1872). https://doi.org/10.1109/EDUCON52537.2022.9766687

9

The Impact of Digital Transformation on the Sustainable Development of Social Innovation, Socio-ecological Resilience and Governance

José G. Vargas-Hernández, M. C. Omar C. Vargas-González, and Leonidas Efthymiou

9.1 Introduction

The concept of Social Innovation (SI) initially relates to national systems and sites of Innovation. It is defined as the improvement in a social system supported by the changes in social relations, political arrangements and governance processes, identified in components of

J. G. Vargas-Hernández (✉)
Postgraduate and Research Division, Tec MM Campus Zapopan. Instituto Tecnológico José Mario Molina Pasquel y Henríquez,
El Bajio, Zapopan, Jalisco, Mexico
e-mail: jose.vargas@zapopan.tecmm.edu.mx

M. C. Omar C. Vargas-González
Instituto Tecnológico de México, Campus Cd. Guzmán,
Cd. Guzman, Jalisco, Mexico
e-mail: omar.vg@cdguzman.tecnm.mx

A. Zarifis et al. (eds.), *Business Digital Transformation*,
https://doi.org/10.1007/978-3-031-33665-2_9

satisfaction of needs, empowerment and social relations reconfiguration (Moulaert et al., 2013). The notion of SI is inherently territorialized and refers to processes such as governance structures, stronger social fabric and new services delivery, operating at multiple spatial scales (Van Dyck & Van den Broeck, 2015). It also refers to modified social structures and revisited ethical norms to meet the socio-ecological needs and social issues related to inequality, power relationships and environmental degradation (Avelino et al., 2015; Vercher et al., 2020).

SI theory and processes contribute to socio-ecological resilience from a socio-political perspective. The dynamic of SI is combined with the socio-ecological perspective, the interactions of natural environments embedded in social systems and a set of governance institutions (Ostrom, 2009). Also, SI strives to meet material and non-material societal needs, assuming vulnerability to environmental risks, through socio-ecological resilience. In addition, secure socio-political environments favor SI in the public sector (Martinelli, 2013; Spijker & Parra, 2018). The socio-political aspects are central to human well-being incorporated into the resilience building process.

Moreover, from a socio-technical perspective, IS integrates and complements technological innovation. By the same token, governments, companies, non-governmental organizations and other entities explore ways to innovate by embracing the implications of digital transformation, and driving better operational performance (Batiz-Lazo et al., 2022; Thrassou et al., 2022a, b). Within this framework, the current chapter explores SI, socio-ecology and governance, amidst the ongoing digital transformation. While such fields attract attention by researchers, we currently lack a comprehensive understanding of the impact of digitization on SI. Therefore, we have to look more closely at SI alongside digital transformation and sustainability. The analysis continues in the next section with a review of SI amidst digitization.

L. Efthymiou
School of Business, University of Nicosia, Nicosia, Cyprus
e-mail: efthymiou.l@unic.ac.cy

9.2 Literature Review

Social Innovation Amidst Digitization

The foundational economic thinking of SI is based on established economy, society and political assumptions (Foundational Economy Collective, 2018). The foundational economy perspective in SI can be juxtaposed with foundational technological sectors, generating a knowledge economy, using knowledge-intensive sectors, similar to the concept of low-tech (Hansen & Winther, 2011). SI contrasts with digitization and technological innovation in a dichotomous manner rather than being in a continuum (Moulaert et al., 2013). This dichotomy between social and technological innovation understates the potential of digitization and the intensity of knowledge to SI and other forms, such as grass-roots innovation in community initiatives, the sharing economy, recycling workshops and more (Seyfang & Smith, 2007).

The foundational economy model of SI in safe, civilized, sound ordinary sectors such as education, health, and housing, including goods and services, contrasts with the conventional innovation models focused on high-technology sectors in knowledge economy (Marques et al., 2018). The foundational economy sectors in SI use digitization in knowledge-intensive sectors and is not antithetical to technology (Hansen & Winther, 2011).

SI has considerable ambiguity in foundational economy. The foundational economy of SI is a positive-sum game in contrast to the zero-sum game, considering that regions and local cities have a stock of employment in sectors that tends to be more than one-third of total employment in lagging regions with a significant function in meeting the human needs (Foundational Economy Collective, 2018). Satisfaction awareness of individual and collective needs are considered to be outcomes of SI processes. The foundational economy considered within the SI perspective is politically challenged by constraints to provide funding for public services, engaged in regulations to deliver foundational services and the active citizenship deemed to become producers of goods and services or collective consumption (Morgan, 2018).

Governments promote mission-driven SI under an age of austerity in an ideological quest to secure a shrinking state as a counter-factual to the challenges of experimentalism in public and societal innovation sectors in the provision of goods and services in public health, food, and energy transport. Such austerity also has an impact on technology adoption. For example, supply-based SI focuses on mapping and collective articulations of organized intermediation processes of unmet needs related to socio-environmental challenges to meet problem-solving innovative capabilities funded and governed across the spaces. Problem-solving in SI incentives are based on entrepreneurial opportunities and articulated demands for solving local problems. Arguably, digital technologies can further enhance such SI incentives, especially in terms of knowledge sharing, communication among stakeholders, and problem solving.

The foundational economy approach to SI is analogous to public goods deemed not rivalrous aimed to promote growth breaking with local tournaments and zero-sum games reducing the scope for territorial competition among countries, regions, local communities, and cities. Some regions of the world are currently suffering from social innovative power, leading to a sluggish economy, public debt, and high rates of unemployment. Local communities can make decisions to act upon SI and make experimental improvements (Long & Long, 1992). Experimentation emphasizes selection and investment in SI opportunities to align supply and demand rather than focusing solely on the supply side of SI systems.

The metrics domain is changing in the SI processes, requiring management to encourage their development, due to the difficulties of identifying relevant impacts of externalities, despite it being costly to measure the impact. SI processes may lead to second-order and unanticipated effects and consequences, such as projects to reduce homelessness resulting in the construction of buildings that increase carbon emissions. Notions of materiality, identification and the ranking of stakeholders' perspectives are among the most significant measures of SI processes. Once again, digitization has a role to place here. Platform infrastructures, including technological measurement equipment, facilitate the implementation of SI processes, integrating transdisciplinary research in order to yield added value in regions and localities (Haberl et al., 2006).

Digitization can also enhance interaction among stakeholders and agents from government and civil society who are sharing knowledge, negotiating, reducing uncertainty, and experiencing SI. It can also facilitate new ways of learning among social actors, including iterative doing-by-learning and learning-by-doing – thereby minimizing the learning gap. Exogenous interventions in SI induce local agents to commit their knowledge resources and energy to untapped potential in their territory and engaging in rent-seeking, using the principles of democratic experimentalism to make local decisions (Sabel & Zeitlin, 2012).

Place-based SI is social in terms of their means and ends, which are good for society and enhance the capacity to act based on the foundational economy (European Commission, 2012). SI capacity is built into adaptive cycles in complex systems to generate social finance thinking and the need to measure the impact between the metrics through reorganization and organizational innovation (Pradhan et al., 1998).

This SI place-based approach has an entrenched nature of the public sector barriers with implications to be addressed through multilevel actions rather than the multiscalar approach. The nature of the SI process is a complex and multi-phased adaptive cycle referred to as developmental impact investing used to build a rationale for an alternative social finance evaluation model. The technology-led developmental approach of SI processes and complex socio-ecological systems feedback ensures change. The foundational economy in SI upgrades employment in conditions of work in sectors of high social value and low in economic reward at the societal level, governments, civil societies and significance to human well-being (Bentham et al., 2013).

Local distribution of goods and services leads to immobile foundational activities of SI from regulations for investments and global competition, planning permission and government contracts (Barbera et al., 2018). Adaptive planning emerged as the synthesis of these opposing perspectives with an emphasis on the normative level, and flexible and innovative changes in the system (Ozbekhan, 1973), which is appropriate for a dual organizational technological and SI. The investment experiment informs capital decisions on allocation, blending diverse types of capital in innovative financial deals to make an impact in complex environmental systems and thereby increasing the likelihood of impacts on the outcomes of SI.

Furthermore, Research and Innovation Strategies for Smart Specializations (RIS 3) states that SI creates new business opportunities that provide perspectives to citizens, and contribute to the modernization of the public sector and also to regional development (European Commission, 2012). Removed from real-world complexities, public sector innovation technologies and labs introduce small-scale innovations into public niche services innovations. These can later be scale up in the transition from local SIs to systemic SIs (Geels et al., 2008; Bugge et al., 2017).

SI processes may emerge within the environmental complexity, co-evolving with the availabiliy of resources. Environmental sustainability warns of the likelihood of damage to the socio-ecological system given the inability of humanity to respond to crises and emergencies (Efthymiou et al., 2023). This is leading to the need for a turning point in the global socio-ecological system, based on technological and SI systems which are looking to establish alternatives in order to ameliorate the impact of external shocks. Digital transformation and changes in investment in the socio-ecological system engage in sensemaking, reframing the system and revealing further opportunities for radical SI. High natural value assets address challenges of socio-ecological systems to ensure SI (Bennett et al., 2016; Fischer et al., 2017).

Complex socio-ecological and SI process systems are ensured to change in a timely manner by the establishment of a developmental approach. The feedback of complex socio-ecological and SI processes is ensured to change through a developmental approach with an impact on an investing cycle. The components of this cycle are the complexity of the socio-ecological system used in the portfolio selection and the benchmark for the development of impacts in the operations of investment niches, limited by the intermediaries at the upper-bound limits. Within this framework, digital transformation leads to SIs, as it brings a new kind of knowledge and expands social benefits among stakeholders and broader society.

Socio-ecological Resilience

The SI perspective is a critical and normative approach to the socio-ecological processes and outcomes, leading to resilience building and offering the elements for societal and political resilience. The socio-ecological and political resilience of complex socio-economic landscapes requires the collaboration of socio-ecosystems, including diversified agro-forests and human-socio-cultural demands from complex landscapes and socio-ecological forms and functions of human-nature geography (Watkins, 2018).

The notion of socio-ecological resilience from the perspective of SI needs a critical revisioning to put forward a socio-centered approach seeking to combine the capacity of resilience theory for interactions between the socio-ecological systems (Folke, 2006). The notion of socio-ecological resilience is an interlinked process between societal, technological and political dynamics in the territories where the underlying crisis phenomena occur (Kaika, 2017; Keck & Sakdapolrak, 2013). The sense of belonging is an element of socio-ecological resilience. The socio-ecological resilience processes enhance the sense of belonging through strong socio-emotional bonding as a source element of the socio-ecological resilient systems, leading to stirring engagement concerned with environmental stewardship (Masterson et al., 2017).

The socio-ecological resilience concept, from a SI perspective, unravels the socio-political and technological dynamics in the building of resilience in socio-ecological systems. A sensitive socio-ecology resilience perspective is a concept related to the SI initiative despite the diverse types of resilience to deal with the complexity of socio-ecological systems. The resilience perspectives aim at interdisciplinary integrated innovation, technology utilization, and adaptation, as part of the environmental sustainability transformative processes of socio-ecological components of a system, as well as the adaptive processes to cope with disturbance.

Socio-ecological transformation and resilience are interconnected concepts quite at odds with one another, responding to the environmental sustainability predicament organized between and withing the liberal capitalist order (Swyngedouw, 2013). Resilience and environmental sustainability are challenges of transformation, innovation and adaptation processes of the interacting concepts that are related to vulnerability and risk (Leach et al., 2012). While new technologies emerge, as part of the ongoing digital transformation, socio-ecological transformation is related to future possibilities for change, while creating and reproducing resilience.

The concepts of SI and socio-ecological resilience in cross-fertilization processes lead to the notion of socio-ecological resilience in the territorial context as a collective engagement process motivating the citizens' active mobilization toward mitigating risks and unveiling vulnerabilities. Resilient territories are described as socio-ecological systems drifting away from the zero-crisis event paradigm, entailing management strategies, risk analysis and mitigation (Otero & Nielsen, 2017; Tedim et al., 2016; European Forest Institute, 2019). Contextual factors of socio-ecological innovation and complex processes of change are the sustainability environment and resilience.

Furthermore, theoretical and empirical foundations of a socio-ecological growth necessary to design and implement a feasible development strategy enable a transition to achieve high levels of well-being, employment, social inclusion, and socio-ecosystems resilience, leading to the fulfilment of global Sustainable Development Goals (SDGs). It also serves a common good, such as a more stable climate (Dimitrova et al., 2013). By the same token, the Black Swan theory sustains reduction in the risks of thresholds and promotes the technological breakthroughs, stimulated by open source information (Farley & Voinov, 2016).

The socio-ecological resilience and SI motivate a progressive paradigm for the long-term prevention of crisis (Birot, 2009; Dunn et al., 2020). Crisis-prone territories with complex socio-ecological systems in the context of human factors intertwined with ecological factors become prominent to building socio-ecological resilience. This is an issue that arises as a policymaking objective (Lelouvier et al., 2021; Leone et al., 2020). Also, socio-ecological resilience is defined by the SI's dimensions based on socio-political issues related to human wellbeing. Building socio-ecological resilience to natural disasters is a continuous process beyond survival, protecting infrastructure and assets. The human capital possessed by rural farms and socio-ecological innovation with livelihood strategies in disaster types affecting the vulnerability of the resilience dimension is one way to achieve sustainability issues and sustainable livelihoods (Rusciano et al., 2020; Cattivelli & Rusciano, 2020; Cisco & Gatto, 2021).

Socio-ecological resilience has as defining characteristics the amount of change sustained by the system and remaining in the same domain of attraction, the capacity of self-organization, and the capacity for learning and adaptation (Berkes et al., 2008). Continuous economic growth is the goal of economic activity assuming price mechanisms that fail the ecological thresholds by ignoring the needs of poor people and technological breakthroughs to ensure resilience (Farley & Voinov, 2016).

Moreover, livelihood resilience is the ability of social systems to respond and recover from disasters, depending on social networks, socio-demographic profiles, and livelihood strategies (Zhou et al., 2021). The socio-ecological resilience approach is robust for studying natural disasters with interrelations and feedback processes between the social and biophysical dimensions to further enhance the analytical resilience theory in order to analyze dynamics and socio-political change (Moritz et al., 2014; Folke, 2006). Also, informal social networks, which often exist on digital platforms, promote sustainability and resilience innovations, adaptations, and transformations in environmental organic farming and agricultural production (Thrassou et al., 2022d)

SI and socio-ecological resilience theories are linked in a socially sensitive and territorial embedded framework used to analyze socio-ecosystems from the grass roots and bottom-up-linked institutional initiatives to operate in territories. The resilience theory combines the socially sensitive capacity of SI perspectives to analyze the interactions with the socio-ecological systems as the framework for societal change and socio-political dynamics aimed to shape, negotiate, and govern territories in which socioeconomic events and contingencies occur (Folke, 2006; Moulaert et al., 2013). Resilience and sustainability strategies require technologies, technical and SIs created by transformation action groups aimed to solve socio-environmental change.

Also, social finance is one of the strategies for generating financial returns from SIs. It is also a practice aiming at providing resources to support SI (Pradhan et al., 1998). Social financing is another useful strategy during times of crises and critical events (Thrassou et al., 2022c; Vrontis et al., 2022). However, to exit an economic crisis, governments must build strengths and upgrade skills and capabilities on SI, toward social inclusiveness, increased resources, and energy productivity. In addition, social finance intermediaries supporting SI need to frame social uncertainties and risks to make defensible allocations of capital. Investment capital projects may propose strategies to scale up activities and manage adaptive cycles of SIs requiring feedback strategies of reorganization and sense-making (Moore et al., 2012).

Finally, the incorporation of capital allocation opportunities between profit and not-for-profit investments expands the diversity of SI opportunities to stimulate it and effect transformative change (Nicholls, 2010). Social finance theory and practice have opportunities and limits in supporting SI with challenges in attempting to capitalize in order to solve complex problems. The adaptive cycle of social finance draws from the conceptual framework of resilience theory used to analyze the dynamic phases of socio-ecological innovation. Lack of SI does not necessarily lead to a lack of productivity, recognizing the multiple values as innovating within a post-productivism alternative. In the next section, the analysis provides links between SI and governance.

SI and Governance

Amidst digital transformation, the mobilization of all interested actors, agents, stakeholders, and collective local actors facilitate participation in experimental governance toward measuring and comparing systematic learning processes (Sabel & Zeitlin, 2012). Smart technologies assist knowledge sharing and help minimize the learning gap. Specific governance mechanisms facilitate the design and implementation of socio-ecological innovation models and innovation development processes. The reconfiguration of social relations is a dynamic process and non-nature SI in social relations and governance (Baker & Mehmood, 2015; Neumeier, 2012; Ray, 2006; Spijker & Parra, 2018). Dynamic SI is suitable for a socio-ecological perspective in interaction with the natural environment embedded in the social system and a specific set of governance institutions and rules (Ostrom, 2009).

Bottom-up initiatives incorporated into structured and formalized systems enhanced by the public sector, such as the creation of coalitions of collaborative partnerships are bottom-linked SI governance (Castro-Arce & Vanclay, 2019). Innovation governance and new forms of co-governance considers the foundational economy of the place-based SI challenging the experimentalism of the regional public sector and local places in the political system (Rodríguez-Pose, 2018). The experimental governance in SI is fueling a precarious economy in spatial social inequality and insecurity. Experimentation of SI governance of economic, social, political, and environmental challenges occurs across the spatial contexts.

The resilience of the socio-ecological innovation system is subject to evolving forms of public and private governance relationships and cooperation in market niches, civil society, and local communities, able to respond to economic, socio-ecological, and political risks. Socio-ecological resilience applied the analysis of civil society engagements, rooted in volunteer groups and solidarity networks conducting prevention and suppression activities. The utilization of technology and digital platforms by these groups, enhances reliance and solidarity even further. Also, "digital transformation, in terms of digital collaboration, joint efforts with internal/external partners to achieve common goals and the adoption of digital tools supporting this practice, affect social innovation capital in the context of small innovative enterprises (SIEs)" (Chierici et al., 2021).

Socio-ecological systems resilience is a core element of inclusive governance systems that address the needs of local communities for learning and innovation (Skrimizea et al., 2021). Collective learning processes are recognized by different joint actors aimed to discuss and co-construct responses to socio-ecological change is crucial for leading to socio-ecological resilience (Cinner & Barnes, 2019). With the diffusion of smart technologies, communication and learning moved from the natural environment to cyberspace; it became richer and more immediate (Roblek et al., 2019). In turn, multi-scale inclusive politics and governance processes became more effective in transforming innovativeness for sustainability. Digital platforms became inclusive spaces for societal dialogue, questioning the status quo and collective action, building socio-ecological resilient systems, generating societal dynamic processes, fulfilling multiple roles, and meeting societal needs.

Adaptive institutions show more bottom-linked participative governance legitimized at the local level, leading to the promotion of creativity and innovation, creating an institutional environment and increasing the socio-ecological systems' resilience (Manyena et al., 2011). Grass-roots organizations with bottom-up initiatives establish bottom-linked institutions to assess socio-ecological resilience contributions in operating territories with a growing number of extreme events, surpassing capacities of a complex socio-ecological issue (Bowman et al., 2009; Howitt, 2014; Moritz et al., 2014)

What's more, urban living labs are relevant in the governance of complex urban green environments and collaborative innovation processes that meet socio-ecological challenges (Buscher et al., 2010; Paskaleva, 2011; Franz, 2014). The formal urban living lab process structures socio-ecological innovation development and the governance of the stakeholders' interactions for knowledge production and transfer. A socially sensitive perspective for socio-ecological resilience concept is related to the SI initiative to contribute in territories where they operate, further reflecting upon the socio-political resilience dimension while contributing to an enhancement of SI in rural areas (Neumeier, 2012; Vercher et al., 2020; Castro-Arce et al., 2019). Resilience of a socio-ecological innovation system enhances the agro-ecological organizations and cooperatives to enable to create and develop evolving collaboration forms with public, private governance relationships in market niches to respond and face economic, social, political, and agro ecological risks.

Rural communities' empowerment through SI must be supported in networking that facilitates cooperation for the capacity building of policymaking among regional and local government agencies and institutions, rural communities, universities and research centers, farmers, etc. aimed at securing knowledge transfer. Socio-ecological innovation in studies of rural communities facing rapid changes focuses on opportunities to enhance the local resilience of marginal indigenous and developing communities (Gadgil et al., 1993; Perevolotsky, 1987; Terashima, 1983). The technological development runaway with the concept of smart cities promises to develop more sustainable and resilient cities.

9.3 Discussion and Conclusions

While reviewing the literature, we came across significant differences in perceptions and attitudes toward digitization. However, a common base amongst most commentators is that digitization has a positive impact on SI. In fact, digital transformation is itself a form of social innovation. This is because digitization facilitates a framework of enhanced communication, problem solving, knowledge sharing and learning amongst stakeholders and the broader society. Within this framework, digital transformation becomes a driver of SI while it enables greater interconnection with socio-ecological resilience and governance.

The impact of digitization is also observed on socio-ecological resilience, including its power relations, and social and governance dynamics. Socio-ecological resilience is restored by economic planned release degrowth. The most relevant challenge of the socio-ecological system is to maintain resilience by reducing the negative impacts of economic activities to the critical ecological thresholds. On the other hand, "governance" for sustainability transformations is a component at different scales and levels of action. The complexity of socio-ecological and socio-cultural process of transformations have, as common components, the governance of sustainability and the transformative action groups.

Technological innovations in socio-ecological sustainability governance are related to local resilience strategies such as specifically to localized manufacturing, yet globally connected, leading to possible economic tradeoffs. Technological innovation and price mechanisms ensure economic growth and resilience of the socio-ecological systems. In addition, digitization enhances cooperation amongst stakeholders, toward co-creating innovation. Various "new age" technologies facilitate better interaction, communication, knowledge sharing, and successful development of innovations. New ways of learning and sharing knowledge are enabled, thus reducing the learning gap among stakeholders. Also, technologies promote labor market integration and the generation of new jobs. Such developments have a positive impact on social innovation and socio-ecological resilience.

As presented in Fig. 9.1, the addition of digital smart technologies in the intersection of SI, socio-ecological resilience and governance enable new ways of learning, enhanced cooperations among stakeholders, knowledge sharing, and knowledge retention, thus contributing to sustainable development. Digitization is deemed as a driver of lasting social change amongst the community, or, in other words "technology-led" sustainable social innovation. Also, the complexities of socio-ecological and socio-cultural transformation are reduced to political processes and transformative action groups as the components of governance of sustainability. But the utilization of digital platforms enhances social dialogue, which exist in inclusive spaces as the result of collective action that questions the status quo of all elements necessary for building socio-ecological resilience.

The future implications of this study are also interesting. Digitization has gradually become fundamental for social innovation, as current generations such as "Gen Z" (also called "iGen") have no experience of life before the Internet. The members of such generations are defined as

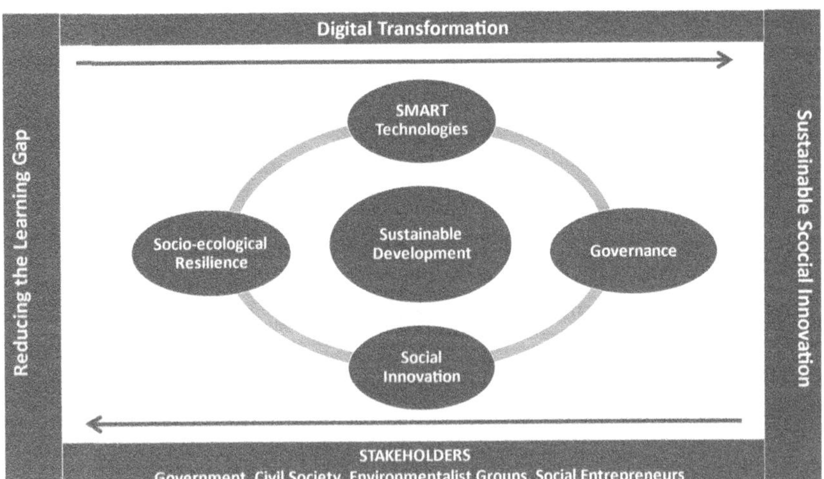

Fig. 9.1 A Digital Framework for Sustainable Social Innovation, Socio-ecological Resilience and Governance

digital natives (Roblek et al., 2019). Members of generations "Z" and "Alpha" live during a period when technology is easily accessible to young people, including in the form of smartphones, tablets, Internet of Things, smart TVs and more. From this point on, as societies' members will be constantly engaged in communication in an online world, sustainable social innovation, socio-ecological resilience and governance will only be possible through means of technology and digitization. Social innovation will be created and shared through smart technologies. This has an impact not only on social innovation, but also on resilience, solidarity, and governance.

References

Avelino, F., Wittmayer, J. M., Pel, B., Weaver, P., Dumitru, A., Haxeltine, A., Kemp, R., Jørgensen, M. S., Bauler, T., Ruijsink, S., & O'Riordan, T. (2015). Transformative SI and (Dis)empowerment. *Technological Forecasting and Social Change*, 0–1. https://doi.org/10.1016/j.techfore.2017.05.002

Baker, S., & Mehmood, A. (2015). SI and the Governance of Sustainable Places. *Local Environment, 20*, 321–334. https://doi.org/10.1080/13549839.2013.842964

Barbera, F., Negri, N., & Salento, A. (2018). From Individual Choice to Collective Voice: Foundational Economy, Local Commons and Citizenship. *Rassegna Italiana di Sociologia, 59*(2), 371–397.

Batiz-Lazo, B., Efthymiou, L., & Davies, K. (2022). The Spread of Artificial Intelligence and Its Impact on Employment: Evidence from the Banking and Accounting Sectors. In A. Thrassou, D. Vrontis, L. Efthymiou, Y. Weber, S. M. R. Shams, & E. Tsoukatos (Eds.), *Business Advancement Through Technology Volume II. Palgrave Studies in Cross-Disciplinary Business Research, In Association with EuroMed Academy of Business*. Palgrave Macmillan. https://doi.org/10.1007/978-3-031-07765-4_7

Bennett, E. M., Solan, M., Biggs, R., et al. (2016). Bright Spots: Seeds of a Good Anthropocene. *Frontiers in Ecology and the Environment, 14*, 441–448.

Bentham, J., Bowman, A., de la Cuesta, M., Engelen, E., Erturk, I., Folkman, P., Froud, J., Johal, S., Law, J., Leaver, A., Moran, M. & Williams, K. (2013). *Manifesto for the Foundational Economy*. CRESC Working Paper 131.

Berkes, F., Colding, J., & Folke, C. (2008). *Introduction Navigating Social-Ecological Systems: Building Resilience for Complexity and Change*. Cambridge University Press.

Birot, Y. (2009). *Convivir con los incendios forestales: Lo que nos revela la ciencia*. European Forest Institute.

Bowman, D. M. J. S., Balch, J. K., Artaxo, P., Bond, W. J., Carlson, J. M., Cochrane, M. A., D'Antonio, C. M., Defries, R. S., Doyle, J. C., Harrison, S. P., Johnston, F. H., Keeley, J. E., Krawchuk, M. A., Kull, C. A., Marston, J. B., Moritz, M. A., Prentice, I. C., Roos, C. I., Scott, A. C., Swetnam, T. W., Van Der Werf, G. R., & Pyne, S. J. (2009). Fire in the Earth System. *Science (80-.), 324*, 481–484.

Bugge, M., Coenen, L., Marques, P., & Morgan, K. (2017). Governing System Innovation: Assisted Living Experiments in the UK and Norway. *European Planning Studies, 25*(12), 2138–2156. https://doi.org/10.1080/09654313.2017.1349078

Buscher, V., Tomordy, M., Ashley, G., & Tabet, M. (2010). *Smart Cities: Transforming the 21st Century City Via the Creative Use of Technology*. Arup IT & Communication Systems.

Castro-Arce, K., & Vanclay, F. (2019). Transformative SI for Sustainable Rural Development: An Analytical Framework to Assist Community-Based Initiatives. *Journal of Rural Studies, 74*, 45–54. https://doi.org/10.1016/j.jrurstud.2019.11.010

Castro-Arce, K., Parra, C., & Vanclay, F. (2019). SI, Sustainability, and the Governance of Protected Areas: Revealing Theory as It Plays Out in Practice in Costa Rica. *Journal of Environmental Planning and Management, 62*(13). https://doi.org/10.1080/09640568.2018.1537976

Cattivelli, V., & Rusciano, V. (2020). SI and Food Provisioning during COVID 19: The Case of Urban–Rural Initiatives in the Province of Naples. *Sustainability, 12*, 4444.

Chierici, R., Tortora, D., Del Giudice, M., & Quacquarelli, B. (2021). Strengthening Digital Collaboration to Enhance Social Innovation Capital: An Analysis of Italian Small Innovative Enterprises. *Journal of Intellectual Capital, 22*(3), 610–632. https://doi.org/10.1108/JIC-02-2020-0058

Cinner, J. E., & Barnes, M. L. (2019). Social Dimensions of Resilience in Social-Ecological Systems. *One Earth, 1*, 51–56. https://doi.org/10.1016/j.oneear.2019.08.003

Cisco, G., & Gatto, A. (2021). Climate Justice in an Intergenerational Sustainability Framework: A Stochastic OLG Model. *Economies, 9*, 47.

Dimitrova, A., et al. (2013). Literature Review on Fundamental Concepts and Definitions, Objectives, and Policy Goals as Well as Instruments Relevant for Socio-ecological Transition, *WWWforEurope Working Paper*, No. 40, WWWforEurope, Vienna.

Dunn, C. J., O'Connor, C. D., Abrams, J., Thompson, M. P., Calkin, D. E., Johnston, J. D., Stratton, R., & Gilbertson-Day, J. (2020). Wildfire Risk Science Facilitates Adaptation of Fire-Prone Social-Ecological Systems to the New Fire Reality. *Environmental Research Letters, 15*. https://doi.org/10.1088/1748-9326/ab6498

Efthymiou, L., Kulshrestha, A., & Kulshrestha, S. A. (2023). Study on Sustainability and ESG in the Service Sector in India: Benefits, Challenges, and Future Implications. *Adm. Sci. 13*, 165. https://doi.org/10.3390/admsci13070165

European Commission. (2012). *Guide to Research and Innovation Strategies for Smart Specialisations (RIS 3)*. Publications Office of the European Union.

European Forest Institute. (2019). *Resilient Landscapes to Face Catastrophic Forest Fires*. Madrid, Spain, 14–15 October. https://www.fs.usda.gov/research/treesearch/treesearch/pubs/download/62430.pdf

Farley, J., & Voinov, A. (2016). Economics, Socio-ecological Resilience and Ecosystem Services. *Journal of Environmental Management, 183*(2), 389–398. https://doi.org/10.1016/j.jenvman.2016.07.065. https://www.sciencedirect.com/science/article/pii/S0301479716305023

Fischer, J., Abson, D. J., Bergsten, A., et al. (2017). Reframing the Food–Biodiversity Challenge. *Trends in Ecology & Evolution, 32*, 335–345.

Folke, C. (2006). Resilience: The Emergence of a Perspective for Social–Ecological Systems Analyses. *Global Environmental Change, 16*, 253–267. https://doi.org/10.1016/J.GLOENVCHA.2006.04.002

Folke, C., Carpenter, S., Walker, B., Scheffer, M., Elmqvist, T., Gunderson, L., & Holling, C. S. (2004). Regime Shifts, Resilience, and Biodiversity in Ecosystem Management. *Annual Review of Ecology Evolution and Systematics, 35*, 557–581.

Folke, C., Biggs, R., Norström, A. V., Reyers, B., & Rockström, J. (2016). Social-Ecological Resilience and Biosphere-Based Sustainability Science. *Ecology and Society, 21*. https://doi.org/10.5751/ES-08748-210341

Foundational Economy Collective. (2018). *Foundational Economy: The Infrastructure of Everyday Life*. Manchester University Press.

Franz, Y. (2014). Chances and Challenges for Social Urban Living Labs in Urban Research. In *ENoLL OpenLivingLab Days 2014 Conference Proceedings* (pp. 105–114). Amsterdam, Netherlands.

Gadgil, M., Berkes, F., & Folke, C. (1993). Indigenous Knowledge for Biodiversity Conservation. *Ambio, 22*, 151–156.

Geels, F. W., Hekkert, M. P., & Jacobsson, S. (2008). The Dynamics of Sustainable Innovation Journeys. *Technology Analysis & Strategic Management, 20*(5), 521–536. https://doi.org/10.1080/09537320802292982

Haberl, H., Winiwarter, V., Andersson, K., et al. (2006). From LTER to LTSER: Conceptualizing the Socio-economic Dimension of Long-Term Socio-ecological Research. *Ecology and Society, 11*, 13. www.ecologyandsociety.org/vol11/iss2/art13/. Viewed 3 Sept 2010.

Hansen, T., & Winther, L. (2011). Innovation, Regional Development, and Relations Between High-and Low-Tech Industries. *European Urban and Regional Studies, 18*(3), 321–339. https://doi.org/10.1177/0969776411403990

Howitt, R. (2014). Coexisting with Fire? A Commentary on the Scale Politics of Adaptation. *Geographical Research, 52*, 61–64. https://doi.org/10.1111/1745-5871.12036

Kaika, M. (2017). "Don't Call Me Resilient Again!": The New Urban Agenda as Immunology … or … What Happens When Communities Refuse to be Vaccinated with "Smart Cities" and Indicators. *Environment & Urbanization, 29*, 89–102. https://doi.org/10.1177/0956247816684763

Keck, M., & Sakdapolrak, P. (2013). What Is Social Resilience? Lessons Learned and Ways Forward. *Erdkunde – Archive for Scientific Geography, 67*, 5–19.

Leach, M. J., Rockström, P., Raskin, I., Scoones, A. C., Stirling, A., Smith, J., et al. (2012). Transforming Innovation for Sustainability. *Ecology and Society, 17*(2), 11. https://doi.org/10.5751/ES-04933-170211

Lelouvier, R., Nuijten, D., Onida, M., & Stoof, C. R. (2021). *Land-Based Wildfire Prevention*. Publications Office of the EU.

Leone, V., Tedim, F., & Xanthopoulos, G. (2020). Fire Smart Territory as an Innovative Approach to Wildfire Risk Reduction. In *Extreme Wildfire Events and Disasters: Root Causes and New Management Strategies*. Elsevier.

Long, N., & Long, A. (1992). *Battlefields of Knowledge: The Interlocking of Theory and Practice in Social Research and Development*. Routledge.

Manyena, B., O'Brien, G., O'Keefe, P., & Rose, J. (2011). Disaster Resilience: A Bounce Back or Bounce Forward Ability? *Local Environment, 16*, 417–424. https://doi.org/10.1080/13549839.2011.583049

Marques, P., Morgan, K., & Richardson, R. (2018). SI in Question: The Theoretical and Practical Implications of a Contested Concept. *Environment and Planning C: Politics and Space, 36*(3), 496–512.

Martinelli, F. (2013). Learning from Case Studies of SI in the Field of Social Services: Creatively Balancing Top-Down Universalism with Bottom-Up Democracy. In *The International Handbook on SI* (pp. 346–360). https://doi.org/10.4337/9781849809993.00044

Masterson, V. A., Stedman, R. C., Enqvist, J., Tengö, M., Giusti, M., Wahl, D., & Svedin, U. (2017). The Contribution of Sense of Place to Social-Ecological Systems Research: A Review and Research Agenda. *Ecology and Society, 22*. https://doi.org/10.5751/ES-08872-220149

Moore, M., Westley, F., Tjornbo, O., & Holroyd, C. (2012). The Loop, The Lens, and The Lesson: Using Resilience Theory to Examine Public Policy and SI. In A. Nicholls & A. Murdock (Eds.), *SI: Blurring Boundaries to Reconfigure Markets* (pp. 114–136). Palgrave Macmillan.

Morgan, K. (2018). *Experimental Governance and Territorial Development*. OECD. https://www.oecd.org/cfe/regional-policy/Morgan(2018)ExperimentalGovernanceAndTerritorialDevelopment_OECD_FINAL.pdf. Accessed 4 Nov 2019.

Moritz, M. A., Batllori, E., Bradstock, R. A., Malcolm Gill, A., Handmer, J., Hessburg, P. F., Leonard, J., McCaffrey, S., Odion, D. C., Schoennagel, T., & Syphard, A. D. (2014). Learning to Coexist with Wildfire. *Nature, 515*, 58–66. https://doi.org/10.1038/nature13946

Moulaert, F., MacCallum, D., Mehmood, A., & Hamdouch, A. (2013). *The International Handbook on SI: Collective Action, Social Learning and Transdisciplinary Research*. Edward Elgar.

Neumeier, S. (2012). Why do SIs in Rural Development Matter and Should They Be Considered More Seriously in Rural Development Research? Proposal for a Stronger Focus on SIs in Rural Development Research. *Sociologia Ruralis, 52*, 48–69. https://doi.org/10.1111/j.1467-9523.2011.00553.x

Nicholls, A. (2010). The Institutionalization of Social Investment: The Interplay of Investment Logics and Investor Rationalities. *Journal of Social Entrepreneurship, 1*(1), 70–100.

Ostrom, E. (2009). A General Framework for Analyzing Sustainability of Social-Ecological Systems. *Science, 80*(325), 419–422. https://doi.org/10.1126/science.1172133

Otero, I., & Nielsen, J. (2017). Coexisting with Wildfire? Achievements and Challenges for a Radical Social-Ecological Transformation in Catalonia (Spain). *Geoforum, 85*, 234–246. https://doi.org/10.1016/j.geoforum.2017.07.020

Ozbekhan, H. (1973). *Thought on the Emerging Methodology of Planning*. University of Pennsylvania.

Paskaleva, K. (2011). The Smart City: A Nexus for Open Innovation? *Intelligent Buildings International, 3*(3), 153–171. https://doi.org/10.1080/17508975.2011.586672

Perevolotsky, A. (1987). Territoriality and Resource Sharing Among the Bedouin of Southern Sinai: A Socio-ecological Interpretation. *Journal of Arid Environments, 13*, 153–161.

Pradhan, B., Roy, P., Saluja, M., & Venkatrum, S. (1998). *Income, Expenditure, and Social Sector Indicators of Households in Rural and Urban India*. Micro Impacts of Macroeconomic and Adjustment Policies, Third Annual Meeting, November 2–6.

Ray, C. (2006). *Neo-endogenous Rural Development in the EU Handbook of Rural Studies* (pp. 278–291). SAGE Publications Inc. https://doi.org/10.4135/9781848608016.n19

Roblek, V., Mesko, M., Dimovski, V., & Peterlin, J. (2019). Smart Technologies as Social Innovation and Complex Social Issues of the Z Generation. *Kybernetes, 48*(1), 91–107.

Rodríguez-Pose, A. (2018). The Revenge of the Places that Don't Matter (And What to Do About It). *Cambridge Journal of Regions, Economy, and Society, 11*(1), 189–209.

Rusciano, V., Civero, G., & Scarpato, D. (2020). Social and Ecological High Influential Factors in Community Gardens Innovation: An Empirical Survey in Italy. *Sustainability, 12*, 4651.

Sabel, C., & Zeitlin, J. (2012). Experimentalist Governance. In D. Levi-Faur (Ed.), *Oxford Handbook of Governance* (pp. 169–183). Oxford University Press.

Seyfang, G., & Smith, A. (2007). Grassroots Innovations for Sustainable Development: Towards a New Research and Policy Agenda. *Environmental Politics, 16*(4), 584–603. https://doi.org/10.1080/09644010701419121

Skrimizea, E., Bakema, M., McCann, P., & Parra, C. (2021). Disaster Governance and Institutional Dynamics in Times of Social-Ecological Change: Insights from New Zealand, The Netherlands and Greece. *Applied Geography, 136*, 102578. https://doi.org/10.1016/j.apgeog.2021.102578

Spijker, S. N., & Parra, C. (2018). Knitting Green Spaces with the Threads of SI in Groningen and London. *Journal of Environmental Planning and Management, 61*, 1011–1032. https://doi.org/10.1080/09640568.2017.1382338

Swyngedouw, E. (2013). The Non-political Politics of Climate Change. *ACME: An International Journal for Critical Geographies, 12*(1), 1–8.

Tedim, F., Leone, V., & Xanthopoulos, G. (2016). A Wildfire Risk Management Concept Based on a Social-Ecological Approach in the European Union: Fire Smart Territory. *International Journal of Disaster Risk Reduction, 18*, 138–153. https://doi.org/10.1016/j.ijdrr.2016.06.005

Terashima, H. (1983). Mota and Other Hunting Activities of the Mbuti Archers: A Socio-ecological Study of Subsistence Technology. *African Study Monographs, 3*, 71–85.

Thrassou, A., Vrontis, D., Efthymiou, L., & Uzunboylu, N. (2022a). An Overview of Business Advancement Through Technology: Markets and Marketing in Transition. In A. Thrassou, D. Vrontis, L. Efthymiou, Y. Weber, S. M. R. Shams, & E. Tsoukatos (Eds.), *Business Advancement Through Technology Volume I. Palgrave Studies in Cross-Disciplinary Business Research, In Association with EuroMed Academy of Business*. Palgrave Macmillan. https://doi.org/10.1007/978-3-031-07769-2_1

Thrassou, A., Vrontis, D., Efthymiou, L., & Uzunboylu, N. (2022b). An Overview of Business Advancement Through Technology: The Changing Landscape of Work and Employment. In A. Thrassou, D. Vrontis, L. Efthymiou, Y. Weber, S. M. R. Shams, & E. Tsoukatos (Eds.), *Business Advancement Through Technology Volume II. Palgrave Studies in Cross-Disciplinary Business Research, In Association with EuroMed Academy of Business*. Palgrave Macmillan. https://doi.org/10.1007/978-3-031-07765-4_1

Thrassou, A., Efthymiou, L., Vrontis, D., Weber, Y., Shams, S. M. R., & Tsoukatos, E. (2022c). Editorial Introduction: Crisis in Context. In D. Vrontis, A. Thrassou, Y. Weber, S. M. R. Shams, E. Tsoukatos, & L. Efthymiou (Eds.), *Business Under Crisis Volume I. Palgrave Studies in Cross-Disciplinary Business Research, In Association with EuroMed Academy of Business*. Palgrave Macmillan. https://doi.org/10.1007/978-3-030-76567-5_1

Thrassou, A., Uzunboylu, N., Efthymiou, L., Vrontis, D., Weber, Y., Shams, S. M., & Tsoukatos, E. (2022d). Editorial Introduction: Business Under Crises: Organizational Adaptations. In D. Vrontis, A. Thrassou, Y. Weber,

S. M. R. Shams, E. Tsoukatos, & L. Efthymiou (Eds.), *Business Under Crisis Volume II. Palgrave Studies in Cross-Disciplinary Business Research, In Association with EuroMed Academy of Business*. Palgrave Macmillan. https://doi.org/10.1007/978-3-030-76575-0_1

Van Dyck, B., & Van den Broeck, P. (2015). SI: A Territorial Process. In *The International Handbook on Social Innovation* (pp. 131–141). https://doi.org/10.4337/9781849809993.00021

Vercher, N., Barlagne, C., Hewitt, R., Nijnik, M., & Esparcia, J. (2020). Whose Narrative Is It Anyway? Narratives of SI in Rural Areas – A Comparative Analysis of Community-Led Initiatives in Scotland and Spain. In *Social Polarization in Post-industrial Metropolises*. https://doi.org/10.1515/9783110878394-015

Vrontis, D., Thrassou, A., Efthymiou, L., Uzunboylu, N., Weber, Y., Shams, R. S. M., & Tsoukatos, E. (2022). Editorial Introduction: Business Under Crisis: Avenues for Innovation, Entrepreneurship and Sustainability. In D. Vrontis, A. Thrassou, Y. Weber, S. M. R. Shams, E. Tsoukatos, & L. Efthymiou (Eds.), *Business Under Crisis Volume III. Palgrave Studies in Cross-disciplinary Business Research, In Association with EuroMed Academy of Business*. Palgrave Macmillan. https://doi.org/10.1007/978-3-030-76583-5_1

Watkins, C. (2018). Landscapes and Resistance in the African Diaspora: Five Centuries of Palm Oil on Bahia's Dendê Coast. *Journal of Rural Studies, 61*, 137–154. https://doi.org/10.1016/j.jrurstud.2018.04.009. https://www.sciencedirect.com/science/article/pii/S0743016717305727

Zhou, W., Guo, S., Deng, X., & Xu, D. (2021). Livelihood Resilience and Strategies of Rural Residents of Earthquake-Threatened Areas in Sichuan Province, China. *Natural Hazards, 106*, 255–275.

Index

A. Zarifis et al. (eds.), *Business Digital Transformation*,
https://doi.org/10.1007/978-3-031-33665-2

The manufacturer's authorised representative in the EU is Springer
Nature Customer Service Centre GmbH, Europaplatz 3, 69115 Heidelberg,
Germany. If you have any concerns regarding our products, please
contact ProductSafety@springernature.com

Printed and bound by CPI Group (UK) Ltd, Croydon, CR0 4YY
30/09/2026
02225311-0003